SPAIN:

The European and International Challenges

Of Related Interest

POLITICS AND POLICY IN DEMOCRATIC SPAIN
No Longer Different?
edited by Paul Heywood

THE EURO-MEDITERRANEAN PARTNERSHIP
Political and Economic Perspectives
edited by Richard Gillespie

THE BARCELONA PROCESS
Building a Euro-Mediterranean Regional Community
edited by Álvaro Vasconcelos and George Joffé

PERSPECTIVES ON DEVELOPMENT
The Euro-Mediterranean Partnership
edited by George Joffé

'EUROPEANISATION' AND THE SOUTHERN PERIPHERY
edited by Kevin Featherstone and George Kazamias

GENDER INEQUALITIES IN SOUTHERN EUROPE
Women, Work and Welfare in the 1990s
edited by María José González, Teresa Jurado and Manuela Naldini

UNEMPLOYMENT IN SOUTHERN EUROPE
Coping with the Consequences
edited by Nancy G. Bermeo

MEDITERRANEAN ISSUES
ISSN 1465-9182

Series Editors: **Richard Gillespie**, University of Liverpool
Claire Spencer, King's College London

Designed to focus interest on an area seen by many as a newly emergent region, besides constituting a core element of the historical experience of the various countries around the Mediterranean Basin.

SPAIN:

The European and International Challenges

Edited by

RICHARD GILLESPIE

and

RICHARD YOUNGS

FRANK CASS
LONDON • PORTLAND, OR

First published in 2001 in Great Britain by
FRANK CASS PUBLISHERS
Newbury House, 900 Eastern Avenue
London IG2 7HH, England

and in the United States of America by
FRANK CASS PUBLISHERS
c/o ISBS
5824 N.E. Hassalo Street
Portland, Oregon 97213–3644

Website: www.frankcass.com

British Library Cataloguing in Publication Data

Spain: the European and international challenges. –
(Mediterranean politics; v. 5; no. 2)
1. Spain – Foreign relations – 1975-
I. Gillespie, Richard II. Youngs, Richard
327.4′6

ISBN 0-7146-5110-9 (cloth)
ISBN 0-7146-8148-2 (paper)
ISSN 1465-9182

Library of Congress Cataloging-in-Publication Data

Spain: the European and international challenges / editors,
Richard Gillespie and Richard Youngs.
   p. cm.
   "This group of studies first appeared in a special issue on
'Spain: the European and international challenges' of
Mediterranean Politics (ISSN 1362-9395), 5/2 (summer 2000)
published by Frank Cass" – T.p. verso.
   Includes bibliographical references and index.
   ISBN 0-7146-5110-9 (cloth) – ISBN 0-7146-8148-2 (pbk.)
   1. Spain – Foreign relations – 1975-   . 2. Spain – Foreign
economic relations. I. Gillespie, Richard, 1952-   . II. Youngs,
Richard, 1968-   .
   DP85.8.S64 2000
   327.46–dc21   00-64378

This group of studies first appeared in a Special Issue on 'Spain: The European and
International Challenges' of *Mediterranean Politics* (ISSN 1362-9395)
5/2 (Summer 2000) published by Frank Cass.

Printed in Great Britain by
Antony Rowe Ltd, Chippenham, Wilts

Contents

Acknowledgements

This volume is the product, not simply of individual research and writing, but of planning, collaboration and discussion among a largely Anglo-Spanish team of researchers and experts. We are grateful to the Centro de Investigación para la Paz (CIP) in Madrid for providing a venue for the original planning meeting, held in September 1999, at which our original outline was given more substance through discussion with Mariano Aguirre and Jesús Núñez. It was then decided to proceed with a workshop so that an assembled team of experts on the diverse aspects of Spain's external relations could obtain critical feedback on the initial drafts of their analyses and exchange views on our framework and the component parts of the project. In selecting this team, we took care to ensure the presence of individuals who, in addition to possessing impeccable academic credentials, had invaluable experience of working for the European Commission in Brussels and could thus offer invaluable insights derived from the world of the policy practitioner.

The result was a most stimulating workshop, entitled 'Spain 2000: The International Challenges', held at Langrish House, Petersfield (Hampshire) on 21–23 January 2000. This event was made possible by financial support from the British Academy and from the Centre for European Studies Research (CESR), University of Portsmouth. We wish to express our gratitude to these institutions and also to various scholars who made valuable points and suggestions at the workshop in their capacity as discussants. Our thanks here go to Dr Ann Matear (University of Portsmouth), Professor Benny Pollack (University of Liverpool), Dr Claire Spencer (King's College, University of London) and Professor Alfred Tovias (Hebrew University, Jerusalem).

Following this meeting, all of the papers were revised in the light of workshop discussion and editorial comments. The result is thus a genuinely collective product, reflecting a meeting of minds on many aspects of Spain's external relations but also identifying key areas of debate through the different emphases placed by contributors on the central issues. The collection is also somewhat innovative in that, in addition to focusing on the major geographical areas prioritized by Spain, the volume also has thematic focuses, enabling it to highlight the emergence of new dimensions in Spanish foreign policy, such as the increasingly significant role played by multinational corporations and by humanitarian missions abroad. We hope that the result rewards the confidence placed in us by all those who facilitated the project in one way or another.

Richard Gillespie
Richard Youngs

Spain's International Challenges at the Turn of the Century

RICHARD GILLESPIE and RICHARD YOUNGS

A new study of Spain's external relations is called for owing to the various international challenges encountered since the end of the cold war. Many of these relate to the European arena (the single currency, eastern enlargement, reform of the EU in preparation for expansion), and to its unstable southern periphery, while others emanate from broader processes of globalization. Spanish foreign policy has become the subject of almost continuous adaptation, with policy preferences determined by an evolving balance and interaction between global, regional and domestic factors. The phase of integration into international bodies is now largely complete, allowing the focus of analysis to shift to consideration of Spain as an actor, concerned to use these bodies to serve its national interests, yet under growing international pressure to take on more responsibility in areas such as development assistance and conflict management.

For much of the twentieth century, Spain occupied a marginal position within the system of international relations. For many decades, the Iberian country 'mostly lived on the tolerance of the Great Powers and on the periphery of their concerns and confrontations...When not a mere plaything of the first-rank powers, she became their playground – or at least their battleground' [Smyth, 1999: 185]. Notwithstanding a degree of exaggeration in this depiction, what is clear is that by the end of the century, there had been an unmistakable qualitative change in Spain's status. During the final quarter century, Spain finally emerged (or re-emerged) as a much more significant actor, deserving attention in its own right. It is thus tempting to join the chorus of voices that hail the evolution of the country's external relations as a simple success story, of Spain going from strength to strength, especially following the death of Franco in 1975. Of course, there *have* been palpable triumphs, yet one should always be wary of triumphalism. While Spanish influence has grown and new opportunities to fulfil national ambitions have been created, the country's international re-emergence has brought with it new responsibilities and challenges that pose new threats to Spain's enhanced status.

This volume is about Spain's responses to the European and other international challenges the country faces at the turn of century. Before further elaborating on the rationale behind such a study, it may be useful to clarify what the volume is *not*. It does not provide an assessment of Spain's foreign policy performance in the twentieth century, a task already undertaken to a greater or lesser extent elsewhere [Balfour and Preston, 1999; Calduch, 1994; Gillespie *et al.*, 1995], although without doing justice to the Nineties. Nor, spurred by the millennial calendar, does it seek to join the ranks of those works that consider how far Spain had progressed as the century came to an end [Alonso Zaldívar and Castells, 1992; Gaviria, 1996, Tusell *et al.*, 1996].¹ While informed by this earlier literature, the present collection of studies focuses much more directly on the 1990s and seeks to place the challenges for Spain in the specific fast-evolving international context in which they have appeared.

Looking back, one can say that by the late 1980s, post-Franco Spain had adapted to the international environment in which it had emerged. The Iberian country had established diplomatic relations with various countries where it lacked them under Franco; it had joined the European Communities, the Council of Europe, NATO and the WEU, and had negotiated a more dignified defence relationship to the United States, under which American military bases were to be scaled down. Momentarily, it seemed as if Spain had successfully 'normalized' its external relations, if by this we mean that it had largely adapted to the dominant pattern of international affiliations characterizing most of the other western European countries. The sensation of success – of having reached a state of harmony with the country's international environment – was soon to evaporate, however, as the world 'moved on'. Starting with the collapse of the Berlin Wall, the international order began to change at a distinctly faster pace, throwing up a succession of new challenges for Spain, particularly within the European arena but also more generally as a result of globalization.

This volume thus addresses Spanish responses to a series of key issues that affected the policy agenda in the 1990s and at the start of the new century. It aims to assess the impact that this crowded end-of-century agenda has had on Spain, as well as the impact that Spain has had on it. The studies presented here of each area of Spain's external relations are informed by a concern to address two broad analytical issues. These underlying themes relate to the fundamental contextual parameters conditioning the nature of Spain's relationship with the external world. First, the volume goes beyond those analyses that have concluded that, by the late 1980s, Spain had succeeded in the aim of fully 'normalizing' its external relations. The broad notion proposed here is that there has been, not one, but rather a succession of adaptations, and thus there is a need to assess Spanish foreign policy in the light of more recent challenges. Second, the contributions seek to reflect the evolving relationships between the different types of factors that affect Spanish foreign policy choices. A central concern of foreign policy analysis in recent years has been to explore the changing balance and interaction between the global, regional and domestic determinants of national policy preferences in the post-cold war period, and this study of Spain's external policies in the latter half of the 1990s seeks to contribute to this ongoing debate. If the first question addresses the impact of an apparent culmination of an internal dynamic upon Spanish policy, the second looks beyond this pattern to changes in the nature and force of internal and external constraints that impinge on governmental decision-making.

The New External Agenda

The external agenda facing Spanish policy-makers since the mid-1990s has been uniquely challenging. Perhaps most crucially, Spain's well-documented general unease over western Europe's adaptation to the end of the cold war has had to be translated into concrete negotiating positions within both the EU's eastern enlargement negotiations themselves and the discussions over the nature of the budgetary and decision-making reforms deemed necessary to prepare the EU for a significant expansion of membership. Clearly, central to any analysis of Spain's place in the world at the turn of the century is an understanding of both the threats and potential benefits to Spanish national interests of central Europe's incorporation into western institutions. Once this incorporation was accepted in principle, the crucial question became the extent to which Spain could withstand the pressure to cede some of the privileges accorded to the EU's cohesion fund recipients; interest here lay in Spain's ability to secure protection for her interests through the new institutional mechanisms that would emerge from the successive Intergovernmental Conferences (IGCs) and through taking advantage of the new markets and additional political allies offered by the opening to the East.

In relation to internal European policy, adjustment to the single market had already given rise to the need to implement a second wave of structural reforms requisite to gaining entry to the single currency. After an apparently inauspicious evolution of economic policy after the Maastricht summit, Spain succeeded in gaining entry to the EU's Economic and Monetary Union (EMU) on 1 January 1999. While this appeared to put to rest fears of a new peripheralization which had surfaced when the EMU project was first drawn up, it also presaged an inevitably difficult period of ensuring that the Spanish economy was equipped to function successfully within the euro. Even as the euro was launched, debates over the next stage of economic integration had appeared on the horizon, obliging Spain to begin to define its preferences and interests in relation to issues such as fiscal harmonization, the external exchange rate policy of the euro and the further convergence of social policy provision.

Beyond Europe, there were also new and ongoing challenges. The unleashing of a host of new ethno-nationalist based conflicts engendered intense debate over the scope and form of new humanitarian and peace-keeping missions. Against the backdrop of Spain's incremental abandonment of its long-standing isolation, questions about participation in new fora of conflict prevention and management had particular resonance in Madrid. In the Mediterranean area, growing socio-economic and political instability, in some countries bringing a reversal of incipient political liberalization, was of particular concern to Spain. The increasingly obvious financial vulnerability, social inequality and bad governance afflicting post-transition Latin America added urgency to a traditional priority area of Spanish policy. The density of European relations not only with Latin America and the Mediterranean but also with the Lomé states and Asia became significantly more marked after 1995, producing both new strains and new opportunities for Spanish policy-making. The rapidly evolving US attitude towards the question of an autonomous European security identity required a revisiting of Spain's particular status and perspectives on defence and security issues, expressed through the 'Spanish model' of participation in NATO. As the EU's new Common Foreign and Security Policy (CFSP) was formally established in 1993, committing member states to more effective and systematic co-operation in foreign policy, Spain faced the challenge of addressing its concerns over the instability beyond Europe's borders in more rigorous concert with its EU partners. This presented the opportunity of adding more effective weight to Spanish national policies, but also raised the prospect of tighter constraints on pursuing national priorities not shared by other EU member states.

New Opportunities and Responsibilities

As highlighted above, the main focus of relevant work on Spain since the mid-1980s has been the gradual 'normalization' of the country's external relations following the years of semi-isolation under Franco. The conscious restructuring of external relations has been explained as simultaneously the effect of, and a contribution to, democratic consolidation [Gillespie *et al.*, 1995]. This normalization was intended as the means to other ends, not as an end in itself. It was seen by policy-makers as having laid the foundations for seeking to fufil national interests through a more germane framework of European and broader international co-operation, rather than, as of the mid-1990s, having secured the desired substantive ends in themselves [Ortega, 1995: 178]. This implies the need for an analysis of the subsequent phase of Spain's external relations, centred on how full integration within the dominant international organizations has changed both Spanish perspectives on the outside world and the outside world's expectations of Spain.

There are a number of factors which, a priori, might be expected to be pertinent to the recent period. If, since the early 1980s, priority had been accorded to the need to convince others that Spain was a 'good European' and a reliable ally in western-dominated financial and security fora, once these credentials were firmly established the question arose of whether Spain would begin to weigh more carefully the benefits and constraints of co-operation at the international level. The willingness to battle hard for national interests had not been completely absent from policy up to the mid-1990s. However, at the latter juncture and particularly in relation to European policy, analysts did claim to witness the beginnings of a more careful consideration of exactly what degree and kind of co-operation were required to maximize perceived national interests. There were the stirrings of a greater self-confidence as Spain sought to use European and other international fora to express specifically national concerns. Would Spain now begin to function in a similar way to France, the UK or the more self-assertive post-unification Germany? Or would securing European unity on external issues still be seen as, in itself, more valuable by Spain than by the more established member states? To what extent was fuller integration encouraging Spain to become more proactive on international issues? While Spain had lobbied hard from the moment of accession into the EU for the latter to upgrade policy toward the Mediterranean and Latin America, it is generally agreed that this effort had been subsumed within the perceived need to develop a profile as a mainstream player within the EU, WEU and even NATO: would Spain subsequently have the assurance to press even harder for more attention to be paid to its own areas of particular concern? Conversely, would one see a broad convergence of Spanish and European perspectives, such that the incentive for enhanced Spanish activism within CFSP would actually diminish? After many years of attention to what international and European fora were doing *to* Spain, by the end of the century it seemed more pertinent to explore Spain's own input into these bodies.

The other side of the coin of international integration was an expectation that the responsibilities placed on Spain, as a firmly established member of western institutions, would increase. Other member states had always seen cohesion funds as a strictly temporary measure to help Mediterranean states (and the Republic of Ireland) through preparations for EMU, and it was thus a crucial issue for Spain how in practice this view would be expressed in the Agenda 2000 negotiations initiated in the mid-1990s [Bastarreche *et al.*, 1999]. Spain's very success in securing entry to EMU and in enhancing its status as a core member state brought with it the expectation that the

Spanish economy would take on the full burden of the monetary discipline underpinning EMU. The imminent eastern enlargement brought home most starkly Spain's conversion from major recipient to potential donor, the relatively quick progression, that is, from Spanish democracy being bolstered and guaranteed by other western European nations to Madrid itself being expected to assume a prominent role in helping strengthen the new democracies of central and eastern Europe, going beyond the simple offer of its political model of democratization.

In relation to international issues beyond Europe, it was widely accepted that by the early 1990s Spain had gained a diplomatic presence and prestige far in excess of its quantitative contribution to international efforts (in terms of finance, hardware and manpower). This raised the question of whether the country would continue to 'punch above its weight', or whether it would be constrained by the expectation that it should take on heavier responsibilities related to international development and conflict management. Having been a firm supporter of strengthened EU 'actorness', or protagonism, on the international stage, how would the nature and extent of Spain's own practical contribution to that enhanced presence evolve? This also raised questions about the effect of European-driven (particularly EMU-related) reforms on Spain's economic strength and, through this, on the vitality of its projection into the wider world.

Levels of Analysis and the Evolution of Spanish External Relations

The post-cold war period has seen intensified debate over the balance between the different levels of influence acting upon government external policies, and the evolution of Spanish external relations must be considered against this background. Here, we refer to the need to address the relative influence of, and relationships between, three levels of influence: European, global and domestic.

The Creep of Europeanization?

By the early 1990s, there was little disagreement over the fact that Spanish foreign policy interests were seen as necessarily and overwhelmingly pursued through European fora. However, it was also recognized that the forces of convergence and divergence at the European level were still finely balanced, with continuing scope for national autonomy when and where this was deemed important in any significant way. Indeed, up to the early 1990s, it was held that Spain had gained particular success from having 'Europeanized' its foreign policy while taking advantage of the scope for national autonomy to accord additional priority to its areas of traditional interest [Gillespie, 1995: 201]. After Maastricht, EU foreign policy co-operation remained intergovernmental, there was only a non-binding aspiration to coordinate national aid policies and several crucial areas of trade policy (services, investment, intellectual property rights) remained outside the scope of the Commission-managed Common Commercial Policy. Meanwhile, in the field of defence and security co-operation, the functioning of the WEU imposed no significant constraints on national governments. However, many analysts argued that the *de facto* dynamics of co-operation in the elaboration of European external policies began to change fundamentally during the mid-1990s.

The perceived change involved the accumulation of a self-sustaining momentum around European foreign and security policy co-operation. A variety of factors, it was suggested, had contributed to this dynamic: the very density of consultation between member states had created national elites that were 'socialized' into thinking at least partly in terms of European rather than purely national interests; the growing *acquis* of largely ineffective joint actions in the foreign policy sphere had generated a stronger determination to ensure that national intransigence ceased to impede more successful co-operation; and the operation of a single market and a (largely) single trade policy, with a single currency imminent, had made divergence in foreign policy increasingly unsustainable [Hill and Wallace, 1996; Edwards and Nuttall, 1994; Allen, 1996]. In short, according to such analysis, the European dimension had become a factor conditioning the very formation of national perspectives on external issues, rather than being simply the arena where standard inter-governmental bargaining occurred, sometimes resulting in compromise, sometimes not. Other analysts rejected this proposition and, taking a more traditionally realist perspective, opined that the degree of convergence of national positions at the European level was still extremely limited, with member states continuing to reason predominantly in terms of nationally-specific interests [Regelsberger and Wessels, 1996; Gordon, 1997; Cameron, 1998; Ginsberg, 1997].

The issue of Europeanization goes beyond that of Spain's normalization as a member state. As the preceding section suggests, it is necessary to analyse whether the fact of attaining normal membership status itself impacted upon Spanish policy decisions. The issue regarding Europeanization is the extent to which the entity within which Spain had normalized its status was itself undergoing change. Assessing the strength of the Europeanizing dynamic is likely to be a key factor in explaining Spanish foreign policy decisions over the latter half of the 1990s. Have the deepening 'norms' of co-operation offset any greater confidence to promote distinctive national interests which might have been accumulating in Madrid (or even in certain Spanish regions)? Have the norms of convergence developed to such a degree that distinctive aspects of Spain's external identity have receded? Or is the 'looseness' of European policy-making procedures sufficient to allow, and even actively encourage, divergence from other member states? This must be a crucial explanatory variable in charting the evolution of those Spanish positions that were characterized by distinctiveness at the start of the decade: the less-than-full membership of NATO; the highly ambivalent attitude towards the United States, surpassed in its prickliness only by that of France; and the ambivalence towards *rapprochement* with eastern Europe. With regard to Latin America and the Mediterranean, Spain's early recognition that the development of its own policies toward these areas required the backing of European resources and diplomatic weight has long rendered an entirely zero-sum perspective (allocating priority either to Europe *or* to the traditional areas) simplistic. However, it clearly is important to assess the impact that changes in the nature of EU 'actorness' have had on the type of policy adopted by Spain in these two areas: has this 'actorness' strengthened to Spain's benefit, or has Madrid in fact gained more from its continuing weaknesses? To the extent that European co-operation has deepened, how has this affected Spain's incentive to secure a distinctive profile in the Mediterranean and Latin America?

Structural Shifts in the International System

Explanations of the evolution of Spain's external relations must also be sought in the nature of changes to the wider global, as opposed to narrower European, environment. The relationship between the process of European integration and trends in the structure of the broader international system is a complex one. Many of the core areas of EU policy have been designed expressly as a reaction to the constraints of globalization. In addition, debates over the remodelling of the western security architecture in the aftermath of the fall of the Berlin Wall flowed directly from overarching geo-strategic shifts. In this sense, many would argue that European integration has proceeded to the extent that member states have sought common reactions to such broad structural factors, rather than by virtue of an internal Europeanizing dynamic itself having any causal impact on national foreign policy choices. In Spain's case, it has commonly been suggested that, up to the early 1990s, what was significant in explanatory terms was the extent to which the basic orientation of Spanish foreign policy was largely predetermined by the international economic constraints upon the Spanish economy (with even the *rapprochement* with NATO being driven as much by the need to gain access to advanced technological projects as by security imperatives themselves) [Heywood, 1995: 268–9].

Much ink has been expended analysing the nature and influence of structural changes to the international economy and state system during the 1990s. The standard parameters set by deepening globalization and the post-cold war restructuring of the international order need no reiteration here. However, it is important to recognize that the period from the mid-1980s to the early 1990s was a period of uniquely intense change, and that external policy choices made in the middle and latter part of the 1990s must be understood as having been elaborated in the shadow of the changes witnessed during this earlier period. The early 1990s witnessed the most spectacular increases in global financial capital flows and were also years dominated by the initial readjustments by governments to the end of the cold war. It was during this period that many of the defining orientations of Spain's external relations were decided: the commitment to EMU; the more active participation in international trade negotiations; the decision to move towards a more mainstream *de facto* involvement in western defence and security operations; and the commitment to a more significant international presence beyond Europe.

This volume seeks to build on works that have analysed these fundamental shifts and itself explores the way in which overarching international constraints filtered through to influence the next stage in Spain's external relations. If international structure is recognized to be primary in explaining the choices made to effect Spain's 'normalization', what sway would these choices hold over the 'post-normalization' period? Had the necessary adaptations to the external environment been made, such that Spain could enjoy more effective autonomy in policy-making? Had Spain become a more aggressive beneficiary of globalization? To what extent had the country been transformed from a passive adaptor to international structural change into a more self-confident and effective shaper of the ongoing shifts in global parameters? Which elements of international structure had become most constraining, and to what extent did these change over the 1990s? Would it be more helpful to analyse Spanish external relations less through the lense of any self-sustaining Europeanizing dynamic and more through that of wider global change, within the context of which European fora were not much less passive players than Spain itself?

Domestic Constraints

A key issue in the study of post-cold war international relations has been the changing relationship between civil society and the policy-making processes of the nation-state. The very breach of the Berlin Wall was widely attributed to the actions of eastern European civil society. For many, this reflected a more generally applicable rise in influence undercutting the autonomy of national governments in relation to foreign policy issues. The empowerment of domestic actors derived from a variety of factors: the greater dissemination of information, permitting a heightened awareness of international issues; technological advances, facilitating the development of transnational networks of civil society groups organized around a concern for particular foreign and developmental policy themes; and a general rise in prominence, in both national policy debate and the orientation of international financial organizations, of issues of transparency and accountability, valued in terms of both democracy and efficiency. The influence of these new actors appeared particularly interesting in relation to the so-called 'new' security issues, such as environmental degradation, demographic change and immigration. By the early 1990s, a number of analysts claimed to detect a greater involvement of such domestic actors, particularly in relation to EU policies, and saw this as an especially significant development given the largely elite-driven nature of European integration hitherto [Moravscik, 1993; Youngs, 1999].

Once again, these developments raised particularly interesting questions for Spain. Prior to the 1990s, Spanish policy-making in external relations had been notably elite-driven. The extent of Spanish NGO activity abroad was extremely limited. Likewise, few Spanish companies had established a significant international profile. History had left Spaniards with an 'isolationist psychology', expressed in their unease over the apparent beginnings of a more active Spanish involvement in international conflict resolution, as heralded by its—albeit still relatively limited—contribution to western operations in the Gulf and in Bosnia [Ortega, 1995: 190]. Eurobarometer polls regularly showed Spaniards to be the population least informed of EU policy developments. As EU policies began to impinge more directly on economic and social conditions in Spain during the mid-1990s, would domestic debate and influence over European policy become more significant? Against this background, the enhanced agency of domestic actors, not least through trans-border networks, would represent an especially significant change to the nature of Spanish external relations. An assessment of the scale and impact of these developments is, therefore, a central concern of this volume.

Previous work has also emphasized the degree of political consensus over foreign policy in Spain, highlighting both a considerable degree of continuity between the Franco regime and subsequent democratic governments [cf. Pollack and Hunter, 1987; Viñas, 1999] and the significant convergence of views between the main political parties from the 1980s onwards. The one notable exception to the post-Franco foreign policy consensus was over the issue of NATO entry, and even here centre-left positions had come largely into line with those of the centre-right by the end of the 1980s, paving the way for full Spanish membership of a reorganized

Alliance from 1999. It is true that, during the first half of the 1990s, the People's Party (PP) under José María Aznar did express criticisms of the Socialist Party (PSOE) government of Felipe González on a range of European and broader international issues. However, while in opposition, the PP did not appear to question the fundamental orientations that governed PSOE foreign policy and remained ambiguous with regard to what it would do itself if it came to power.

When the PP was elected to office in March 1996 it was, thus, not entirely clear what kind of balance between change and continuity would develop under its administration. The replacement of one of Europe's longest-serving governments, in power for over 13 years, was a potentially significant watershed for issues relating to the further consolidation of Spanish democracy and the nature of Spain's international profile. Before long, there were discernible changes in the intensity of certain bilateral relations.[2] But would the change of government really signify a substantial change in external relations? The different contributions to this volume compare the first Aznar government's external policies with those of its PSOE predecessor, in order to assess this question at the end of a full term of PP administration.

Other dimensions of domestic influence may emerge in the future. In particular, the devolution of power to Spain's regions may come to complicate the Spanish external relations agenda owing to the political evolution of certain regions and the more general rethinking of the role of regions within the EU. However, proposals to enhance the role of regional governments within Spain were still in the air as the twenty-first century began.[3] Developments of this kind had been hinted at from 1993, with the PSOE and the PP successively depending on Catalan nationalist support for their parliamentary majorities in Madrid. The incomplete transfer of powers under the existing (1979) Catalan autonomy statute, together with broad satisfaction over the central government's European and economic policies, for a while gave rise to easy political trading between Madrid and Barcelona. None the less, the European initiatives of regional governments proliferated rapidly during the 1990s, on occasions implicitly challenging the central government's constitutional monopoly on foreign policy. As the decade drew to an end, Catalan nationalists were calling for a re-reading of the existing constitution while their Basque counterparts were seeking to raise the issue of 'sovereignty' much more directly. The present volume does not seek to downplay these trends and developments, but inevitably reflects the fact that their outcome remains unsure at the time of writing, notwithstanding the PP's outright victory in the election of March 2000.[4] Only from the vantage point of the future will one be able to assess their significance with any degree of certainty.

This introduction has suggested a range of questions pertinent to the study of Spain's European and international relations as these have evolved since the early 1990s. These questions, it has been argued, derived from the interaction of the specific characteristics of the historical trajectory of Spain's external relations with new developments at the global, European and domestic levels. It is this analytical framework that informs the contributions that follow, examining the main thematic issues constituting Spain's international and European challenges.

NOTES

1. Still less does the present volume seek to compare this *fin de siècle* and previous ones, for which see the volume of essays edited by Raymond Carr [1999].
2. Under the Socialist governments, Spain managed to achieve good relations simultaneously with both France and Germany, perceived in Madrid as forming a 'strategic axis' of the EU. Under the PP, relations with France continued to strengthen and co-operation grew in several areas of mutual interest, including counter-terrorism; however, relations with Germany became more difficult, not least owing to tension over German efforts to shift European aid from the poorer southern European member states to the eastern European countries that were being prepared for membership. Only towards the end of Aznar's first term as prime minister were there signs of a relaunching of Hispano-German relations, facilitated by a new German interest in the Mediterranean. Meanwhile, recurrent tensions over Gibraltar notwithstanding, Aznar's government also began to work with the UK in an attempt to exert joint influence over EU decision-making in areas such as employment policy. Elsewhere in the world, the main impact of the change of government upon international relations was a sudden chilling of Spain's relations with Cuba, which led to normal diplomatic relations being suspended from 1996 to 1998. On the evolution of Spain's key bilateral relationships in the 1990s, see especially Barbé [1999] and CIDOB [1990-2000].
3. Proposals to move Spain further in the direction towards federalism appeared in the joint programme agreed by the PSOE and the United Left for the general election in March 2000.
4. Regionally-based nationalist parties continued to increase their parliamentary presence as a result of this eighth post-Franco general election, but their leverage *vis-à-vis* the Spanish government suffered a reversal, owing to the PP winning an absolute majority of the seats in both houses of the Cortes.

REFERENCES

Allen, D. (1996): 'Conclusions: The European Rescue of National Foreign Policy?', in C. Hill [1996].

Alonso Zaldívar, C. and M. Castells (eds.) (1992): *España, fin de siglo*, Madrid: Alianza.

Balfour, S. and P. Preston (eds.) (1999): *Spain and the Great Powers in the Twentieth Century*, London: Routledge.

Barbé, E. (1999): *La política europea de España*, Barcelona: Ariel.

Bastarreche, C., Cordero, G., Cobo R. and J.V. Bellver (1999): *España y la agenda 2000*, Madrid: Cuadernos del CERI, 3–4.

Calduch, R. (ed.) (1994): *La política exterior española en el siglo XX*, Madrid: Ediciones Ciencias Sociales.

Cameron, F. (1998): 'Building a Common Foreign Policy: Do Institutions Matter?', in J. Peterson and H. Sjursen (eds.), *A Common Foreign Policy for Europe? Competing Visions of the CFSP*, London: Routledge.

Carr, R. (ed.) (1999): *Visiones de fin de siglo*, Madrid, Taurus.

CIDOB (1990–2000): *Anuario Internacional CIDOB*, Barcelona: Centre d'Informació i Documentació Internacionals a Barcelona (yearbook).

Edwards, G. and S. Nuttall (1994): 'Common Foreign and Security Policy', in A. Duff, J. Pinder and R. Pryce (eds.), *Maastricht and Beyond: Building the European Union*, London: Routledge.

Gaviria, M. (1996): *La séptima potencia: España en el mundo*, Barcelona: Ediciones B.

Gillespie, R., F. Rodrigo and J. Story (eds.) (1995): *Democratic Spain: Reshaping External Relations in a Changing World*, London: Routledge.

Ginsberg, R. (1997): *Foreign Policy Actions of the European Community*, Boulder, CO: Lynne Rienner.

Gordon, P. (1997): 'Europe's Uncommon Foreign Policy', *International Security* 22/3, pp.74–100.

Heywood, P. (1995): *The Politics and Government of Spain*, London: Routledge.

Hill, C. (ed.) (1996): *The Actors in Europe's Foreign Policy*, London: Routledge.

Hill, C. and W. Wallace (1996): 'Introduction: Actors and Actions', in Hill [1996].

Moravscik, A. (1993): 'Preferences and Power in the European Community: A Liberal Intergovernmentalist Approach', *Journal of Common Market Studies* 31/4, pp.473–524.

Ortega, A. (1995): 'Spain in the Post-Cold War World', in Gillespie *et al.* [1995].

Pollack, B. and G. Hunter (1987): *The Paradox of Spanish Foreign Policy: Spain's International Relations from Franco to Democracy*, London: Pinter.

Regelsberger, E. and W. Wessels (1996): 'The CFSP Institutions and Procedures: A Third Way for the Second Pillar?', *European Foreign Affairs Review* 1/1, pp.29– 54.

Smyth, D. (1999): 'Franco and the Allies in the Second World War', in Balfour and Preston [1999].

Tusell, J., Lamo de Espinosa, E. and R. Pardo (eds.) (1996): *Entre dos siglos: Reflexiones sobre la democracia española*, Madrid: Alianza.

Viñas, A. (1999): 'Breaking the Shackles from the Past: Spanish Foreign Policy from Franco to Felipe González', in Balfour and Preston [1999].

Youngs, R. (1999): 'The Domestic Politics of Spanish European Economic Policy 1986–94', *Southern European Society and Politics* 4/1, pp.48-70.

Spain and Europe

The Spanish Economy: From the Single Market to EMU

KEITH SALMON

Between the establishment of the Single Market in 1993 and the end of the first year of EMU membership in 1999, the Spanish economy emerged from one of the deepest recessions in the European Union to become one of the fastest growing economies. Technological change, further liberalization and globalization drove economic restructuring. Deeper European integration and further regional devolution blurred the role of the state in managing the economy. Inside the domestic economy, the trend continued towards an increasing dependence on services. Economic development, as in the past, was geographically uneven. New mega-corporations emerged as powerful poles of economic and political power. A new dynamic from within society became more visible, that of shrinking birth rates and demographic ageing. Externally, there was a surge in foreign direct investment in Latin America, creating an architecture of globalization that was asymmetric: focused on the European Union and a new Iberian cultural realm embracing the Iberian peninsula and Latin America. In this 'new economy' with permeable boundaries, domestic economic development and foreign policy were inextricably linked.

During the last decade of the twentieth century, Spain became more deeply embedded in the dynamic network of flows and relationships that constituted the European Union and, beyond that, the global economy. Globalization was accompanied by further changes in the regulatory environment, notably liberalization, and by technological developments that were beginning to revolutionize economic activity. At the beginning of the twenty-first century the boundaries of the Spanish economy were dissolving, merging foreign policy with domestic economic management.

This discussion documents key features in the development of the Spanish economy during the last decade of the twentieth century, spanning the period from the formal establishment of the European Single Market to the end of the first year of Spain's membership of Economic and Monetary Union (EMU) at the beginning of the twenty-first century. It seeks to set this development against the background of the changing economic environment and thus illustrate something of the economic context of Spanish foreign policy challenges.

The discussion first traces the pattern of economic growth through an upward swing in the economic cycle. It then looks inside the domestic economy, identifying key characteristics at the beginning of the twenty-first century: the industrial structure, diversity, the formation of major Spanish-controlled companies, the growth of new poles of economic power and business governance. The analysis also emphasizes the importance of demographic factors, especially their impact on the labour market and the provision of social services. Then the external economic relations of the economy are considered, in particular the position of Spain in the process of globalization, thereby illustrating the asymmetry around the European Union and Latin America. The discussion concludes with a review of economic policy and the regulatory environment.

Evolution of the Economy

Growth slowed in the early 1990s before giving way to recession in 1993. Signs of growth began to reappear in 1994, building into accelerating growth in the late 1990s (see Figure 1). The pattern looked like part of a classic economic cycle with growth previously having accelerated out of the recession of the early 1980s into the boom of the late 1980s [García Delgado, 1999b; Lieberman, 1995]. As in the 1980s, recession was broken by an export-led recovery (preceded by devaluation of the currency) followed by the expansion of domestic demand. As in the previous boom, the one at the end of the 1990s was beginning to show signs of imbalances, notably in inflation and on the current account of the balance of payments, only this time monetary policy and devaluation were not available to rectify the situation. Yet there were also prospects of an extended period of sustained growth [OECD, 2000a].

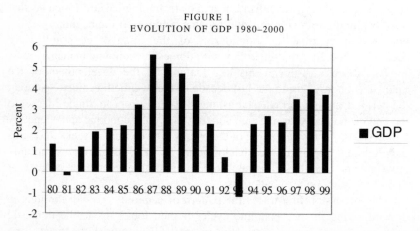

FIGURE 1
EVOLUTION OF GDP 1980–2000

Source: Based on Banco de España [1999b].

With the exception of 1993, when the economy contracted, from 1994 to the end of 1999 the economy grew at an average annual rate of above three per cent. This was above the European Union average, enabling Spain to achieve further real convergence. By the turn of the century the gap in Gross Domestic Product (GDP) per capita, measured in purchasing power parities, had been narrowed to some 18 percentage points of the EU average.[1]

Recession and Economic Crisis, 1992–94

Economic growth decelerated sharply through 1991. The economy then plunged into recession in mid-1992, roughly at the same time as the rest of OECD Europe. In 1993 GDP fell by over one per cent, the sharpest decline in 30 years. It was a hard landing from the earlier economic boom, which had been prolonged by high levels of public spending.

In the domestic market demand was finally punctured by high interest rates and growing debt servicing costs. Government consumption and investment also fell sharply following the completion by mid-1992 of infrastructure projects associated with the Barcelona Olympic Games and the Seville International Exhibition, and in recognition of the difficulties of financing the rising government deficit [OECD, 1993]. Falling external demand added to the overall picture of slowing demand. A vicious circle of contraction had been triggered. Moreover, there was a decline in the net inflow of foreign investment as multinational companies moved to improve cash flows by reducing inward investment and increasing disinvestment. The bleak picture was compounded by concerns over the ramifications of the Maastricht Treaty.

Contraction was most visible in the labour market. Employment started to decline in the second half of 1991, reinforced by the steep long-term decline in the number of farm workers. Job losses exceeded all previous records, with the shake-out particularly strong in the second half of 1992. Following the net creation of two million jobs between mid-1985 and mid-1991, employment contracted by one million net jobs during the 1992–93 recession [OECD, 1996]. The decline in employment coupled with continued growth in the labour force led to a sharp rise in unemployment. After falling to 16 per cent in mid-1991 (the lowest level since 1982), the unemployment rate climbed to almost 24 per cent by the end of 1993. Youth unemployment (among those aged 16-24) soared to around 50 per cent. Nevertheless, wage pressure remained strong.

Against this background, and in the context of more liberal capital markets, turbulence broke out in European foreign exchange markets. Membership of the Exchange Rate Mechanism (ERM) committed member states to exchange rates fixed within defined fluctuation bands. In September 1992 speculative capital movements forced the pound sterling and the Italian lira out of the ERM. The peseta was devalued by five per cent against the Ecu and then devalued again by six per cent in late November 1992. The peseta was devalued again in May 1993, this time by eight per cent [Salmon, 1995a]. By August 1993, continued speculative pressure on European currencies forced a revision of the whole ERM with wide bands of fluctuation being set for all member currencies.

Economic Recovery and the Late 1990s Boom, 1994–99

Economic growth returned in 1994. After pausing at two to three per cent between 1994 and 1996, growth accelerated to between 3.5 and 4.0 per cent in the last three years of the century. This performance led the OECD to state that 'Spain is achieving its finest economic performance since the late 1980s. Growth is strong and broadly based, job creation rapid, inflation low, and the current account broadly in balance' [OECD, 1998a: 1; 2000a: 19] and that 'Spain's economic performance has been impressive'.

Devaluation gave Spanish exports a competitive advantage and laid the foundations for another export-led recovery. Subsequently, growth was driven by domestic demand as the external sector faltered in the face of slow growth in many European economies, the economic crisis in South-East Asia and the reverberations of this crisis around the world.

Domestic demand was initially led by a strong upswing in private sector investment as business profits grew. Investment levels remained high throughout the late 1990s, marked by record levels of construction activity. Domestic consumption, initially held back by uncertainty over the employment market, interest rates and inflation, picked up steam as confidence recovered in 1996. In the following years, consumption grew to become the main engine of growth, lubricated by rapidly falling interest rates (from nine per cent in January 1996 to 2.5 per cent in April 1999), inflation (falling to virtually zero at the beginning of 1999, helped by a collapse in oil prices and weak raw material prices) and unemployment (from nearly 25 per cent in 1994 to 15 per cent at the end of 1999), and rising employment (from the last quarter of 1994) and disposable incomes. Another virtuous circle of growth had been established, reinforced at the turn of the century by stronger growth in Europe and the world economy, and threatened primarily by rising inflation and any collapse in the remarkable United States economy.

The lack of serious economic imbalances at the end of the 1990s led economic commentators to speculate about the possibility of a 'new economy' in which growth was sustainable. The arguments were derived from observations of the United States where the economy continued to record high growth with low inflation and low unemployment (but very high private sector debt and an enormous current account deficit [Economist, 2000a: 22–24].

There was no doubt that the structure of the Spanish economy had changed and that there was a different economic environment. The currency was fixed within the euro-zone. Interest rates were determined by the European Central Bank (ECB). The labour market was more flexible. There had been important shifts in the locus of economic decision-making and control. Business costs had been reduced by continued improvements in infrastructure. The whole economy was more deeply embedded in the world economy and it was suggested that the economic cycle in Spain had become more closely synchronized with that of the other major economies in the European Union (especially those of France and Italy) [Ortega, 1999]. Moreover, the whole economy was experiencing rapid technological change and arguably a technological revolution based on information and communication technologies [Castells, 1996; Leadbeater, 1999].

Inside the Domestic Economy

Structures in the domestic economy evolved with changes in the economic environment. These structures were also deeply embedded in the cultural fabric. They were at once a contributor to cultural change and a result of that change [Crang, 1997]. This section highlights some of the 'new' elements in the domestic economy and looks specifically at two aspects of the cultural fabric associated with business governance and demographics.[2]

A Service Economy

As in other OECD economies, the shift of employment towards the service sector and away from manufacturing industry and the primary sector continued. Whereas in 1990 only some 63 per cent of the occupied population were in services and construction, by 1999 the proportion had risen to almost 75 per cent [INE, 1999a]. Given that a large part of the black economy operated in services and construction, the proportion of the population occupied in this area almost certainly exceeded three-quarters of the total. In contrast, the proportion occupied in agriculture, forestry and fishing dwindled over the same period from almost 13 to around seven per cent. In industry (including mining) the proportion declined from about 24 to 20 per cent. Where the service sector was weak was in the large number of jobs in 'traditional' services and in the provision of enough skilled full-time employment to match the aspirations of those emerging from the education system [Cuadrado Roura, 1999a; 1999b].

Traditional heavy manufacturing industries, such as iron and steel, shipbuilding and heavy engineering, continued their path of long term decline but there remained a substantial volume of employment in other traditional industries such as ceramics, food and drink, leather goods, shoes, textiles and clothing, toys and wood products. Throughout Spain small family-owned manufacturing businesses persisted. These appeared to remain competitive through informal flexible work practices, local agglomeration economies and brand loyalty, as well as through increased capital intensification. Spain also attracted inward investment in more modern industries, especially in motor-vehicles. Where the industrial structure remained weak was in Spanish-owned high technology manufacturing industry and in research and development [Molero and Buesa, 1998a, 1998b].

Agriculture, forestry and fishing continued to contract in both employment and in their contribution to GDP to levels more similar to those of Spain's northern European neighbours. Reforms in the Common Agricultural Policy (CAP) were slowly exposing agriculture to further competition, forcing further job losses, the use of contract labour and immigrant labour, and increased specialization around the fruit and vegetable sector [Colino, 1996]. For horticulture to continue to develop, solutions would have to be found to water supply problems. The large fishing fleet in Spain was also facing further decline as the European Union and other fishery organizations struggled to maintain fish stocks. As fewer people depended on these primary activities their significance in national economic policy diminished.

A Diverse Economy

Economic development was uneven, proceeding further and faster in some sectors and geographical areas of the economy than in others [Paralleda, 1999]. Great spatial contrasts continued to exist in per capita incomes, access to employment opportunities, patterns of economic activity and provision of infrastructure. According to the Banco Bilbao Vizcaya, GDP per capita in 1998 varied from 126 per cent of the European Union average in the Balearic Islands to 59 per cent in Andalucía [BBV, 1999]. The Balearic Islands, the Mediterranean arc from the French frontier to the Straits of Gibraltar, the Ebro valley and the north-east quadrant of Spain, including Madrid, registered GDP per capita above the European Union average. In contrast, the north, north-west, the south and the centre (outside Madrid) recorded GDP per capita below the European Union average. Such diversity meant that economic policies and processes would have a differential impact across Spain and thus generate different regional responses [Villaverde, 1999].

Formation of Large Spanish-controlled Companies (National Champions)

Out of the processes of industrial restructuring at the end of the twentieth century, a number of major Spanish-controlled business groups emerged to dominate the domestic business scene and raise the profile of Spanish companies on the world stage [Durán, 1999]. This was part of a general process of business concentration in which ever larger corporations were being formed (although atomization remained the distinguishing characteristic of business, with over 90 per cent of an estimated 2.5 million businesses employing less than six people [Consejo Superior de Cámaras, 2000]).

One of the objectives of the governments of both the Socialist Party (PSOE) and the People's Party (PP) was to ensure the formation of large Spanish-controlled companies able to remain independent and to compete in international markets. This was achieved through encouraging Spanish companies to merge and—during the privatization process—through the reorganization of companies prior to their sale, selection of companies in trade sales and specific privatization strategies and legal arrangements such as the formation of stable shareholder groups (*núcleos duros*) and the use of the 'golden share' (*acción de oro*). Examples of these companies include the three leading financial groups – Banco Bilbao Vizcaya Argentaria (BBVA), Banco Santander Central Hispano (BSCH) and La Caixa – , the electricity utility Endesa, the oil and gas group Repsol-YPF and the hotel group Sol-Meliá. The telecoms group Telefónica deserves special mention because of its sheer size in the domestic economy. In February 2000 companies in this group constituted over one-third of the stock market capitalization of the blue chip index, the Ibex 35, with the prospect of this proportion rising to over 50 per cent before the end of the year.

New Poles of Economic and Political Power

The growth of giant transnational corporations implied an increased concentration of power in their hands, challenging the power of state, regional and local governments [Dicken, 1992, 1998]. In relation to Spanish companies, the major financial groups not only grew in size but extended their influence far beyond financial markets into energy, telecoms, the media, urban and environmental services, construction, real estate and transport. They partly replaced the government in the process of orchestrating industrial restructuring.

Yet, in an increasingly open global economy, even large companies remained vulnerable to acquisition. Moreover, as companies became more truly transnational, activities associated with proximity to the headquarters, and even the operational headquarters themselves, could be shifted away from the national base. Nation states were faced with more fluid business loyalties and even threats to their tax base [*Economist, 2000b*].

Business Governance

One aspect of business closely associated with the cultural fabric related to business governance. Traditionally business practice was idiosyncratic and marked by a lack of transparency, of independent advisors, and generally of any person to counterbalance the power of the executive president, while jobs were frequently given to friends or were political appointments. This situation arose partly from the extent of family ownership and the lack of public capital. The hostile takeover was almost unknown.

Many companies continued to operate under the tutelage of banks, as was common practice elsewhere in continental Europe. This practice was extended by the creation of stable groups of shareholders in privatized companies. Arguably, this provided more stable long-term finance and some insulation from the 'short-termism' of financial markets. But as with the government's practice of retaining a golden share in 'strategic' privatized companies, it cushioned these companies from market forces and therefore ran counter to the general trend towards liberalization.

Business relations in the 1990s were further complicated by numerous strategic alliances, cross-shareholdings, and interests and pacts between business owners. Complex interrelationships were exacerbated as companies diversified and their interests converged around the exploitation of similar technologies and synergies from the exploitation of physical infrastructure and customer databases. This created paradoxes in which companies had common interests in some areas and yet competed in others [Noceda and Rivera, 1999]. The shifting sands of acquisitions, mergers and alliances further complicated a business scene where competition could be frustrated.

Many of these business practices ran counter to the trend towards more transparent governance recommended in a series of influential reports during the 1990s [Cadbury Report, 1992; Greenbury Report, 1995; Hampel Report, 1998]. Even among businesses quoted on the Stock Market, there was only partial compliance with the recommendations on good business governance made in the Olivencia Report commissioned by the Madrid Stock Market Council [CNMV, 1998; Gómez, 2000]. In the non-quoted sector, traditional practices lingered on and remained common.

Demographics and the Economy

Cultural change was intertwined with economic change. This was expressed particularly strongly in changing demographics and their consequences for the labour market and other aspects of the economy, particularly the provision of social services. From the mid-1970s to the beginning of the twenty-first century, fertility rates plummeted from being among the highest in Europe to being among the lowest in the world. The average number of children born to women of reproductive age fell from 2.89 to 1.07 [INE, 1999b]. In 1974 there were 698,711 births, in 1986 438,750, in 1992 about 400,000 and in 1998 only 361,930 [INE, 1999c].

Population growth ground to a halt, at just below 40 million, raising the possibility of future population decline and drastically modifying the population structure. By the beginning of the twenty-first century the population bulge had passed into the population of working age and there were substantially smaller numbers of children. The process of demographic ageing was firmly established but provision for the elderly, especially in terms of retirement pensions, gained temporary relief from the relatively small numbers of people reaching retirement age as a consequence of low birth rates in the 1930s and 1940s.

The impact of demographic change on the labour force was that throughout the 1980s and 1990s the population of working age increased substantially, swelling the potential population looking for employment (the economically active population). In 1986 the national population survey [*Padrón*, 1986] recorded a total population of 38,473,332, in 1996 the survey recorded 39,669,392 [*Padrón*, 1996]. In contrast to this population increase of almost 1.2 million (three per cent), the population of working age rose by around two million from 24.5 to 26.5 million (an increase of eight per cent).

The growth of the economically active population was driven also by significant cultural changes, which included the changing role of women in society. Throughout the 1980s and 1990s an increasing proportion of women of working age sought employment. By the beginning of the twenty-first century there were more women than men enrolled on degree programmes in Spain and female economic activity rates among young people were probably only lower than those for males because of the disincentive constituted by continuing high female youth unemployment. Feminization of the labour force was well established.

Exceptionally high unemployment characterized the final two decades of the twentieth century. According to the official survey figures (*Encuesta de la Población Activa*), unemployment stood at over 21 per cent in 1986; it then fell in the late 1980s to a minimum of around 16 per cent, only to rebound to 25 per cent in 1994. From 1994 unemployment declined to 15 per cent at the turn of the century. The reasons for high unemployment (whatever the real figures might have been, and they were almost certainly several percentage points below the figures quoted) lay in the labour supply factors outlined above and in substantial structural change, including the continuous decline of employment in the primary sectors of agriculture, fishing, forestry and mining, in the contraction of traditional manufacturing industries and in a general shake-out of employment as businesses were exposed to competition [OECD, 1996].

At the beginning of the twenty-first century the labour market picture was changing. Although the general economic activity rate had some way to rise to bring it into line with other EU member states, the labour supply pressure on employment was falling. In the first decade of the century, unemployment will remain an important issue, especially among the young, the unskilled, among women, in the less affluent districts of urban areas and across the South, but it will be increasingly tinged with cases of labour shortages. These shortages could be filled in part by immigrant labour, which is likely to become a more serious political issue [Kennedy, 1993; King and Black, 1997; OECD, 2000b].

Flexibility in the labour market increased as a result of new labour legislation and the decline of traditional industries with their accompanying traditional working practices. A dual employment market of indefinite and fixed duration contracts emerged following labour market reforms in the mid-1980s. Since that time people working on fixed-term contracts came to represent over one-third of those in employment, the highest proportion in OECD Europe. The proportion was even higher among the young, women and the unskilled. If those employed in the black economy were added, then around half those in employment were working under very flexible arrangements at the beginning of the twenty-first century. The other half of the labour force continued working within a more rigid labour market framework. Although successive reforms during the 1990s (especially those agreed in 1997) sought to increase the flexibility of indefinite duration contracts and reduce the coverage of sectoral collective wage agreements, there was still some distance to go before this was achieved.

Greater flexibility in the labour market had long been espoused by international institutions, including the OECD, as a means of achieving more rapid job creation and enabling businesses to adjust more quickly in times of economic contraction [OECD, 1998a; 2000a]. But it also implied more rapid job destruction in periods of economic contraction, greater employment uncertainty and greater geographical mobility of labour, which would be reflected in social change and consumer behaviour.

The changing structure of the population also had critical implications for the provision of social services. An ageing population would place increasing strains on the health service and require a much larger provision for pensions, while some resources for the young would become redundant. Simultaneously, neo-liberalism implied a retreat from the welfare state, the emblematic feature of the post-Second World War model of development in Europe and a fundamental feature of the evolution of the Spanish economy in the 1980s.

Like many other EU countries, Spain operated a pension system in which the contributions of those currently in employment paid the pension bill: a 'pay-as-you-go' system. With a shrinking population of working age and an economic philosophy that implied lower income taxes and no overall increase in tax pressure, continued state provision of social services and pensions was coming under greater scrutiny. Reforms implemented under the *Pacto de Toledo* (1996), together with those contemplated in the budget for the year 2000, recognized the concerns over the long-term viability of the pension system. Nevertheless a serious problem of resourcing hung over the system in the twenty-first century [Angel Rojo, quoted by Casamayor, 1999; OECD 1998a; 2000a].

As in other European countries, new mechanisms will have to be found to guarantee people support into old age and to provide social services. This will probably involve increased private provision. Whatever system is chosen will prove the focus of intense debate.

Integration into Europe and the Global Economy

Throughout the 1990s the Spanish economy became more deeply integrated into Europe and the global economy [Antonio Alonso and Doñoso, 1999]. Integration was marked by quantitative changes, such as increasing international flows of trade, capital, information and people. But more especially it was marked by qualitative changes characterized by a deeper form of integration labelled as globalization. This process was made possible by the growth of information and communication technologies, which compressed time and space [Harvey, 1989], and by the progressive liberalization of markets. In addition, the market economy spread to embrace a larger proportion of the world economy. More open markets blurred the boundaries between local, regional, national and supranational markets and increased exposure to the 'creative winds of destruction' of capitalism [Schumpeter, 1943].

Globalization embraced the opening of markets and the continued restructuring of companies. Ever larger companies emerged. Value-added chains and marketing were organized on an increasingly global scale and the ownership of companies passed to people and organizations, in many countries transforming national and multinational corporations into transnationals [Dicken, 1998]. Supranational economic systems demanded supranational governmental institutions and a reconsideration of the roles of existing institutions such as the World Bank, the International Monetary Fund and the World Trade Organization. Simultaneously, both transnational corporations and supranational institutions were increasingly seen to challenge the autonomy and authority of nation states. Few of these changes were entirely new, but together they contributed to a qualitative change in the economic environment.

Integration implied a domestic economy more open to Europe and the world; a more permeable state. External growth impulses and external shocks could be more rapidly transmitted to the domestic economy. Thus the economic crises in South-East Asia in 1997 rapidly spread throughout that region and thence to Latin America. The effects of these external problems reverberated throughout European economies, including Spain, in 1998 and 1999. The fact that Europe was not affected more adversely reflected the extent to which it had become a sub-system within the global economy, plus the continued economic strength of the United States.

Although Spain was enveloped in the processes of globalization, the geography of this process was asymmetric. Globalization was Euro-centric and skewed towards a growing business involvement in Latin America. An Iberian–South Atlantic axis in the global economy was formed.

Integration into a Changing Europe

The dominant dimension of external integration was into the European Union, signified by accession to the European Community in 1986 and the adoption of the Single Market Act in the same year, leading to the formal establishment of a 'Single European Market' from 1 January 1993 [Martín, 1997; Tovias, 1995]. A further step towards integration was taken with the signing of the Maastricht Treaty in December 1991, committing Spain to the convergence criteria in the Treaty. Arguably, membership of the European Monetary Union from 1 January 1999 completed the 'European project', aimed at taking Spain to the heart of Europe. However, the European Union was evolving with changes in the *acquis communautaire* (regulatory regimes) and eastward enlargement.

An important element of integration was that into the network of European Union budgetary transfers. Throughout the period from Spain's accession to the EU to the end of the twentieth century, Spain was a net beneficiary of these transfers. Generally, reforms worked in its favour: for example, the shift towards a larger proportion of EU budget income being derived directly from member states in proportion to their GNP, the increased proportion of budget spending allocated to the Structural Funds (Spain receiving over a quarter of this funding) following the Edinburgh summit in 1992 and the adoption of the Delors II package, and the adoption of the Cohesion Fund for those countries with per capita incomes (measured in purchasing power parities) of less than 90 per cent of the EU average. The 1999 EU budget was the last one covered by the Edinburgh financial perspective, marking the end of the Delors II package and the transition to Agenda 2000. In that year structural operations accounted for some 40 per cent of all EU expenditure and the CAP (Guarantee section) some 42 per cent [European Commission, 1999].

From the moment of accession, payments from the EU contributed towards subsidizing agricultural production, replacing the previous national system of protection. By the late 1990s it was estimated that one-quarter of declared agricultural incomes in Spain arose from EU transfers, figures which rose to half in the case of olives, linseed, sunflowers and tobacco [Maté, 1999]. The principal sector mainly outside the framework of protection was fruit and vegetables.

Similarly, Structural Fund transfers became an established component of regional development, contributing to a transformation in infrastructure provision and channelling development along the lines set by the Structural Fund criteria. Objective 1 regions (those with per capita incomes measured in purchasing power parities of less than 75 per cent of the EU average) were the greatest beneficiaries (Andalucía, Asturias, Canarias, Cantabria, Castilla-La Mancha, Castilla y León, Extremadura, Galicia, Murcia, the Comunidad Valenciana, Ceuta and Melilla).

Between 1994 and 1999, Structural Fund transfers to Spain (including the Cohesion Funds) amounted to an annual average of Euro 7.7 billion, or roughly 1.6 per cent of Spain's GDP. Agricultural transfers were equivalent to between 1.0 and 1.3 per cent of GDP (France being the largest beneficiary). While Structural Fund transfers represented a redistribution of income from more wealthy to less prosperous regions, agricultural price-support payments benefited most those farmers with the largest volumes of subsidized production.

The Agenda 2000 financial perspective (agreed at the Berlin Conference in March 1999) established the budgetary framework for the period 2000 to 2006. It was agreed to fix a financial ceiling on the EU budget of 1.27 per cent of EU GDP. As a proportion of total expenditure, agriculture was to remain at roughly its 1999 levels, while the Structural Funds would contract slightly to allow for spending under new headings. Reform of the CAP continued to make only slow progress with price support levels being lowered and funding moving towards direct support for farm incomes. Despite powerful criticisms, the CAP had survived into the twenty-first century [Swinbank, 1999].

For existing member states, including Spain, funding until the end of 2006 was secure (although Cantabria lost its Objective 1 status for this period, qualifying instead for transitional funding). Beyond 2006, with EU enlargement, Spain was likely to lose its access to the Cohesion Funds as its per capita income (measured in purchasing power parities) would rise above the threshold of 90 per cent of the EU average. Further allocations under the Structural Funds and agricultural operations would depend on the process of enlargement and the nature of the political economy in Europe in the lead-in to the next funding period. What was certain was that the present funding arrangements and levels of allocation to Spain could not continue in a greatly enlarged European Union.

Trade Creation

As in other OECD economies, the growth of Spain's international trade in the 1990s was faster than national economic growth, reflecting a more open trading economy. By 1992 the Spanish economy had already opened up significantly in merchandise trade and services [Salmon, 1995a]. As a percentage of GDP, exports and imports of goods and services rose from 38 per cent in 1990 to 48 per cent in 1995 and to over 55 per cent by the end of the century [Banco de España, 1999b], bringing Spain broadly into line with other EU economies. Spain's trade also grew faster than the world average, rising to two per cent of world trade.

Structural Concentration of Trade

Although the growth of merchandise exports was commendable, about one-quarter of exports arose from the motor-vehicle sector and thus from a small number of foreign multinational companies. In 1999 some 80 per cent of all motor-vehicle production in Spain was exported. Exports of services were even more heavily reliant on a single sector, tourism, which contributed more than 60 per cent of all income from service exports in the 1990s. The large annual surplus on the travel and tourism account contrasted with the annual deficits recorded on the rest of the service account and helped to offset the annual deficits in merchandise trade.

Throughout the 1990s a number of factors contributed to buoyant inbound tourism, which saw the number of foreign visitors increase from 55 million in 1992 to 74 million in 1999. According to the World Tourism Organization, in 1999 Spain was the world's second destination ranked by number of tourists (52 million) and by tourism income (Pta.5,000 billion) [WTO, 2000]. Apart from devaluation of the currency, instability in other areas around the Mediterranean helped divert tourists to Spain. Although a considerable effort went into diversification of the tourism product in Spain, the prospect that remained was that greater political stability elsewhere in the Mediterranean might in the near future result in a slowing down of further growth.

On the import side, the main weakness remained the high dependence on imported energy, with almost all oil and gas being imported. As the domestic coal mining industry contracted, imports of coal were likely to rise. Of most concern was the future of nuclear energy. At the beginning of the twenty-first century, this contributed one-third of domestic electricity production. With no further nuclear power stations planned, the energy from existing nuclear power stations would have to be replaced. Although substantial progress had been made in developing renewable energy sources, reliance on imported energy was set to increase.

Spatial Concentration of Trade

Trade creation in the 1990s was accompanied by the concentration of trade on the European Union. Trade became concentrated on this region in the late 1980s and had already reached about three-quarters of exports and two-thirds of imports (closer to three-quarters of non-oil imports) by the early 1990s [Salmon, 1995a]. It then remained at around this level throughout the rest of the decade [IMF, 1999]. The dominant trading partners were France, Germany, Italy and Britain, which together accounted for over half of all merchandise exports and imports. If tourism trade was added, then the concentration on the European Union was even greater. Over 90 per cent of all visitors came from other EU member states.

Outside of the European Union, trade with other parts of the world remained relatively small. Only around five per cent of exports and imports were with Latin America and a similarly low proportion with the United States and with South-East Asia. In Latin America, the main trading partners were Argentina, Brazil and Mexico. In South-East Asia the main trading partner was Japan. In Africa, excluding the important oil trade with Algeria and Nigeria, the dominant trading partner through the 1990s was Morocco, accounting for over one-quarter of all Spanish merchandise exports to African countries [IMF, 1999].

Integration of Iberian Economies

Trade integration within the Iberian Peninsula, forming part of a wider process of economic integration between Spain and Portugal, is also worth noting [Corkill, 1999]. Trade with Portugal grew strongly following the accession of both countries to the European Union in 1986. By 1999 Portugal accounted for over nine per cent of all Spanish merchandise exports and around three per cent of imports. In travel and tourism, Portugal was the second largest source of visitors after France. For Portugal, trade relations with Spain were considerably more important. In 1990 around 15 per cent of exports and imports were with Spain. In 1998 while roughly the same proportion of exports went to Spain, imports from Spain had risen to almost one-quarter [IMF, 1999].

Integration through Capital Transactions

Although growth in trade was the most visible feature of the opening of the economy, integration was more far reaching in relation to capital transactions [Salmon, 1995a, 1995b]. What distinguished these flows from those of trade was that they involved the transfer of ownership and control over assets and thus a shift in the locus of economic power in the economy.

Portfolio Investment and Speculative Capital Movements

Portfolio investment became the largest item of outward foreign investment in the late 1990s [Banco de España, 1999a; ICE 1999b]. Initially swamped by inward flows, the volume of Spanish outward portfolio investment (especially in bonds and other corporate and government debt) grew sharply in the late 1990s to exceed inward flows in 1997 and 1998 [Banco de España, 1999a]. Outward flows were driven by investments by insurance companies, pension funds and mutual funds as savings were switched out of bank deposits [ibid.: 66] and in response to the limited market in these investment vehicles in Spain. The majority of portfolio investment both into and out of Spain was with the European Union (in 1998, 80 per cent) [ibid.: 67]. A much closer link was thus forged between the performance of world stock markets (especially those in Europe and New York) and the Spanish economy.

Foreign Direct Investment

At a global level there was a strong expansion of foreign direct investment (FDI) in the 1990s, with the total value of flows setting new records in each consecutive year from 1997 to 1999 inclusive. Spain occupied a significant position in this process. In terms of cumulative flows involving OECD countries in 1990–98, Spain occupied sixth position with regard to inflows and twelfth position for outflows [OECD, 1999b]. According to the OECD:

> The strong expansion of FDI flows in the 1990s [was] driven by several inter-related factors: rapid technological change, trade and investment liberalisation at a national, regional and global level, privatisation, deregulation, demonopolisation and the switch in emphasis by firms from product to geographical diversification, involving a more balanced   global distribution of production and sales by each company. A large number of stock market listings have also facilitated the sale of domestic companies to foreign investors [OECD, 1999b: 111].

Inward Foreign Direct Investment

Inward FDI escalated following Spain's membership of the European Community in 1986 and the subsequent opening up of capital markets [Salmon, 1995a, 1995b]. Foreign companies, predominantly European ones, scrambled to acquire access to markets in Spain and in some instances to establish export platforms. By 1992 large chunks of Spanish industry, including most of the motor-vehicle industry, had been acquired by foreign capital. Inflows dropped in the mid-1990s as the profits of European businesses were squeezed by a downturn in European markets. Towards the end of the 1990s, inflows increased again as new sectors of the economy were opened-up to foreign capital, especially through privatization. But the magnitude of these inflows did not match the record levels reached at the beginning of the decade.

A large slice of inward investment at the end of the decade was going into strengthening existing investments, thus marking the maturing of the earlier cycle of investment associated with acquisitions in the late 1980s and early 1990s. This pattern of FDI contrasted with the record levels of FDI being recorded generally among OECD countries. Nevertheless, at the beginning of the twenty-first century a large slice of control over businesses in Spain had passed to foreign-based decision makers, mainly elsewhere in Europe or in the United States. This pattern was set to continue as more markets were liberalized, especially in services.

Outward Foreign Direct Investment

The defining feature of foreign direct investment during the 1990s was the sudden expansion of Spanish outward investment at the end of the decade to exceed volumes of inflows in the three years 1997 to 1999 inclusive. Although only ranked twelfth in terms of outflows over the period 1990–98 [OECD, 1999b], in 1999 it was ranked fifth [UNCTAD, 2000]. In the late 1990s, Spain became one of the leading sources of foreign investment to Latin America and the leading investor in 1999 [ECLAC, 2000]. During the late 1990s, Latin America far exceeded the European Union as the dominant destination of Spanish outward foreign direct investment.

Outside of Latin America, the European Union was the other major destination for outward FDI during the early and mid-1990s. After slowing in the mid-1990s, investment into this region picked up momentum towards the end of the decade, reflecting the general growth in that part of FDI associated with merger and acquisition activity, as integration within the region gained a further stimulus from monetary union. In general terms, however, at the end of the 1990s mergers and acquisitions in Europe were being driven 'as much by global industrial logic as by regional integration' [OECD, 1999b: 126]. The most high profile actors in this area were the two major Spanish banks seeking to strengthen their position within the European banking and financial services sector. Further economic integration appeared inevitable, with national interests, as in the example of the bid by the Spanish BSCH group to acquire the Portuguese Champalimaud group, able to divert but not to stop the tide.

Within Europe, investment in Portugal is again worth noting. Although frequently opposed by national interests in Portugal (and for that matter in Spain, where inward investment was concerned), Spain built up significant investments in banking and financial services, telecoms and energy. The main incentive for cross-border investments was the industrial logic of providing goods and services across the peninsular, access to markets and access to cheap labour in Portugal. There was also the added incentive of building bridges to the Brazilian market, the largest in Latin America.

Foreign Direct Investment in Latin America:

The surge in outward foreign investment in the late 1990s reflected the internationalization of Spanish business. It was characterized by a specific concentration on Latin America, which was the leading destination. This region accounted for two-thirds of gross direct investment abroad in 1998 [ICE, 1999] and over three-quarters in 1999 (author estimate).

Substantial investments by Spanish companies in Latin America first emerged in the early 1990s, principally by the leading Spanish private banks and the partly privatized Telefónica. The rush of investment towards the end of the decade embraced continued high investment by the banks and Telefónica, plus major investments by Spanish energy, construction and hotel companies. These investments coincided with changing conditions in both domestic and foreign markets. In Spain outward FDI was stimulated by high levels of corporate profitability, privatization, the prospect of increased competition and relatively slow long-term growth in the domestic market. Simultaneously global markets were being opened up, especially through privatization, providing opportunities for investment and the potential in emerging markets for more rapid long-term growth. Spanish companies, especially the banks and newly privatized companies, opted overwhelmingly for investment in Latin America where the crucial competitive advantage lay in a shared cultural heritage and where – via Mexico – there were opportunities to penetrate the United States market through the North American Free Trade Association (NAFTA). In 1998, on the centenary of Spain's final withdrawal from its colonial empire, Spanish businesses were energetically rebuilding a Spanish cultural realm.

Government Policy and the Regulatory Environment

Underlying the evolution of the Spanish economy were shifts in economic 'ideology' towards an acceptance of a greater role for market forces in allocating resources, coupled with changes in the institutional position of the state. The latter involved joining the European Union and other international organizations, thereby trading some direct control over the economy for indirect control through a voice in these organizations. Further central government autonomy was relinquished through the devolution of power downwards to lower tiers of government. The results of this shift in economic thinking and the changing institutional position of the state were reflected in changes in government policy, the regulatory environment and the way in which the economy was managed.

Neo-liberalism became the dominant ideology of the late twentieth century, championed by the United States, Britain and many international institutions including the World Bank and the Organization for Economic Co-operation and Development (OECD). This reflected the hegemonic position built by the United States through the success of its model of economic growth and its accompanying political and military power. The challenge of communism collapsed, the South-East Asian model appeared fatally flawed and the European model was being reconstructed.

Successive governments in Spain were strongly influenced by these currents in economic thought. The shift towards a neo-liberal approach in managing the economy was evident under the PSOE from the mid-1980s. Following the election to office of the right-of-centre Partido Popular minority government in 1996, there was no radical change of policy, only a strengthening of neo-liberal policies as they were put on a firmer ideological footing.

Membership of supranational organizations redefined the way in which the state managed the economy. No longer was it in an autonomous position over a wide range of decisions [Cerny, 1996; McVeigh, 1999; Strange, 1996]. The state now worked through supranational organizations to influence their decisions, which were then applied to the domestic economy. In relation to the European Union, an enormous volume of legislation was passed, much of it designed to harmonize market conditions and to promote competition, thereby radically changing the business environment in Spain [Martín, 1997]. In addition, economic relations beyond the European Union were shaped by EU economic policy towards non-EU states [Tovias, 1995].

The devolution of government authority from the centre to the regions continued. This too constrained the state's management of the economy and once again required the state to engage in a more consultative process in developing economic policy. It also added an extra dimension to control over public expenditure.

Regional governments were given responsibility for a wide range of activities, including the promotion of their own regional economic development, the development of regional infrastructure, education and health services. They also actively encouraged the merger of local savings banks to create strong regionally-based entities over which they had control. This, and other regional government actions, sometimes appeared to run counter to the central government policy of liberalization. The regions also had direct channels of communication with the European Commission, by-passing the central government.

In contrast to the transfer of these responsibilities for expenditure, income remained tied largely to transfers from the state to meet the cost of providing the services that were transferred. However, there continued to be calls for greater fiscal autonomy and there was already some regional fragmentation of the tax system. Any such development would challenge the principle of regional solidarity.

Macro-economic Policy in the 1990s

During the 1980s economic policy became dominated by measures to achieve European integration [Holman, 1996; Tovias, 1995]. Despite these pressures, PSOE governments held back from radical measures to reform the labour market, fully privatize leading companies or open up the remaining areas of the economy that were still subject to protection. Nevertheless, the gradual adoption of more liberal policies created a growing rift between successive PSOE governments and their socialist roots.

External constraints on economic policy became more explicit following the agreement on the first phase of monetary union reached in Madrid in June 1989 and the simultaneous entry of Spain into the Exchange Rate Mechanism (ERM) of the European Monetary System. In joining the ERM, Spain hoped to gain a monetary discipline inside which inflation could be contained, and a place at the heart of Europe. In return, it became committed to maintaining the exchange rate within the limits fixed by the wide band of the ERM (+/- 6 per cent of its central rate). The Spanish government thereby relinquished its previous autonomy over monetary policy and limited its room for manoeuvre on broader economic policy issues such as economic growth and unemployment [Salmon, 1995a].

The external constraints on economic policy were tightened following the signing of the Maastricht Treaty in December 1991, committing Spain to the convergence criteria in the Treaty. To achieve these criteria, a Convergence Plan was agreed in March 1992 under which macro-economic policy was refocused and structural measures pursued more vigorously. Whereas 'up to 1991 interest rate policy [in Spain] was largely dictated by domestic considerations' [OECD, 1993: 33], in 1992 it became overshadowed by external considerations and the need to keep the peseta in the ERM. External factors were dictating economic policy, especially an economic policy in Germany of maintaining high interest rates in order to contain the inflation generated by German reunification. Because of the limitations placed on monetary policy by the ERM and a failure to reach an incomes policy with the unions (the unsuccessful *Pacto de Competitividad* in 1991), the economic policy emphasis had to be placed on budgetary and fiscal policy. Hence there were tax increases and public expenditure cuts [Salmon, 1995a]. High interest rates and clear indications of a tight budget were required by the capital markets as the price of maintaining the peseta inside the ERM. Concern grew over the contradiction of maintaining high interest rates while the economy entered recession, inflation was falling and unemployment was over 20 per cent and rising [Sebastián, 1992].

The election to government of the Partido Popular in 1996, with support from the Catalan and Basque parties (CiU and PNV), removed the ideological barriers to the introduction of more radical measures to liberalize the economy and reduce public spending. Tight budgetary measures were carried forward, more sweeping structural reforms introduced to increase flexibility in the labour market and liberalize product markets, and the privatization programme accelerated.

In the climate of relatively weak growth, it was possible to relax monetary policy and reduce interest rates to meet the convergence criteria. However, as the economy began to gain strength, the Bank of Spain's dilemma became obvious: it was reducing interest rates in the face of accelerating growth and renewed inflationary pressures simply to meet the Maastricht targets. On 1 January 1999 its dilemma was lifted as responsibility for the setting of interest rates was passed over to the European Central Bank. Inside EMU, interest rates were set according to the inflation position across the member states, dominated by the position in the two largest economies, Germany and France. With inflation very low in these countries, and unemployment high and growth weak in Germany, interest rates remained low throughout 1999. For Spain this meant living with low but rising inflation.

A strengthening economy brought increased government revenues, allowing the government to raise public spending. This fuelled economic growth, which was driven by expanding consumer demand, buoyed-up by income tax reforms in 1998. Despite strong growth and signs of renewed inflation, the budget for the year 2000 was not restrictive. One of the few measures the government still had to manage the economy and control inflation, budgetary and fiscal policy, was neutralized by the approach of a general election.

Liberalization

The dominant theme behind economic policy in the 1990s was liberalization. This implied the removal of all those forms of protection that inhibited the operation of market forces and a withdrawal of the state from direct involvement in the economy. The process proceeded furthest within the European Union under the banner of 'single market' initiatives. Liberalization involved the dismantling of barriers to trade, capital movements, movement of people (inside the European Union) and information, generally opening up product markets to competition. In the labour market, it involved increasing the variety of employment contracts and forms of employment. In business governance, it meant an easing of restraints on business acquisitions and an increase in transparency.

A considerable degree of market liberalization occurred. But a European single market was still incomplete, protection remaining for example in some areas of service provision, with respect to tax harmonization and a single European currency. Problems of access slowed the introduction of real competition in Spain in some sectors, which continued to be dominated by monopoly or oligopoly suppliers. However, where existing market distortions were dismantled by deregulation, the private sector frequently created new anti-competitive structures, thus forcing the government into re-regulation.

Overall, liberalization contributed to a more flexible economy. Looked at from another perspective, it brought increased exposure to volatility in financial markets, challenging the ability of existing systems of economic governance to manage change and threatening the sovereignty of the state. A question mark hung over the extent to which liberalization and the accompanying globalization process would be allowed to proceed, a question mark underlined by the failure of the World Trade Conference in Seattle at the end of 1999.

Privatization

The defining feature of industrial policy during the 1990s was the ambitious programme of privatization initiated by the PSOE and accelerated by the PP [Fanjul and Mañas, 1994; Gámir, 1999]. Although many public enterprises remained, as well as many more at regional and local level, the pace and magnitude of state privatization was greater than in most other countries in the world. Transfer of ownership, embracing some of Spain's largest companies, contributed to a redrawing of the business environment and a further redefinition of the role of the state in the economy [Wright, 1994]. Driving the process was the requirement to reduce public sector debt and deficits (notably to gain entry to EMU), the increasing weight of argument pointing to efficiency gains through privatization, and general pressures coming from the evolving business environment and new regulatory regimes.

Privatization was very much a political process: 'The decision to privatise, what to privatise and how to privatise are driven by political as well as economic considerations' [Parker, 1998: 7]. Each of the political parties built political influence into business through their control over the regulatory authorities, political appointments to head the state holding companies, designation of the chairmen of public enterprises, and their influence in securing their own supporters as the heads of key businesses and business institutions. In making these decisions, and those relating to which companies should be allowed to participate in or acquire companies being sold directly to the private sector, the PP had to take into account the demands of its coalition partners and their regional constituencies.

Renovation of the management of public enterprises under the PP brought government and business closer together. But giving people from employers' organizations key political posts and placing political figures at the heart of businesses resulted in some questionable interlocking of business and political roles [Estefanía, 1996]. With political influence built into business, there was a risk that companies would be used as political instruments and thus dilute business strategy, and that companies would use their political connections to manipulate government policy for their own purposes.

Overall, the process of privatization, and the broader one of liberalization, had fundamental consequences for the structure of business in Spain: launching major private sector companies, creating new poles of economic power, contributing to the internationalization of Spanish companies, providing opportunities for foreign capital to penetrate the Spanish economy and redistributing power between the state and the regions. It also contributed to the creation of a more flexible economy. The government distanced itself from labour markets, easing the passage of labour market reforms. Government supply chains were changing as they were required to open up supply contracts to competitive tendering. In business the logistics of supply chain organization and marketing arrangements could be developed independently of government interference.

Although the process of privatization advanced a long way, there remained some important questions relating to further progress. State privatization in the 1990s was accompanied by the formation of an increasing number of public enterprises in lower tiers of government. State industrial public enterprises were concentrated in the less prosperous parts of Spain. Closure of these would exacerbate local unemployment problems. There was a growing debate over the future of public services such as the post office, the railways, the water companies and the radio and TV channels (most of which had already been subject to significant restructuring). Even more contentious was any discussion on the future of the services of the welfare state: hospitals, schools and social services.

Conclusion

From the inauguration of the European Single Market to Economic and Monetary Union, the Spanish economy was bound more closely into Europe and the global economy. By the beginning of the twenty-first century, it had been moulded into a distinctively western European economy: displaying many common attributes of other western European economies while retaining its own distinctive cultural features. Spanish business had also capitalized on its cultural heritage to rebuild investment in Latin America. The economy was riding a wave of success, but beneath the surface there remained some serious structural vulnerabilities.

As in other European countries, the population was ageing. Rapid technological developments were changing the nature of economic activity. Development was uneven, there being both income and spatial inequalities. Polarization was evident in the emergence of larger corporations. There were also processes of dispersion as new technologies and improved communications enabled new economic spaces to develop and new types of small business to emerge. Globalization was accompanied by new forces of localization. Economic change was creating economic, social and political tensions that formed part of the political reality in which foreign policy was framed.

Integration into the European Union was at the heart of many of the processes generating change. The boundaries of the state became more permeable as barriers between states were dismantled, extending domestic networks into Europe and increasing intra-European flows [Castells, 1996]. Regulatory regimes were harmonized and a more uniform system of governance was established. Nevertheless, deeply embedded structures and practices continued to inhibit competition.

Two critical strategic decisions were taken during the 1990s, one by government and one by private capital. They were to join Economic and Monetary Union and to concentrate investment outside the EU on Latin America. These decisions will have long-lasting implications and be the source of many foreign policy challenges in the twenty-first century.

EMU membership gave Spain a voice in the determination of monetary policy in the European Union. It reduced transaction costs and provided a more stable planning environment for companies operating within the euro-zone. Above all it provided greater security against financial and economic turbulence. But living with the euro also meant accepting uniform economic policies across economies which retained different structural characteristics, where growth cycles were still not synchronized and where geography still mattered to its citizens. Higher unemployment might have to take the strain of inflationary pressures [Friedman, 1997; Tsoukalis, 1997]. Moreover, in a two-tier Union, countries outside the euro (including new member states) could gain competitive advantage through devaluation (although the reverse occurred in 1999).

Economic relations beyond the EU in the 1990s were dominated by the huge investment of Spanish businesses in Latin America, marking an asymmetric pattern of globalization and creating an Iberian-South Atlantic axis. Spanish banking, telecommunications and energy businesses expanded rapidly to become leaders in the region. Simultaneously, the size of these businesses established them as vital national interests demanding foreign policy responses.

At the beginning of the twenty-first century, the economic boundaries of the state were dissolving, intertwining management of the domestic economy with foreign policy. Both were undertaken within the context of evolving networks and shifting alliances. State economic policy alone no longer determined the path of economic development. Macro-economic policy was constrained by international obligations and the reaction of international financial markets. The foreign exchange rate within the euro-zone was fixed, interest rates were determined by the European Central Bank, budgetary policy was restricted by the 'Stability Pact' and fiscal policy by international tax competition and political realities. There were also other major decision makers influencing the path of development: the regions with their own development goals and, more crucially, transnational capital with its ability to move resources around the world in pursuit of its own corporate goals.

NOTES

1. My own estimate, based on BBV [1999] and Eurostat [2000].
2. For a fuller account of the characteristics of the domestic economy, see García Delgado [1999a] and Salmon [1995b].

REFERENCES

Antonio Alonso, J. and V. Doñoso (1999): 'Relaciones con el exterior e integración española en la Unión Europea', in García Delgado [1999b].
Banco de España (1999a): *Balanza de pagos de España, 1998*, Madrid.
Banco de España (1999b): *Financial Accounts of the Spanish Economy 1989–98*, Madrid.
BBV (1999): *Renta Nacional de España*, Bilbao: Fundación Banco Bilbao Vizcaya.
Cadbury Report (1992): *Report of the Committee on the Financial Aspects of Corporate Governance (Report with Code of Best Practice)*, London: Gee Publishing.
Casamayor, R. (1999): 'Luis Angel Rojo alerta de "problemas muy serios" en las pensiones', *El País*, 23 Nov.
Castells, M. (1996): *The Information Age: Economy, Society and Culture*, Vol.1: 'The Rise of the Network Society', Oxford: Blackwell.
Cerny, P. (1996): 'What Next for the State?', in E. Kofman and G. Youngs (eds.), *Globalization: Theory and Practice*, London: Pinter.
CNMV (1998): *The Governance of Listed Companies*, Madrid: Comisión Nacional del Mercado de Valores.
Colino, J. (1996): 'El impacto de la integración sobre la agricultura española', in J. Velarde, J. García Delgado and A. Pedreño (eds.), *España en la Unión Europea*, Madrid: Civitas.
Consejo Superior de Cámaras de Comercio (2000): *Informe anual*, Madrid.
Corkill, D. (1999): *Development of the Portuguese Economy*, London: Routledge.
Crang, P. (1997): 'Introduction: Cultural Turns and the (Re)constitution of Economic

Geography', in R. Lee and J. Wills (eds.), *Geographies of Economies*, London: Arnold.

Cuadrado Roura, J. (1999a): *El sector servicios y el empleo: Evolución reciente y perspectivas de futuro*, Bilbao: Fundación Banco Bilbao Vizcaya.

Cuadrado Roura, J. (1999b): 'Sector servicios: una visión del conjunto', in García Delgado [1999a].

Dicken, P. (1992): 'International Production in a Volatile Regulatory Environment', *Geoforum* 23/3, pp.303-16.

Dicken, P. (1998): *Global Shift: Transforming the World Economy*, third edn., London: Paul Chapman Publishing.

Durán, J. (1999): *Multinacionales españolas en Iberoamérica, valor estratégico*, Madrid: Pirámide.

ECLAC (2000): *Foreign Investment in Latin America and the Caribbean*, Economic Commission for Latin America and the Caribbean, Annual Report 1999, Santiago de Chile: United Nations.

Economist (2000a): 'Debt in Japan and America', *The Economist* 354/8154, pp.22–4.

Economist (2000b): 'Globalisation and Tax', *The Economist* 354/8155, special survey.

Encuesta de la Población Activa: quarterly labour force survey, Madrid: Instituto Nacional de Estadística.

Estefanía, J. (1996): 'La obscenidad del poder', *El País*, 9 June.

European Commission (1999): *General Budget of the European Union for the Financial Year 1999*, Luxembourg: Office for Official Publications of the European Communities.

Eurostat (2000): 'Regional GDP for 1995–1997 according to ESA95', News Releases No. 18/2000, 3 February. Luxembourg.

Fanjul, O. and L. Mañas (1994): 'Privatisation in Spain: The Absence of a Policy', in Wright [1994].

Friedman, M. (1997): 'Why Europe can't afford the euro', *Financial Times*, 19 Nov.

Gámir, L. (1999): *Las privatizaciones en España*, Madrid: Editorial Pirámide.

García Delgado, J. (ed.) (1999a): *España, economía: ante el siglo XXI*, Madrid: Espasa Calpe.

García Delgado, J. (ed.) (1999b): *Lecciones de la economía española*, Fourth Edition, Madrid: Espasa Calpe.

Gillespie, R., Rodrigo, F. and J. Story (eds.) (1995): *Democratic Spain: Reshaping External Relations in a Changing World*, London: Routledge.

Gómez, C. (2000): 'Las sociedades se saltan el código', *El País*, sección negócios, 23 Jan.

Greenbury Report (1995): *Directors' Remuneration*, report of a study group chaired by Sir David Greenbury, London: Gee Publishing.

Hampel Report (1998): *Committee on Corporate Governance: Final Report*, London: Gee Publishing.

Harvey, D. (1989): *The Condition of Post-modernity*, Oxford: Blackwell.

Holman, O. (1996): *Integrating Southern Europe: EC Expansion and the Transnationalization of Spain*, London: Routledge.

ICE (1999): 'El sector exterior español en 1998 (II)', *Boletín Económico de ICE* (Información Comercial Española, Madrid) 2609, pp.3–7.

IMF (1999): *Direction of Trade Statistics, 1998*, Washington, DC: International Monetary Fund.

INE (1999a): *Encuesta de la Población Activa*, tercer trimestre 1999, Madrid: Instituto Nacional de Estadística.

INE (1999b): *Avance de la Encuesta de Facundidad 1999*, Madrid: Instituto Nacional de Estadística.

INE (1999c): *Movimiento Natural de la Población*, Madrid: Instituto Nacional de Estadística.

Kennedy, P. (1993): *Preparing for the Twenty-first Century*, New York: Random House.

King, R. and R. Black (eds.) (1997): *Southern Europe and the New Immigrations*, Brighton: Sussex University Press.

Leadbeater, C. (1999): *Living on Thin Air: The New Economy*, London: Viking.

Lieberman, S. (1995): *Growth and Crisis in the Spanish Economy 1940-93*, London: Routledge.

McVeigh, P. (1999): 'Globalization and National Economic Strategy: The Case of Spain', *Journal of European Area Studies* 7/1, pp.73–90.

Martín, C. (1997): *España en la nueva Europa*, Madrid: Alianza Editorial.

Maté, V. (1999): 'Las ayudas comunitarias suponen más del 25% de los ingresos anuales del sector agrario', *El País*, 24 May.

Molero, J. and M. Buesa (1998a): *Economía industrial de España: organización, tecnología e internacionalización*, Madrid: Civitas.

Molero, J. and M. Buesa (1998b): 'Inovación y cambio tecnológico', in García Delgado (ed.) [1995b].

Noceda, M. and J. Rivera (1999): 'Intereses cruzados', *El País*, 6 June.

OECD, (1993): *OECD Economic Surveys 1992–1993: Spain*, Paris: Organization for Economic Co-operation and Development.

OECD (1996): *OECD Economic Surveys 1995–1996: Spain*, Paris: Organization for Economic Co-operation and Development.

OECD (1998a): *OECD Economic Surveys 1997–1998: Spain*, Paris: Organization for Economic Co-operation and Development.

OECD (1999b): 'Recent Trends in Foreign Direct Investment', *Financial Market Trends* 73, Paris: Organization for Economic Co-operation and Development.

OECD (2000a): *OECD Economic Surveys 1999-2000: Spain*, Paris: Organization for Economic Co-operation and Development.

OECD (2000b): *Globalisation, Migration and Development*, Paris: Organization for Economic Co-operation and Development.

Ortega, E. (1999): 'The Spanish Business Cycle and its Relationship to Europe', Documento de Trabajo 9819, Madrid: Banco de España, Servicio de Estudios.

Padrón: local authority-based count of the population, Madrid: Instituto Nacional de Estadística.

Parker, D. (ed.) (1998): *Privatisation in the European Union: Theory and Policy Perspectives*, London: Routledge.

Paralleda, M. (1999): 'Distribución territorial de la renta', in García Delgado [1995b].

Salmon, K. (1995a): 'Spain in the World Economy', in Gillespie, Rodrigo and Story [1995].

Salmon, K. (1995b): *The Modern Spanish Economy*, London: Pinter.

Schumpeter, J. (1943): *Capitalism, Socialism and Democracy*, London: Allen & Unwin.

Sebastián, L. de (1992): 'El Barça, Induráin y Maastricht', *El País*, 2 June.

Strange, S. (1996): *The Retreat of the State: The Diffusion of Power in the World Economy*, Cambridge: Cambridge University Press.

Swinbank, A. (1999): 'CAP Reform and the WTO: Compatibility and Developments', *European Review of Agricultural Economics* 26/3, pp.389–407.

Tovias, A. (1995): 'Spain in the European Community', in Gillespie, Rodrigo and Story [1995].

Tsoukalis, L. (1997): *The New European Economy Revisited*, Oxford: Oxford University Press.

UNCTAD (2000): Press release TAD/INF 2837, 8 Feb., Geneva: Conference on Trade and Development.

Villaverde, J. (1999): *Diferencias regionales en España y Unión Monetaria Europea*, Madrid: Pirámide.

Wright, V. (ed.) (1994): *Industrial Privatisation in Western Europe: Pressures, Problems and Paradoxes*, London: Pinter.

WTO (2000): 'Asia/Pacific comes back to drive world tourism', press release, 25 Jan., Madrid: World Tourism Organization.

Spain and CFSP: The Emergence of a 'Major Player'?

ESTHER BARBÉ

An active participation in CFSP during the 1990s helped enhance Spain's diplomatic status. By the latter half of the decade there were no issues of fundamental principle at stake for Spain in relation to CFSP. Rather, the focus was on securing modest improvements to EU foreign policy instruments. In this respect, Spain was increasingly cautious, favouring intergovernmental procedures and only a very gradual, incremental development of European foreign policy cooperation. Such caution emerged during the PSOE administration, but became more notable under the first PP government. CFSP produced different effects depending on the policy area: in the Mediterranean it facilitated a Europeanization of Spain's strategic interests; in Russia it allowed Spain to let other EU states take the lead in protecting European interests; in Latin America it was insufficient for Spanish objectives, the latter having to be pursued through national policies. Spain became a more mainstream and influential actor within CFSP, but still fell short of enjoying major player status.

The visibility problem of European foreign policy has existed for many years. Who represents the European Union in the world? For the first time since the early years of European construction in the 1950s, a figure has been created that goes some way to fulfilling this role. The Treaty of Amsterdam (Art. 18.3) established the function of a High Representative for the Common Foreign and Security Policy (CFSP) and the European Council in June 1999 nominated Javier Solana as the first holder of this office. The visible image of CFSP is thus Spanish, which gives rise to the question: what attitude has Spain had in relation to CFSP in order to obtain such honours? Does CFSP occupy a prominent place on the Spanish European agenda?

It will be argued here that, contrary to what the nomination of Javier Solana implies, CFSP is not a priority on the Spanish foreign policy agenda. This was illustrated at the European Council of Turin in March 1996, where the then Spanish prime minister Felipe González defined Spain's main European priorities as being to enter European Economic Monetary Union (EMU) and maintain Spain's cohesion fund receipts in the face of the imminent eastern enlargement. In this sense, González set the agenda for the

The author would like to thank Pablo Aguiar and Elisabeth Johansson for their technical assistance in the elaboration of this contribution.

incoming administration headed by José María Aznar, with CFSP continuing to be relatively low priority for the PP government

By 1996, CFSP had ceased to involve issues of fundamental principle and instead became predominantly an issue of policy management. In sharp contrast with Spanish policy in the early 1990s, Spain currently sees the European common foreign and security policy as a means and not as an end. In the debate that surrounded the creation of CFSP at the beginning of the 1990s, Spain defended its establishment. In the mid-1990s, when the European discussion circled around the essence of CFSP, Spain handled the issue in an orthodox fashion by refusing to accept the notion of a Europe à la carte – a battle which it would loose. In contrast, by the late 1990s the CFSP agenda had, for Spain, become primarily a matter of improving policy instruments. This pragmatic vision has meant leaving behind other more far-reaching aims relating to the model of European construction that Spain previously defended. Spain's pragmatism has resulted from the fact that, since the entry into force of the Treaty of Amsterdam in May 1999, Madrid has been largely content with the CFSP mechanisms already in existence. Two main factors explain this satisfaction. On the one hand, the CFSP reforms have been oriented largely in the direction sought by Madrid throughout the 1990s. On the other hand, Spain's adaptation to the changes of the 1990s at the global level (the end of the cold war), at the European level (enlargement to 15) and at the Euro-Atlantic level (new relations with the United States and with NATO) has facilitated the convergence of Spanish policies with those of its European neighbours. This indicates that the policy of the González administration towards CFSP has continued under Aznar. In spite of some changes in Spanish diplomatic orientation, which will be explained below, there has been broad continuity in terms of Spain's perspectives on CFSP.

This is the context in which one must consider whether Spain may be considered a 'major player' within CFSP. A number of questions need to be addressed here. What use has Spain made of CFSP? What institutional structure has Spain advocated for CFSP? In what ways are Spain's vital interests converging with European interests? How does Spain facilitate or obstruct the formation of European interests?

The Benefits of CFSP

Ever since Spain became a member of the European Community in 1986, it has been a staunch proponent of the development of a European diplomacy. This was evident from the very beginning in Spain's support for CFSP's predecessor, European Political Co-operation (EPC).[1] What are the benefits derived from this position? The answers are many and affect the role of the

Spanish government in the international system, its influence over the communitarian system and its domestic politics.

At the international level, Spain's status has been reinforced through belonging to the EU in general, and CFSP in particular. This reality is in full agreement with the expectations of foreign policy analysts who maintain that CFSP participation enhances a small state's international status in diplomatic terms [Wallace, 1983]. Thus, holding the rotating presidency of the CFSP is very important for smaller countries. Spain has held the presidency on two occasions (in 1989 and 1995) and both periods were characterized by considerable foreign policy activity [Barbé, 1995; OID, 1995].

Beyond such benefits to the diplomatic status of Spain – benefits applicable to most European countries – CFSP has, more specifically, helped overcome the trauma of the period of Francoist isolation. It is significant that in 1988 Spanish public opinion held that the greatest benefit for the country from joining the EC was in terms of the diplomatic context (as a means of enhancing Spain's role in the international system) and not in the domestic sphere (democratization, modernization, economic development, and so on) [Almarcha Barbado, 1993: 278]. The combination of this historical factor with the benefit of augmented diplomatic weight explains why CFSP was doubly valuable for Spain.

Spain's support for political union also has been beneficial to the country in its relations with other European partners. In effect, Spain's strategy in the European political framework has given it greater influence within the EU, in excess of that accorded by its relatively limited economic weight. One might infer that the development of political union has been one of the means used by Spain to emerge as a mayor player in the Union. The desire to achieve a greater impact in the Community was evident in the early years of the 1990s, when Spain applied two main strategies to attain this objective.

First, the activism on the part of the Spanish delegation during the negotiations for the Maastricht Treaty, demonstrated through a prolific presentation of proposals, was complemented by a clear willingness to place Spain on an equal level with the leaders of European political construction, France and Germany. In this way, Spain sought major player status in the Union. Some Spanish diplomats have interpreted high-level meetings between France, Germany and Spain, such as that held between the foreign ministers of these three countries in October 1991 (without the participation of the Dutch presidency) with the aim of unblocking the process of creating a common foreign and security policy, as a sign of Spain's status as a major player [Peña, 1994: 416].

Second, Spain's strategy has translated into a Europeanization of its national foreign policy agenda, the most prominent example being policy towards the Mediterranean. After the fall of the Berlin Wall, there was a feeling in Madrid that Spain was increasingly being relegated to a new periphery in Europe. This sentiment catalysed the creation of a Spanish policy towards the Mediterranean, which was subsequently transplanted onto the agenda of the European Union. Spain's aim of balancing the EU's eastern and southern dimensions, a goal shared by the European Commission, would result in 1995 in the establishment of the Euro-Mediterranean Partnership [Barbé, 1998]. The leadership exercised by González in this area of policy during the European Councils at Essen (December 1994) and Cannes (June 1995) gave Spain the profile of a major player in the Union [Barbé, 2000a]. This reaffirms the idea of CFSP being beneficial for Spain as a means of achieving a superior status at the core of the Union. Nevertheless, in the second half of the 1990s Spain's major player profile has clearly been diminished owing to the predominance of internal economic issues, in particular EMU, on the European agenda.

At the domestic level, CFSP provides an evident benefit for smaller countries, derived from participation in a network of diplomatic information (the 'politics of scale'). In the Spanish case, participation in EPC from 1986 had a double effect. On the one hand, it gave access to a degree of knowledge about the world that was unavailable at the national level. On the other hand, Spain's diplomacy saw itself immersed in a rapid process of modernization, above all in the area of diplomatic communications [Barbé, 1996b]. CFSP has also helped Spanish governments to bolster their own domestic position. The stronger international projection which Spain achieves through belonging to CFSP is emphasized internally to increase the government's prestige in the eyes of the population. For example, the last González administration made ample use of the EU Presidency, held by Spain in the second half of 1995, as a primary instrument to attain his domestic political salvation [Barbé, 1999: 168]. González's official visits abroad and those he received in Madrid were aimed at transmitting an image of a successful country engaged in world affairs, while Spain was passing through a moment of internal crisis. The Barcelona Conference in November 1995, which brought together ministers from EU member countries and partner countries in the Mediterranean, also assisted the González administration's effort to attain internal prestige. More recently, Aznar's official visit to Bethlehem during Christmas 1999 was also aimed at increasing the prestige of the prime minister among Spaniards, in particular through his appearance at the side of Yassir Arafat. This was a symbolic gesture with reference to the Arab–Israeli conflict, opted for in the framework of Spanish policies traditionally characterized by principled politics [Salomón, 1996: 98]. Governments may also use CFSP as a 'shield' to justify decisions that are likely to be badly received by public opinion. An example was when the González administration sought to defend its diplomatic recognition of Israel to the Spanish public in 1986 [Regelsberger, 1989].

Spain in the CFSP Debate: Realist Europeanism

Spain has actively participated in the process of defining the CFSP since its inception. In contrast to other dimensions of European integration that were formulated before Spanish entry into the European Community, CFSP was 'virgin territory'. Thus, Spain could influence the shaping of this policy area from the very beginning, rather than having to adapt to an already existing policy.

Well before the end of the cold war, Felipe González had established the Spanish position on a potential common foreign and security policy within the framework of a future European Union. González argued that CFSP, together with monetary union and 'European citizenship', should be one of the pillars of the Union [González, 1988]. In other words, when the post-cold war debate began over the need for political union in the Europe of the Twelve, Spain had already defined the creation of CFSP as a central objective on its agenda. As a result, Spain has been an active participant in the definition of CFSP from the first debates on this subject in 1990 through to the reforms introduced by the Treaty of Amsterdam in 1997. Spain's contributions to this process may be characterized as 'realist Europeanism'. Throughout the last decade, Spain has been Europeanist in its objectives, intergovernmentalist in its methods and gradualist in terms of the processes adopted.

Since Spain's accession to the EC, Spanish Europeanism has translated into staunch support for the creation of a common foreign and security policy. This fact was contrary to the desire of some of Spain's European partners, who advocated the maintenance of an intergovernmental accord as a means of co-ordinating the diplomacy of the Twelve. When the Berlin Wall came down, Spain aligned itself with the project of political union proposed by Helmut Köhl and François Mitterrand in April 1990, favouring the development of CFSP and perhaps above all the development of a common defence policy. Consequently, in a letter sent in May 1990 to the EC presidency of the day, Spain gave its full support to the calling of an intergovernmental conference (IGC) with a view to the establishment of a political union among the Twelve. One may infer that Spanish Europeanism can be distilled into two basic ideas: first, that CFSP is fundamental in order to further the process of broader European integration; and second, it is necessary to establish the instruments capable of giving Europeans greater initiative in international affairs.

However, although Spain's attitude during the IGC negotiations of 1991 indicated that in general it favoured the creation of CFSP, Spain was prudent over issues of methodology. Thus, in 1991 Spain joined the majority of EU members in rejecting the Dutch presidency's proposal for full integration of CFSP into the Community (communitarization). The basic ideas of the Spanish government were cautious over CFSP's institutional mechanisms [MAE, 1990]. In this respect, Spain's position was resolutely intergovernmentalist, defending the central role of the European Council and the Council, although supporting the right of initiative of the Commission.

On the issue of decision-making mechanisms, Spain joined the cautious, albeit not immobile, group. In other words, Spain supported the introduction of qualified majority voting only for the implementation of policies (joint actions) adopted previously by unanimity. The minister for foreign affairs, Francisco Fernández Ordóñez, justified this caution to the Spanish parliament by arguing that it would protect the areas of Spain's vital interests, such as Latin America [Fernández Ordóñez, 1990: 5087]. Even so, Madrid's approach was too daring for some of Spain's European partners, such as Great Britain. Thus, the Treaty of Maastricht adopted the qualified majority vote for the operational dimension of CFSP, but gave member states a right of veto over its use. This compromise arose, according to Felipe González, from one of González's own proposals at Maastricht [González, 1991: 7788]. This supports the notion of Spanish activism in the creation of CFSP.

The prudent realism that characterized Spanish positions in the formation of CFSP was expressed in Spanish IGC documents favouring a gradualist approach to the policy process. The notion of gradualism has always been present in Spanish governmental documents, ever since the early days of Spain's Community membership. Spanish political proposals should thus be perceived as creating 'a stage in the gradual development of the European Union' [MAE, 1990]. This incrementalist approach also marked Spanish preparation for the IGC that gave rise to the Treaty of Amsterdam. Gradualism has been evident in many Spanish proposals since 1995, for example, over the role of the Western European Union (WEU) and the broader process of European integration [MAE, 1995a, 1995b]. Spain's incrementalism is representative of its philosophical attitude towards European integration as an ongoing process with an open destiny, but is also typical of the Spanish policy style. In fact, Spain had to adapt its vision of European integration and CFSP to the changes that the EU went through as a result of the signing of the Maastricht Treaty (the Danish referendum and enlargement to include the EFTA countries). The realist notion of gradualism replaced the orthodoxy advocated by Spain up to 1992, which consisted of defending the Maastricht model and refusing to accept the notion of opting out or of a Europe à la carte. Spain renounced this orthodoxy only in exchange for specific benefits. Thus, at the Edinburgh European Council in December 1992, González accepted a trade-off, agreeing to an opt-out clause for Denmark in the area of defence policy in return for a generous increase in cohesion funds. The abandonment of the Maastricht model became further evident when Spain accepted that the three new EU members (Austria, Finland and Sweden) would not have to join the WEU. The very logic of a bloc of neutral countries within the EU was contrary to the Spanish vision based on the orthodoxy of Maastricht. Hence, with this change, a more flexible course in Spanish European policy could be discerned.

Spain's acceptance of the new reality was evident during the Spanish presidency of the EU in 1995, during which the government assumed the function of 'manager of diversity' rather than 'policy creator'. The documents elaborated by Spain clarifying its positions at the 1996–97 IGC illustrate this notion well [MAE, 1995a; 1995b; 1996]. This was the case, for example, in relation to the European Security and Defence Identity (ESDI). Spain supported the development of this area, but as an open-ended process without concrete dates for the incorporation of the WEU into the EU. With a great measure of realism, Spain showed itself favourable to advancing the process of converting the WEU into the operative defence instrument of the EU, while highlighting the existing difficulties given the lack of consensus among the Fifteen [MAE, 1995b].

The positions maintained by Spain during the IGC that ended in Amsterdam in June 1997 were reached consensually by all the political forces in the Spanish parliament [Cortes, 1995]. Spain's aims for CFSP centred on the improvement of decision-making processes and implementation mechanisms. Madrid's proposals were in line with the final accords of the Treaty of Amsterdam in relation to the creation of a planning and analysis unit, the double function of the Secretary General of the Council and High Representative for CFSP, and the use of constructive abstention in the Council. Spain's position during the Amsterdam IGC itself was prudent. Its representatives pragmatically defended, among other issues, the establishment of a permanent organ for CFSP planning and analysis, the centralization of the CFSP in the Secretary General of the Council, a provision for humanitarian, diplomatic and military actions to be undertaken by a group of countries inside the EU and, finally, the maintenance of unanimity for decision-making but with the introduction of constructive abstention.

During the IGC of 1996–97, the importance attached by Spain to the second pillar reforms was minor compared to that accorded to issues in the first (such as the weighting of voting in the Council) or third (terrorism and political asylum) pillars. For Spain, debate on CFSP was by now a question of instruments rather than essence. This facilitated Spain's continuing adherence to the European mainstream when it came to give more detailed shape to CFSP in the framework of the Treaty of Amsterdam. In addition, it is worth noting that Spanish activism on CFSP during the IGC in 1996 was much weaker than during the Maastricht IGC in the early 1990s.

The Dynamic Equilibrium between Europe and Spain

Article 13.2 of the Treaty of Amsterdam states: 'the European Council will determine the common strategies that the Union should apply in the areas in which the Member States have important interests in common.' How do Spain's vital interests compare with those of Europe in general?

The approach adopted here follows Hill's suggestion that 'CFSP should be seen as a collaborative framework of increasing solidarity, whose strength partly derives from the very fact that it permits national policies to continue in parallel. In the long run, by virtue of the fact that there are few rivals to structuration capability, it may lead to those national positions being so redefined in common terms that they fade almost to nothing. For the present, the national and collective tendencies exist in a condition of more or less dynamic equilibrium' [Hill, 1997: 96].

To evaluate the dynamic balance between Spanish national interests and the nascent common European interest, one must begin by identifying what each of these interests consists of. In the case of the EU, as indicated by Art. 13.2 of the Treaty on European Union (TEU), such interests are the basis for the definition of common strategies. Following the entry into force of the Treaty of Amsterdam, the European Council adopted two common strategies, the first on Russia, at the Cologne European Council in June 1999, and the second on Ukraine, at the Helsinki European Council in December 1999. A third common strategy dealing with the Mediterranean was expected to be adopted during 2000.

Spain's vital interests can be identified in the policy declarations of the Spanish prime minister and foreign minister.[2] The four consecutive socialist administrations (1982–96) defined three priority areas for Spanish foreign policy: Europe, Latin America and the Mediterranean. The first conservative administration under prime minister José María Aznar (1996–2000) maintained these three priority areas, defining them as permanent interests [Matutes, 1996]. In fact, Spain's permanent interests can be envisaged as a triangle, with Europe occupying the top of the triangle, dominating and determining the relationship with the other two geographical spheres. Thus, it is important to analyse the degree to which

Spanish interests (the Mediterranean and Latin America) have converged with European interests (Russia/Ukraine).

Hill's 'dynamic equilibrium' between CFSP and national foreign policies implies that, as the convergence of interests at the European level increases, there will be less need for an independent Spanish foreign policy. The question of whether or not this dynamic equilibrium between Spanish and European interests exists requires us to examine more closely each of the three areas mentioned: the Mediterranean, Russia/Ukraine and Latin America. These themes have had, in qualitative and quantitative terms (the number of common positions and actions), a different weight on the CFSP agenda since 1993 (see Table 1). In qualitative terms, one must remember that since the Treaty of Amsterdam came into effect, the new 'common strategy' instrument has only been used towards Russia and Ukraine.

TABLE 1
CFSP ACTIVITY UNDER THE TREATY OF MAASTRICHT, NOVEMBER 1993
TO APRIL 1999

Regions of Interest	Joint Actions	Common Positions	Declarations
Mediterranean	6 (Middle East)	2 (Libya)	65
Ex-USSR (European)	1 (Russia)	2 (Ukraine, Belarus)	78
Latin America	0	2 (Cuba, Haiti)	53

Source: Author's compilation.

Converging Interests in the Mediterranean

A different balance between the Spanish national interest and the incipient European interest has been evident in each of the three areas cited: the Mediterranean, Russia[3] and Latin America. In the case of the Mediterranean, we find an area where the convergence between the Spanish and European agenda is considerable, given that it is a zone of priority interest both for Spain and for the European Union. For the EU, the Mediterranean constitutes a region of strategic proximity to countries without the prospect of accession to the EU. Apart from central and eastern Europe (candidates for EU membership), it is the geographical (the case of the Mediterranean) and colonial (the case of the Lomé countries) factors that determine the areas in which the Union has a priority interest. The EU's interest in the Mediterranean was first made explicit at the Essen European Council in December 1994 and later confirmed after the accession of the EFTA states. Several northern European countries, such as Denmark,

Sweden, Austria and Belgium, define the Mediterranean as an area of national interest [Wessels, 1998: 21].

Spain's interest in the Mediterranean region has been expressed through an independent foreign policy, above all for the Maghreb, using diplomatic instruments such as treaties of friendship, good neighbourliness and co-operation (signed with Morocco and Tunisia) and political dialogue [Larramendi and Núñez, 1996]. Moreover, Spain and Morocco maintain regular meetings similar to those Spain holds with its most important European neighbours (France, Germany, Italy and Portugal).

When it comes to favouring the convergence of the interests of European member states towards the Mediterranean region, the Spanish role has been noteworthy [Gillespie, 2000]. Indeed one can speak of leadership exercised (albeit not exclusively) by Spain over EU Mediterranean policies, in particular in relation to the creation of the Euro-Mediterranean Partnership. Madrid's initiatives for the Mediterranean area have served to increase Spain's general profile in the Union. In accordance with some analysts' assertion that 'governments use CFSP to pursue national interests' [Ginsberg, 1999: 439], Spain has in this way seen one of its fundamental objectives for the Mediterranean region realized, namely that the EU should assume the responsibility of increasing the resources destined for Mediterranean co-operation (through the MEDA programme).

The degree of convergence among the Fifteen in relation to the Mediterranean is high. This has been possible owing to a common perception of the importance of the Mediterranean for member states' respective strategic interests. This high degree of convergence between Spain and its European partners does not prevent the existence of manifest tensions and divergence, as, for example, over the Arab–Israeli conflict. The peace process between the Israelis and Palestinians is the issue that has generated most CFSP activity, giving rise to six CFSP joint actions. It is noteworthy that one of these joint actions, the creation of a special envoy to observe the peace process, has been undertaken by a Spaniard, Miguel Ángel Moratinos. The Spanish attitude has been to actively defend the rights of the Palestinians. Spain's stand on this issue has been contested by other European Union members (in particular, Germany and the Netherlands) which have lacked the inclination to press the Israeli government to make progress in the peace process. However, the proposal of Spain and other southern EU members to establish a common strategy for the Mediterranean, which was to be adopted by the end of 2000, offered the future prospect of increased convergence among the Fifteen on Middle East peace process issues.

To summarize, the Mediterranean constitutes a Spanish, as well as European, interest on the CFSP agenda. Spain has contributed significantly to the development of CFSP in this geographical area. From this one might infer that the Mediterranean is a good example of the complementary role that CFSP has for Spanish foreign policy. However, this has not impeded, somewhat paradoxically, the development of a strong national Spanish policy towards the area. Bilateral relations with Morocco have been particularly significant.

Convergence and Divergence: Russia and Latin America

In the case of Russia, convergence between European and Spanish policies has been facilitated by the lack of any significant Spanish national policy in relation to this issue. Thus, when it comes to Russia, Spain lets itself be guided by mainstream EU policy thinking. Like the Mediterranean, Russia is part of the EU's strategic vicinity, which explains the CFSP interest in Russia – in both quantitative (the number of actions and positions taken) and qualitative (Russia being the subject of the first common strategy) terms.

The absence of Spanish policies towards Russia is explained by the fact that Russia is perceived by Spain to be neither a partner nor a threat [Campo, 1998]. Opinion polls reveal that the majority of Spanish citizens do not consider Russia a significant security concern, in contrast to the perception of threat that stems from having Morocco as a neighbour. Spain's relations with Russia are scarce: in 1998, Russia provided only 0.81 per cent of Spanish imports and took only 0.63 per cent of its exports. Bilateral interaction improved slightly in 1998, when Spain for the first time established a co-operation programme with the former eastern bloc countries, including Russia. Diplomatic exchanges between Spain and Russia have not been very extensive, although in this context it is opportune to point out that Spain did not re-establish diplomatic relations with the USSR until 1977. Neither the González administration nor the first Aznar government cultivated the development of closer relations with Russia, and González did not even undertake a bilateral official visit to Moscow until May 1999.

Thus, Russia is not held to be an important country in terms of Spanish national interests [Barbé, 2000b]. In contrast, Russia constitutes a key focus of interest for the CFSP agenda. The lack of a defined Spanish interest towards Russia facilitates Spain's alignment with the collective CFSP tendency and the adoption of a policy of principles (promoting democracy and human rights). An example of this was the Spanish decision, during the Council celebrated on 24 January 2000, to join the EU countries in favour of sanctioning Russia for its intervention in Chechnya. This example shows how CFSP can have a strengthening influence on national foreign policy.

In the case of Latin America, there is a pattern of clear divergence between the Spanish and European agendas. By the end of the 1990s, Latin

America had become a vital interest for Spain, above even the Mediterranean. Two factors explain the priority given to Latin America on the Spanish agenda: first, cultural affinity (language, common history); second, the economic factor. In 1998, Spain was the largest European investor in Latin America. However, Spanish interest in this area has obtained little resonance at the European level. CFSP activity towards Latin America has been limited, due to the primary focus on the two regions mentioned above. This is logical if one keeps in mind that, in contrast to the two previous cases, no strategic geographical proximity factor exists in the case of Latin America.

Given the significant Spanish interest in the region, it is evident that convergence with EU policies is going to be more difficult than in the former cases. When the CFSP of the Union was created, Spain made it clear that it would not accept a generalized system of qualified majority voting and, as noted before, the fundamental reason behind this was its desire to defend vital interests in Latin America. The stronger interests of Spain in this continent explain why Madrid is more indulgent than its European partners when it comes to condemning Latin American governments that fail to respect human rights. This causes divergence between Spain and those EU members pressing for a more systematic CFSP focus on democratic and human rights principles in Latin America.

In this context, we will briefly examine Spanish foreign policy towards Latin America as a whole, as opposed to its individual bilateral relations there. Spain's diplomacy has created an instrument designed to enhance its profile within Latin America as a whole, as well as internationally: the Ibero-American Community. This is an institution intended to co-ordinate policies between Spain and the countries of the region. In addition, Spain has made a radical choice in the area of development co-operation by allocating half of Spanish ODA to Latin America. With these gestures, Spain wants to 'compensate for the limited attention that the EU lends to this region' [Gómez Galán and Sanahuja, 1999: 202]. In the words of a Spanish diplomat, the Spanish government's Latin American policy intends to 'enhance our [diplomatic] weight outside the Union and in the international community as a whole' [Montobbio, 1998–99: 31].

The idea of a CFSP common position on Cuba (agreed in December 1996) was proposed by the Aznar government, which maintained an 'anti-Castro' stance during the years 1996–98. However, the position of the Spanish government was later reversed, when this policy started to affect Spanish commercial interests on the island (in particular, tourist investments). Some of Spain's European partners (for example, Holland in November 1999) have called for a tougher CFSP stance towards the non-democratic Castro regime, with Spain opposing such a move.

From the above discussion, one can infer that Latin America is a place where it is particularly easy to perceive divergence between Spanish national interests and the interests of other EU members. Given that Latin America is not an area of strategic proximity, nor plagued by tragic conflicts as is Africa, it seems reasonable to conclude that the Latin American continent will remain one of the least represented on Europe's agenda. However, this does not necessarily translate into something immediately negative for Spain, in that it provides a wider margin for Spanish political manoeuvring to further its own Latin American interests. However, notwithstanding this analysis, there are recurrent demands by Spanish political forces for CFSP to devote more attention to Latin American issues [Cortes, 1995; 1997]. In sum, Latin America currently does not constitute a major European interest on the developing CFSP agenda, in contrast to the Mediterranean and Russia. The CFSP collective expression towards Latin America is based to a large extent on a policy of principles (human rights etc.). In contrast, Spain's interests in the region are more vital, for many reasons. From this, one may infer that Latin America is a good example of where CFSP policy harmonization may in fact constrain Spanish foreign policy.

A Good CFSP Pupil, Working for Unity

When Spain became a member of the Community, some analysts expected it to become an *enfant terrible* in EPC, in the sense that Spanish foreign policy would obstruct the elaboration of common European positions on international issues. Spain soon proved this assumption to be unwarranted [Regelsberger, 1989]. Spain has consistently favoured common decision-making at the European level. This positive Spanish position stems from, on the one hand, the support of national public opinion (the domestic factor) and, on the other hand, centripetal forces (the European factor).

In general, Spanish public opinion approved of the foreign policy carried out by the different Spanish governments during the 1990s. In 1997, only 9.4 per cent of Spaniards considered that their government's handling of this policy was bad or very bad [Campo, 1998: 42].[4]

During the 1990s, there was a lively debate about the centrifugal forces that endanger convergence in foreign and security policy between the Fifteen. The tendency towards foreign policy renationalization illustrates this phenomenon. Nevertheless, paradoxically, significant centripetal forces have accumulated at the same time, reinforcing the unity of European foreign policy. These forces have been noticeable in relation to both mechanisms and substantive issues. One of the best indicators of converging and diverging tendencies between the EU member states at the international level is the voting pattern in the UN General Assembly. In the period 1995–99, the member states voted identically (or abstained) in 82.64 per cent of the votes in the General Assembly [Johansson, 2000]. This represents an increase from only 45 per cent in 1990 [Strömvik, 1998]. Spain has consistently acted to facilitate this harmonization of the 'European vote' in the General Assembly.[5]

After the end of the cold war, convergence among the Fifteen was favoured by two factors: first, the centrality that 'soft' security concerns attained on the international agenda; and second, the relaxation of the Europeanist-Atlanticist tension that previously had hindered the formulation of common positions in the Union. These factors helped Spain join the mainstream of European foreign policy interests. In turn, Spanish foreign policy has itself reinforced the convergence between Europeans. There has been a mutual reinforcement between the changes in the international system and Spanish policy.

First, Spanish policy in the 1990s favoured a strengthening of the EU in the field of civil power [Duchêne, 1972]. In spite of outbreaks of armed conflict in the European theatre, the multi-dimensional vision of security, focused among other things on issues of economic development, cultural identity, human rights and the environment, has become a topic of convergence between EU member states. Spain, for its part, has collaborated in the formation of a common European policy space through its initiative for a new Mediterranean policy. The Spanish government's discourse on 'soft' security, which pursues the creation of security for the Mediterranean region through European instruments of economic co-operation, is supported by national public opinion. During the negotiation of the Treaty of Amsterdam, polls showed that the Spanish people favoured co-operation with the Third World being made an EU competence (78 per cent being in favour). Nevertheless, Spaniards were less favourable when it came to converting relations with other countries (69 per cent in favour) or defence (54 per cent) into EU competences [Eurobarométre, 1997].

Second, the Europeanist-Atlanticist fracture which had long divided the Europeans over relations with the United States and questions of security and defence diminished in the post-cold war era. This facilitated closer ties between Spain and the European mainstream. With the exception of *Izquierda Unida,* Spanish political forces have accepted the gradual modification of Spain's position over defence matters and relations with the United States.

In respect of security and defence issues, it is worth noting that Spain has seen itself favoured by the new context (NATO reform, development of the ESDI, Petersberg missions, etc.). Spain has thus managed to erase the negative image of being a 'reluctant partner' [Gil and Tulchin, 1988], which was attributed to the country during the 1980s due to its desire to stay on the margins of the NATO military structure. The changes in the 1990s have produced a different Spain. On the one hand, Spain has been very active in the operative terrain, through its participation in the Gulf War, in UN peacekeeping operations, in NATO forces in Bosnia, in the Italian-directed operation in Albania and in the NATO bombing of Serbia. On the other hand, in the institutional terrain, Spain has defended the creation of an ESDI at the same time as it has reinforced the Alliance through its full incorporation into NATO at the Atlantic Council in Madrid in July 1997. The result of all this is a normalized Spain, which fulfils the necessary conditions to form part of the hard core of the EU in matters of security and defence: being a member of NATO and of the WEU and a supporter of the creation of a Common European Security and Defence Policy (CESDP). Spain's current position is the product of a long process initiated under the González administration and consolidated under Aznar, something which allows one to speak of a certain continuity in Spanish policy.

The occasion for progress in the creation of a CESDP came after the Treaty of Amsterdam came into effect. The UK's decision to support the creation of an EU force capable of realizing Petersberg tasks completely changed the Europeanist-Atlanticist logic that had hitherto impeded or slowed down the creation of European forces. In the second half of 1998, a political process was initiated between the four largest EU states (through a Franco-British communiqué, an Italian–British communiqué and a Franco-German communiqué) and this led at the Helsinki European Council in December 1999 to agreement on the establishment of military forces for the prevention of conflict and for crisis management.

The Spanish government joined this process of creating an EU military force [Aznar, 1999], although this time without having a role as one of the main promoters of the project. This marked a difference with what occurred during the negotiations on the Treaty of Maastricht, when Spain played the role of a major player in relation to the foreign, security and defence policy agenda. This diminished role was partly, but not entirely, the product of Spanish policy choices. The change in the broad context was also important. Thus, for example, the replacement of the traditional Franco-German axis by a British 'motor' is new. The effects on Spain are fairly clear: Spain has joined the hard core (armed forces participation) but without having performed the function of political motor, the traditional function of the major players.

In terms of its relations with the United States, Spain has joined the mainstream of EU countries in accepting Washington's leadership since the cold war. European acceptance of US leadership in Bosnia and in Kosovo, in spite of doubts about the legality of the NATO bombing, is a good example. In this case, the attitude of the Spanish government under Aznar did not necessarily favour European convergence. Aznar's administration joined the Atlanticist group (today basically reduced to contain only Great Britain) at those moments when the Europeanist-Atlanticist friction temporarily reappeared. This was the case in relation to the bombings carried out by the US and Great Britain over Iraq in 1998. Faced with European criticism of these attacks, prime minister Aznar defended the policy of Spain's 'allies'. This alignment with the Anglo-Saxon bloc represents a change in terms of the Spanish policy established by the PSOE governments, which joined the continental Franco-German bloc in such cases. This behaviour, if it is consolidated, constitutes an element of divergence in the formulation of a common European policy [Barbé, 1999: 175], in any case inevitable owing to the position of Great Britain.

Conclusion

The question posed above was whether or not Spain is emerging as a major player in CFSP. Analysts of CFSP often use the term 'major player' without supplying a concrete definition of the concept, instead simply naming those states perceived to be major players. However, two criteria of a major player can be identified. The most restrictive one defines the major players as those states enjoying an independent status as great powers outside their membership of the EU. France and Great Britain are the only two countries that meet this criterion (as permanent members of the UN Security Council). The less restrictive criterion equates a major player in CFSP to being a big state, in the terms used in the communitarian-institutional context. This includes France, Germany, Great Britain and Italy.[6] This criterion was used by Hill [1983] in a collective work which analysed the relation between the national foreign policies of the then Nine and EPC. However, the same author later modified his criterion in an update of this first book [Hill, 1996]. By using the criterion of major actor set out in Hill's latter work, the 'big four', plus Spain and the European Commission would be defined as major players.

The reasons that explain this identification of Spain as a major actor have been examined above. There are two main reasons. First, the political will of the Spanish government to play a significant role in the process of European integration, with the intent to participate in the *directoire* of the big states. Here one must mention Spain's meeting with France and Germany in October 1991 to promote the creation of CFSP and Spain's participation in the 1993 '4+1 accord' on Bosnia, arrived at in the framework of the Security Council, outside EU channels. The most evident manifestation of Spain's ambition to play the role of a major actor is found in González's proposal in May 1992 for a *directoire* structure incorporating the five big states to deal with Community issues and CFSP [Barbé, 1996b: 271]. Second, the definition of Spain as a major player in this period is also explained by other EU states' impressions of Spanish activism. The context of the immediate post-cold war period benefited Spain since this placed the political agenda of Europe in prime position. For example, the support that González quickly gave to German unification gained him favours from Köhl. The support given by Germany to Spain in return boosted the stature of Spain in Europe. This, together with Spanish dynamism in relation to Mediterranean policy, created an ideal situation for Spain in the European political framework. This explains, in part, how Spanish diplomacy managed to influence the development of the European Union as an international political actor through prominent nominations: Carlos Westerndorp in Bosnia, Ricardo Pérez Casado in Mostar, Miguel Ángel Moratinos in the Middle East and Javier Solana as 'Mr. CFSP'. The current substitution of political Europe for economic Europe (EMU) has reduced Spain's role in the process of European integration.

Has Spain ceased to be a major actor, then? Was it ever one? Despite Spain's suggested inclusion as a major actor, analysts have often defined Spain's status in the CFSP framework as that of a 'middle power' [Barbé, 1996a: 121; Hill, 1997: 89]. If this is so, what is necessary in order for it to be considered a major player? Wallace and Hill [1996: 14] indicate that, in the absence of a federal foreign policy in Europe, it has to be the co-ordinated leadership of the major players that permits the development of CFSP. This brings us back to an issue addressed earlier, namely the lack of Spanish leadership in the CFSP sphere during the second part of the 1990s in terms of advancing the institutional process.

Currently, one may not speak of Spain as a major actor in CFSP, although Spain does indeed strengthen the development of CFSP through the formulation of many collective interests, by participating in the operational dimension and through joining the hard core of the development of a CESDP. All this situates Spain in a prominent position within CFSP, but its role is not that of a major player. In comparative terms, Spain lacks the economic, diplomatic and military power that are necessary in order to exercise this function, above all when it comes to Spain's relatively limited contributions towards the creation of the CESDP (as witnessed in 2000). Nevertheless, the future development of the EU and CFSP are unknown, especially given the uncertainty surrounding the effect of future EU enlargements. Thus, one day Spain may return to play the role of a major player in the common foreign and security policy of the European Union.

NOTES

1. European Political Co-operation (EPC) functioned between 1970 until the coming into effect of the Treaty on European Union (TEU), which gave rise to CFSP, in 1993. For practical reasons, the term 'CFSP' is used here generically, that is, both when referring to the current foreign policy of the European Union as well as the EPC. None the less, the term EPC will be used when the chronological order calls for it. For more on the EPC, see Nutall [1992].
2. Their presentations of policy and programmes, contained in speeches to the Spanish Parliament (Cortes), are published by the Ministerio de Asuntos Exteriores, Oficina de Información Diplomática, in annual volumes of *Actividades, textos y documentos de la política exterior española*. For a recent example, see the formal declaration (*declaración solemne*) by José María Aznar during the act of investiture in Parliament, 3–4 May 1996.
3. The Ukraine is excluded from this discussion since it does not provide relevant evidence, given the lack of Spanish policies towards this area of Europe.
4. The figures are similar for the whole decade, with the exception of the last González administration, when the country's internal crisis was reflected in a negative public opinion that left its mark on all aspects of Spanish policy including foreign policy. Thus in 1995, 20.3 per cent of Spanish citizens considered the government's handling of foreign policy bad or very bad. This was also noticeable in the public's perception of the work of the Ministry of Foreign Affairs. In 1992, 60.6 per cent deemed the work guided by foreign minister Fernández Ordóñez good or very good. However, in 1995 only 21 per cent thought the performance of foreign minister Javier Solana good or very good. In 1997, under the conservative administration of the Partido Popular (PP), 32.8 per cent of the Spanish public thought that the performance of the Ministry under Abel Matutes was good or very good [Campo, 1998: 42–3].
5. In the period 1995–99, Spain maintained high levels of convergence with most of its European neighbours in the General Assembly votes: 98.4 per cent with Portugal, 96 per cent with Denmark (surprisingly enough), and 95.98 per cent with Germany. The lowest convergence experienced by Spain was that with Great Britain at 87.9 per cent [Johansson, 2000].
6. The analysts of intergovernmental institutionalism, who explain the progress of European construction in terms of intergovernmental negotiation among the big states, apply this category only to France, Germany and Great Britain [Keohane and Hoffmann, 1991].

REFERENCES

Almarcha Barbado, A. (ed.) (1993): *Spain and EC Membership Evaluated*, London: Pinter.
Aznar, J. M. (1999): *Conferencia del presidente del Gobierno, José María Aznar, en la Escuela Superior de las Fuerzas Armadas (Madrid, October 27)*, http//www.mde.es/mde/docs/discur08.htm.
Barbé, E. (1995): 'European Political Cooperation: The Upgrading of Spanish Foreign Policy', in R. Gillespie, F. Rodrigo and J. Story (eds.), *Democratic Spain: Reshaping External Relations in a Changing World*, London: Routledge.
Barbé, E. (1996a): 'Spain: The Uses of Foreign Policy Cooperation', in Hill (ed.) [1996].
Barbé, E. (1996b): 'Spain: Realist Integrationism', in F. Algieri and E. Regelsberger (eds.), *Synergy at Work: Spain and Portugal in European Foreign Policy*, Bonn: Europa Union Verlag.
Barbé, E. (1998): 'Balancing Europe's Eastern and Southern Dimensions', in J. Zielonka (ed.), *Paradoxes of European Foreign Policy*, The Hague: Kluwer Law International.
Barbé, E. (1999): *La política europea de España*, Barcelona: Ariel.
Barbé, E. (2000a): 'The European Union, the Mediterranean and the Barcelona Process: A Case of a Capability-Expectations Gap', in G. Edwards and E. Regelsberger (eds.), *Europe's Global Links: Group to Group Dialogues*, London: Cassell (forthcoming).
Barbé, E. (2000b): 'Spain: A View from Southern Europe', in M. Jopp and T. Vaahtoranta (eds.), *The Northern Security Dimension of the European Union: Comparative Views of Member*

States, Helsinki/Bonn: Ulkopoliittinen Instituutti & Institut für Europäische Politik (forthcoming).

Campo, S. del (1998): *La opinión pública española y la política exterior. Informe Incipe 1998*, Madrid: Instituto de Cuestiones Internacionales y de Política Exterior.

Cortes (1995): 'Dictamen de la Comisión Mixta para la Ponencia Europea en relación con el informe elaborado por la ponencia sobre consecuencias para España de la ampliación de la Unión Europea y reformas institucionales (Conferencia Intergubernamental, 1996)', *Boletín Oficial de las Cortes Generales*, Sección Cortes Generales, series A, no. 82, 29 December.

Cortes (1997): 'Informe de la Subcomisión especial de seguimiento, encargada de estudiar y discutir el proceso abierto por la Conferencia Intergubernamental (154/000001), aprobado a su vez por la Comisión Mixta para la Unión Europea en su sesión del 29 de mayo de 1997', *Boletín Oficial de las Cortes Generales*, Sección Cortes Generales, series A, no. 89, 4 June.

Duchêne, F. (1972): 'Europe's Role in World Peace', in R. Mayne (ed.), *European Tomorrow: Sixteen Europeans Look Ahead*, London: Fontana.

Eurobaromètre (1997): *Eurobaromètre*, 47, Brussels.

Fernández Ordóñez, F. (1990): *Diario de Sesiones del Congreso de los Diputados. Comisiones Mixtas para las Comunidades Europeas* 169, 8 Nov.

Gil, F. G. and J. S. Tulchin (eds.) (1988): *Spain's Entry into NATO*, Boulder, CO: Lynne Rienner.

Gillespie, R. (2000): *Spain and the Mediterranean: Developing a European Policy towards the South*, Houndmills: Macmillan.

Ginsberg, R.H. (1999): 'Conceptualizing the European Union as an International Actor: Narrowing the International Theoretical Capability-Expectations Gap', *Journal of Common Market Studies* 37/3, pp.429–54.

Gómez Galán, M. and J.A. Sanahuja (1999): *El sistema internacional de cooperación al desarrollo. Una aproximación a sus actores e instrumentos*, Madrid: Cideal.

González, F. (1988), 'Discurso de Felipe González en *Les Grandes Conférences Catholiques*, Brussels, 12 December', *Actividades, textos y documentos de la política exterior española*, Madrid: Ministerio de Asuntos Exteriores, Oficina de Información Diplomática.

González, F. (1991): *Diario de Sesiones del Congreso de los Diputados* 155, 17 Dec.

Hill, C. (ed.) (1983): *National Foreign Policies and European Political Cooperation*, London: Allen & Unwin.

Hill, C. (ed.) (1996): *The Actors in Europe's Foreign Policy*, London: Routledge.

Hill, C. and W. Wallace (1996): 'Introduction: Actors and Actions', in Hill [1996].

Hill, C. (1997): 'The Actors Involved: National Perspectives', in E. Regelsberger, P. de Schoutheete and W. Wessels (eds.), *Foreign Policy of the European Union: From EPC to CFSP and Beyond*, Boulder, CO: Lynne Rienner.

Johansson, E. (2000): 'The Voting Practice of the Fifteeen in the UN General Assembly: Convergence and Divergence', working paper, Barcelona: Universitat Autònoma de Barcelona (forthcoming).

Keohane, R.O. and Hoffmann, S. (1991): *The New European Community: Decisionmaking and Institutional Change*, Boulder, CO: Westview Press.

Larramendi, M. H. de and J. A. Núñez (1996): *La política exterior y de cooperación de España en el Magreb*, Madrid: Los Libros de la Catarata.

Matutes, A. (1996): 'España en Europa', *Política Exterior* 10/52, pp.95–105.

MAE (1990): *Política Exterior y de Seguridad Común. Contribución española*, Madrid: Ministerio de Asuntos Exteriores, 26 Nov.

MAE (1995a): *La Conferencia Intergubernamental de 1996. Bases para una reflexión*, Madrid: Ministerio de Asuntos Exteriores, 2 March.

MAE (1995b): *Reflexion Document on the WEU Contribution to the Intergovernmental Conference of 1996*, Madrid: Ministerio de Asuntos Exteriores, 4 July.

MAE (1996): *Elementos para una posición española en la Conferencia Intergubernamental de 1996*, Madrid: Ministerio de Asuntos Exteriores, March.

Montobbio, M. (1998-99): 'La política exterior española y las relaciones Unión Europea-América Latina', *Revista Española de Desarrollo y Cooperación* 3, pp.17–32.

Nutall, S. (1992): *European Political Co-operation*, Oxford: Clarendon Press.

OID (1995): *La Política Exterior y de Seguridad Común (PESC) durante la presidencia española de la Unión Europea*, Madrid: Ministerio de Asuntos Exteriores, Oficina de Información Diplomática.

Peña, L.F. de la (1994): 'La política exterior y de seguridad común', in *España y el Tratado de la Unión Europea. Una aproximación al Tratado elaborada por el equipo negociador español en las Conferencias Intergubernamentales sobre la Unión Política y la Unión Económica y Monetaria*, Madrid: Colex.

Regelsberger, E. (1989): 'Spain and the EPC, No Enfant Terrible', *The International Spectator* 24, pp.118–24.

Salomón, M. (1996): 'Spain: Scope Enlargement towards the Arab World and the Maghreb', in F. Algieri and E. Regelsberger (eds.), *Synergy at Work. Spain and Portugal in European Foreign Policy*, Bonn: Europa Union Verlag.

Strömvik, M. (1998): 'Fifteen Votes and One Voice: The CFSP and Changing Voting Alignments in the UN', *Statsvetenskaplig Fidskrift* 101/2, pp.75–95.

Wallace, W. (1983): 'Introduction: Cooperation and Convergence in European Foreign Policy', in Hill [1983].

Wessels, W. (1998): *National vs. EU Foreign Policy Interests. Mapping 'Important' National Interests*, Final Report of a collective project by TEPSA and member institutes, Brussels: Trans-European Policy Studies Association.

Europe's Evolving Economic Identity: Spain's Role

FRANCISCO GRANELL

Since entering the EC in January 1986, Spain has influenced Community life in a range of policy sectors, being particularly engaged in debates over agriculture, structural and cohesion funds, fisheries, external relations with Latin America and the Mediterranean, the concept of European citizenship, the Schengen provisions and asylum matters. After a difficult process of nominal convergence, Spain secured entry into the euro in January 1999 and has sought further economic integration in areas such as fiscal harmonization. This is part of its broader strategy of seeking to avoid enlargement leading to a dilution of European integration. It is in this context that Spain has pressed for a larger EU budget and institutional reforms. More recently, as the Aznar government has grown in confidence, it has sought more eagerly to influence European economic policy, with the aim of Europeanizing its own domestic free market reforms in areas such as privatization, competitiveness and tax cutting.

European integration is in a permanent process of quantitative and qualitative development, within which Spain is fully involved. The European Union is the most advanced scheme of regional integration in the world. At the beginning of the year 2000, the EU was an economic union composed of 15 member states, eleven of which had adopted a common currency. Progress was made during the 1990s towards creating a political entity, with a new Common Foreign and Security Policy (CFSP) and more systematic co-operation in justice and home affairs. The purpose of this study is to assess Spain's role in the economic dimension of this evolving European identity.

Spain and the Current *Acquis Communautaire*

Spain entered into the EC as a full member on 1 January 1986. This means that Spain has been involved in the richest phase of creation of the European *acquis*, which has taken place since the mid-1980s, and has embraced the creation of the single market and EMU. It would be absurd to claim that the acceleration in the creation of the EU's *acquis* during this period can be explained primarily by Spain's presence in the European institutions,

The findings, interpretation and conclusions are those of the author and do not necessarily represent the views of the European Commission.

although the close relationships between Felipe González and Helmut Köhl, François Mitterrand and Jacques Delors made a significant contribution to that growth. In a number of cases, Spain actively promoted quantitative and qualitative developments in the EU's *acquis* in conjunction with other member states and European institutions.

It would be erroneous to think that Spain was completely without influence in the EC prior to its own accession. A number of internal debates within the EC were the consequence of Spanish moves in relation to the Community. For example, it was Spain that provoked debate over whether the EC should open its doors to European countries with non-democratic political systems. In response to the membership application presented by the government of General Franco in February 1962, the European Parliament created a doctrine on the topic of democracy and membership through the Birkelbach Report. The EEC–Spain Agreement signed on 29 June 1970 stated, in article 1, that:

> the progressive elimination of obstacles to the main body of trade between the EEC and Spain shall be brought about in two stages. The first stage shall last not less than six years. Transition from the first to the second stage shall be effected by mutual agreement between the contracting parties if the conditions for it have been satisfied.

What such 'conditions' meant in political and economic terms was a matter of some controversy. Apart from the issue of democracy, it was Spain's (and Israel's) agreement with the EC that both reflected and drove the development of a new European Mediterranean Policy – prior to this moment a very underdeveloped area of EC policy.

Democratic Spain applied for membership of the EC in July 1977, 25 months after Greece and four months after Portugal. These three applications obliged the EC to reflect on the impact the new members would have on the Common Agricultural Policy, regional policy within the EC and other issues connected with the special situation of countries not fully prepared for free competition but needing to consolidate still fragile democracy.

After 1986 Spain participated fully in Community life, in particular by guiding notable developments in European integration during the Socialist government's two terms in the Presidency (January to June 1989 and July to December 1995). A number of Spaniards secured top jobs in the EU's institutions: two presidents of the European Parliament (Enrique Barón and José María Gil Robles), one president of the Court of Justice (Gil Carlos Rodríguez Iglesias), one president of the Economic and Social Committee (Carlos Ferrer Salat) and one president of the Committee of the Regions (Pasqual Maragall). The first ever High Representative for the CFSP was also a Spaniard, former NATO Secretary General Javier Solana. Spaniards also quickly began to occupy key posts at the level of senior civil servants, a move that many had not expected from a country that had lived outside world affairs for many years.

The first Spanish presidency of the Council achieved considerable progress in the regulations necessary to complete the internal market in accordance with the principles established by the Single European Act. The Delors Report on EMU received approval at the informal ECOFIN meeting at S'Agaró and the European Council in Madrid. Spain also reinforced co-operation with Latin America. This first presidency was also important in showing other member states that Spain had become a reliable partner, with the necessary skills to conduct European affairs in a satisfactory way.

During the second Spanish presidency in 1995, Spain was responsible for preparing the Intergovernmental Conference of 1996; through the work of the Reflection Group presided over by Carlos Westendorp. Felipe González campaigned hard to avoid preparations for future enlargements of the EU weakening the European integration process. At the Madrid European Council in December 1995, it was decided that the new European single currency foreseen in the Maastricht Treaty would be called the euro. The ministerial conference in Barcelona launched the Euro-Mediterranean Partnership. Agreements were signed with the United States, Morocco, Mercosur and the ACP group, and new momentum was given to relations with Mexico, Chile and Cuba.

In addition to the work carried out during its presidencies, Spain has participated actively in all the major EU developments. Spain has sought to establish itself as one of the 'hard-core' members of the EU, while recognizing the challenge involved in this given the limitations imposed by its size, its comparatively low level of economic development in terms of income and unemployment and the country's status as a large net beneficiary of the EU budget.

Felipe González was firm over the establishment of the EU's Economic and Cohesion Policy, first introduced by the Single European Act, and the creation of the new Cohesion Fund at Maastricht. Spain pushed hard for an increase in the budgetary ceilings adopted at the 1992 Edinburgh European Council, arguing that this pressure was in line with Spain's permanent demand for 'more Europe' as well as in terms of its own financial interests.

The change of government in March 1996 did not change the Spanish position regarding the qualitative developments of the European Union. Both the Socialist and PP governments have always been favourable to moves enhancing European integration and against the lack of ambition for further integration. The PP government expressed its disappointment over the limited nature of the reforms agreed in the Amsterdam Treaty and over member states' reluctance to increase the EU budget to meet the increased ambitions of the Union, particularly eastern enlargement.

During the negotiations over the Maastricht and Amsterdam treaties and in the discussions over the Agenda 2000 reform package, Spain defended the new dynamics of European integration and the concept of greater solidarity between member states, expressed in the form of economic and social cohesion and redistributive regional policies. It also defended the need for a sound Common Agricultural Policy. In line with the national Spanish interest, the PP government defended larger expenditure ceilings for the European budget beyond the levels agreed at the Edinburgh European Council of 1992.

When discussing how to avoid 'monetary dumping' and competitive devaluations inside the single market, Spain always favoured the concept of monetary union, despite appreciating the risks of asymmetric shocks and the potential inflationary dangers that would flow from the low interest rates that the more advanced EMU members would be likely to insist upon. Spain also supported the creation of common EU standards to remove technical barriers to internal European trade and strengthen consumer protection. When discussing budgetary discipline, fiscal harmonization or macroeconomic convergence plans, Madrid has accepted that EU 'rules of the game' are better than the alternative, given Spain's recent historical performance in taxation, inflation and public sector deficits. Spain has not applied for opt-outs and has been particularly careful in making sure that it has been in the first wave of key EU developments and initiatives.

While Spain has had disputes with European authorities over subsidies for shipbuilding and coal (both highly sensitive industries because of their social importance in depressed areas), the latest report monitoring the application of Community law points out that Spain is the second best performer in the implementation of single market directives (after Denmark).

In sum, Spain has never adopted a nationalistic approach to Community negotiations. It has defended basic national interests, but within an overall strongly Europhile approach to integration.

National Interests and Deepening Integration: EMU, Structural Funds and the CAP

Initially, the Socialist governments' aspirations concerning EU integration were based on a broad political agenda for Europe more than on a cool-headed look at Spain's economic needs. After the Maastricht Treaty, both the Socialist administration and, after 1996, the Peoples' Party government moved from idealism to a more balanced position, defending the national interest with greater vigour. Spanish positions on the ERM and the euro, on the budget and on reform to the Common Agricultural Policy illustrate this change in the management of key EU debates.

The ERM-Euro Case

For Spain, the question of the euro was initially not solely about the single currency itself, but about moving towards Europeanized economic governance with a centralized political system. In addition, Spain's commitment to the euro was motivated by the desire to show other countries that Spain was a credible economic partner, in addition, of course, to the need to create more solid and favourable macro- and micro-economic conditions. Many sectors of the Spanish economy claimed that there was a risk that, outside the common currency, they would gradually lose access to the single market. Public opinion did not accept the argument that economic conditions were not appropriate for Spain entering the common currency, given that – with the exception of a number of Spanish exporters – they viewed the experience of Spain's participation in the ERM to have been positive.

The peseta joined the ERM on 19 June 1989 with a central parity of 65 pesetas to the deutschmark and a fluctuation band of six per cent. Given the inflation rate at that moment (7.1 per cent compared to an EC average of 5.2 per cent), the entry level was chosen in order to introduce strict anti-inflationary discipline. Many felt the parity to be somewhat overvalued from a longer-term perspective. In the short term, the peseta actually strengthened due to an intensification of capital inflows, which resulted from the high interest rate differentials with other ERM currencies. This made life for Spanish exporters even harder. After the Spanish Convergence Programme was presented to the EC in March 1992 and pressure began to build up in foreign exchange markets in June 1992 (after the Danish 'no' vote), the peseta weakened and finally was devalued by five per cent on 17 September 1992 and then by six per cent on 23 November. A third devaluation, of a further eight per cent on 13 May 1993, took the peseta to a new central parity of 79.12 to the deutschmark.

One of the reasons why the Spanish authorities decided to join the ERM was to enhance the credibility of their anti-inflationary policy. In practice, Spain's performance between 1989 and 1992 was in this respect unsatisfactory: with persistent inflation and a fixed exchange rate, Spanish firms lost competitiveness, compounding the economic downturn of the early 1990s (although these effects were tempered somewhat by the euphoria surrounding the Barcelona Olympic Games, the Seville Expo and Madrid's European Cultural Year). This highly negative experience influenced Spanish positions concerning EMU during the 1995 enlargement negotiations.

Given that EMU was a prerequisite to, and driving force for, promoting balanced and sustainable social progress and political integration, Spain was strongly committed to not being excluded when EMU finally started. During the Intergovernmental Conference on EMU, Spain had pressed for a long transition period, with a view to ensuring that the largest possible number of member states would participate from the start in the third stage of EMU. Spain accepted the convergence criteria agreed at Maastricht (setting targets for price stability, government deficits, ERM fluctuation margins and interest rates), believing that the most likely start date for the third stage of EMU would be 1999, given that the conditions for it to start before then (if a majority of states had met the convergence criteria by 1997) would be difficult to achieve. Given Spain's poor economic performance during this period, it needed as much time as possible before stage three so as to reduce the risk of being excluded from EMU's 'first train'.

Spain feared that the accession of the EFTA countries would increase the likelihood of the third stage starting before 1999 (as good economic performers, these states would make it more likely that a majority of states would have the convergence criteria fulfilled by 1997) and that consequently Spain would face a higher risk of being excluded from the first group of EMU countries. If this were to happen, Spain's Socialist government would appear to have been a failure and the credibility of Spanish economic policy would be significantly undermined. Hence, at the Foreign Affairs Council of 20 December 1993, Spain requested that the EFTA countries should be excluded from decisions about the move to the third stage of EMU, to be taken in 1996. The Spanish proposal risked reopening a discussion on fundamental issues related to the passage to the third stage of EMU. Spain finally lifted its reserve on the subject after receiving guarantees over the political elements that would be considered at the time of the possible move to stage three in 1997.

In the event, as the economic situation improved, Spain finally met the convergence criteria, making it eligible to join the first group of countries entering the euro on 1 January 1999. The exchange rate to the euro was fixed at 166.386 pesetas, equivalent to a conversion rate to the deutschmark of 85.07 pesetas. Even though interest rates would no longer be set in Madrid in accordance with Spanish needs in terms of job creation, full participation in the euro was not a divisive issue within Spain. Some economists argued that Spanish investment flows to Latin America would be greatly facilitated by the country's participation in the euro. Spain's updated Convergence Programme of February 2000 highlighted the fact that macroeconomic projections for 1999–2003 were in line with the requirements of the EU's Stability and Growth Pact and the Economic

Policy Guidelines agreed at the Cardiff European Council. The debt to GDP ratio was expected to fall to 55.8 per cent in 2003. Economic growth was expected to be around 3.7 per cent a year, putting Spain back on track to catch up with the average level of EU wealth. However, Spain received a warning from the European Commission that it must keep inflation in check, as its inflation rate rose well above the ECB's target ceiling of two per cent during the euro's first year. At the same time, despite the country's credible performance with regard to its public accounts, Spain was urged to continue to trim its deficit and debt levels and to implement more far-reaching structural reforms.

The Budget and Structural Funds

As a large net beneficiary, Spain has always been in favour of increasing the EU budget, in particular the structural funds designed to compensate poorer regions. Unemployment in Spain has been five times higher than that in Luxembourg and the Spanish agricultural sector is larger than in other EU member states. These facts explain Spain's constant pressure for the Community budget – within which agricultural support and structural funds together consume more than 80 per cent of expenditure – to be increased. While the amount of fiscal transfers from Brussels to Spain is actually relatively small compared with Spain's national and regional budgets, these flows are important politically, as Spanish public opinion considers them to be crucial to compensate for the opening of Spain's markets to the exports of more advanced European partners. Given that Spain has had both a growing trade deficit with the rest of the EU and lower levels of income, Spanish policy-makers have been influenced by the judgement that Spanish public opinion would not accept being a net contributor to the Community budget even in an eastern enlarged EU.

The relative backwardness of Spanish infrastructures led to the state authorities undertaking significant investment in this area in the years following accession to the EC. Community structural funds have provided vital support for the development of infrastructure and human resources, with their focus on strengthening economic and social cohesion between the EU's regions. As Spanish GDP per head has always been below the threshold established for a country to qualify for structural funds, Spain has been a net recipient of these funds since its accession and the largest recipient of cohesion funds since Felipe González obtained the creation of this fund in exchange for agreement to enlargement at the 1992 Edinburgh European Council.

During the 1995 enlargement negotiations, Spain was concerned to avoid the *acquis communautaire* on the structural funds being interpreted with too much flexibility to the benefit of the candidate countries. It therefore proposed a new criterion (Objective Six of the funds) to meet the special situation of the newcomers, namely support for sparsely populated regions, in a way that would not reduce the amounts available for Spain. At the same time, it was agreed as part of the enlargement negotiations that the commitments relating to the EEA Agreement, under which Spain was a beneficiary of the separate EEA Cohesion Fund (which it had insisted on in the 1991 EEA negotiations), would be incorporated into the EU. In preparation for the enlargement negotiations with central and eastern Europe and in the Agenda 2000 budgetary discussions, Spain continued its robust defence of its structural and cohesion fund receipts, linking these into the broader debate over EU finances within the soon-to-be-enlarged Union.

The Reform of the Common Agricultural Policy

Spain has disagreed with the opinion that the Union should seize the opportunity presented by eastern enlargement to review the Common Agricultural Policy so as to reduce high intervention prices and direct payments to farmers. Since its foundation in 1962, the Common Agricultural Policy has been continuously adapted and reformed. In 1962 the CAP was mainly aimed at achieving self-sufficiency in food products and stabilizing agricultural markets. In the Agenda 2000 proposals presented by the European Commission in 1997, the stated aim was for the CAP to guarantee the protection of farmers' livelihoods, the existence of a working countryside and the EU's rural heritage. At the same time, it was considered necessary to rethink a number of issues, with the need for WTO-compatibility of support mechanisms in mind. It was acknowledged that the EU should reduce over-production and ensure greater equity in the way that the European Agricultural Guarantee and Guidance Fund (EAGGF) budget was distributed among farmers.

If Spain had joined the EC in the early 1960s, the most important problems for the economy would have been those pertaining to the agricultural sector, which was of prime importance in the Spanish economy at that time. With the decreasing importance of agriculture, Spain has had many agricultural concerns that have been fully in line with those of the rest of the EU: the social costs of the adjustment of agricultural production, the modernization of farms, the need for new professional training for farmers, the tighter control of agricultural expenditure, an improvement in production and marketing structures, as well as health, safety and environmental concerns. In this context, Spain fully supported the bulk of the European Commission reform proposals of 1988, 1992 and 1999. However, it adopted a tough stance on the question of the ceiling for the CAP budget, as well as on specific questions affecting Mediterranean products, including: guaranteed quantities of production; the extent of price cuts to bring the prices of Mediterranean products closer to world market levels; the size of compensatory direct payments; and the modalities of allocating such payments. In sum, Spain has acquiesced in the general process of opening agricultural sectors to more global competition, but has insisted on an adequate level of protection being guaranteed to farmers and rural economies as a contribution to the broader cohesion of the Union as a whole.

Spain and the Future of Europe

At a moment when many EU member states are insisting on the primacy of the nation state against the Brussels 'federalists', the decision of all 14 of the other EU members to condemn the inclusion of Haider's extreme right party in the Austrian government showed, arguably for the first time, the existence of a real 'community of values'. The European Commission President, Romano Prodi, argued that Europe now faced the difficult task of moving to a single economy and political unity, having already moved from the single market to a single currency. The European Union, as it currently exists, represents a triumph of pragmatism, by having taken steps towards greater unity without defining the ultimate objective of the process of integration. It is such uncertainty that makes it difficult to assess the positions that Spain will adopt and exactly how it will seek to combine the defence of its national interests with support for further advances in integration.

In general terms, Spain has supported the notion of further enlargement of the EU. Such support has been rooted in the fact that EU accession helped Spain itself consolidate democracy in the 1980s after 40 years of authoritarian rule and international isolation. However, eastern enlargement will undoubtedly involve far-reaching challenges for Spain. The widening of the EU to the east will be far more problematic to Spain than the accession of the EFTA states was: the EFTA countries were net contributors to the EU budget, were not direct commercial competitors of Spanish goods and offered wealthy markets for Spain's own exports. Eastern European states' low cost manufacturing bases will constitute a more direct threat to Spanish production – although the Spanish government recognizes that, regardless of enlargement, the process of globalization will bring new competitive pressures anyway. In addition, Spain acknowledges that the financial package agreed at the Berlin European Council is likely to be the last that secures large-scale cohesion receipts for Spain.

In view of eastern enlargement, Spain has stated that it is willing to accept some institutional changes in order to improve the efficiency of governance in the future Europe. Spain has been ready to agree to a limited expansion of qualified majority voting (as advocated by Romano Prodi), while continuing to defend the veto in those areas of policy of particular concern to Spain. Moreover, any expansion of majority voting has been, for Spain, conditional on the re-weighting of votes within the Council in favour of the larger states, so as to make it impossible for the latter to be outvoted by a coalition of small states within an enlarged EU. Although the experience of the 'Euro 11' and Schengen has proved that some policies are possible without the full participation of all the EU members, Spain has continued to oppose the concept of 'variable geometry'. Nor has it supported the slightly different notion of a provision for 'enhanced co-operation', in which Spain has seen a danger of some states being excluded from deeper co-operation against their will.

Given the distribution of responsibilities among different levels of power in Spain, Romano Prodi's advocacy of 'networking arrangements', embracing national, regional and European authorities, is of special relevance to Spain. The idea of enabling all levels of governance to participate more fully in shaping, proposing, implementing and monitoring policy, may serve to improve relations between Madrid and the regional governments. In the economic domain, the PP government argued that the euro's first year had been successful and that the further deepening of co-operation towards a more comprehensive economic union was still desirable. The government claimed that the early functioning of EMU had been strongly to Spain's advantage: finance minister Rodrigo Rato claimed that the euro was 'a great European success that has brought stability, integration and prosperity'. Even after sliding in value during its first year of operation, the euro was still helping Spain to master its economic fundamentals, such as the budget deficit, debt reduction, fiscal consolidation and inflation.

Spain warmly welcomed the economic reform targets discussed during the March 2000 Lisbon summit dealing with unemployment, poverty and the completion of the single market in financial services, energy and telecommunications. It also supported the concept of more harmonized taxation and the range of other co-operative initiatives focused on helping to make Europe the world's most competitive economy by 2010. A particular focus of José María Aznar was the need to prioritize a knowledge-based society and an entrepreneurial culture. Spain acknowledged the need for the EU to take a new look at not only the quantity but also the quality of its public spending and taxation.

Because of the problem of terrorism at home, Spain has been a key player in developing the Union as an area of freedom, security and justice by making full use of the possibilities offered by the Treaty of Amsterdam and the Vienna and Tampere European Council texts. Because of its domestic situation, Spain has been the state most concerned to ensure that terrorists and criminals should not be able to exploit differences between member states' judicial and asylum systems. As a member of the Schengen area, Spain has been concerned about the prospect that the removal of controls at internal EU borders might make it easier for undocumented workers and potential miscreants to enter the country. As a consequence, Spain has been supportive of the development of the Schengen Area *acquis* so as to guard against such possibilities.

While emphasizing the defence of national interests during much of his first administration, more recently José María Aznar has sought to adopt a broader perspective on European policy and to strengthen Spain's contribution to leadership within the EU. Aznar has been bolstered by Spain's strong economy and the strong mandate he received from the Spanish population in the 12 March 2000 elections. Aznar has also come to gain greater prominence as leader of the coalition of European centre-right parties. Hence, increasingly the PP leader has come to seek the kind of role and influence enjoyed at the European level by Felipe González during the 1980s and early 1990s. This has led to more emphasis being put on building up the kind of strong bilateral alliances that González established with key European leaders. The more self-confident PP has taken an increasingly pro-active role in shaping future economic policy in the EU, criticizing the economic policies of some EU members as still driven too much by out-moded and inappropriate interventionist economic management. In the coming years, it is reasonable to expect this PP philosophy to have a strong influence over reforms to the traditional 'welfare state' model, not only in Spain itself but also at EU level.

REFERENCES

Almarcha, A. (1993): *Spain and EC Membership Evaluated*, London: Pinter.

Areilza, J.M. (1999): *España y las Transformaciones de la UE*, Madrid: Fundación para el Análisis y los Estudios Sociales.

Assemblée Parlementaire Européenne (1962): *Rapport sur les aspects politiques et institutionnels de l'adhésion ou de l'association à la Communauté (Rapport Birkelbach)*, European Parliament.

Aznar, J. M. (2000): 'Fear of the Future in Europe', interview published in the *International Herald Tribune*, 31 Jan.

Barbé, E. (1999): *La Política Europea de España*, Barcelona: Ariel.

Barón, E. (1999): *Europa en el Alba del Milenio*, Madrid: Acento.

Bassols, R. (1995): *España en Europa: Historia de la adhesión a la CEE 1957-85*, Madrid: Estudios de Política Exterior.

Bastarreche, C. *et al.* (1999): *España y la Agenda 2000*, Madrid: Cuadernos CERI 3-4.

Commission of the EC (1978): 'Enlargement of the Community: General Considerations, Transitional Period and Institutional Implications, and Economic and Sectoral Aspects',

Bulletin of the EC, supplement 1/3.

Commission of the EC (1992): 'Europe and the Challenge of Enlargement', *Bulletin of the EC*, supplement 3.

Commission of the EC (1978): 'Opinion on Spain's Application for Membership', *Bulletin of the EC*, supplement 9.

Cuadrado, J. R. and T. Mancha (1996): *España frente a la UEM*, Madrid: Civitas.

Elorza, J. (1997): 'El Tratado de Amsterdam: valoración para España', *El Sol de Bélgica*, 47, 17 July.

Fernández Ordóñez, F. (1989): 'The EC Presidency Experience of Spain', *European Affairs* 3.

Gasòliba, C. (1996): *1986–1996, Deu Anys d'integració*, Barcelona: Vicens Vives.

Gillespie, R., Rodrigo, F. and J. Story (eds.) (1995): *Democratic Spain: Reshaping External Relations in a Changing World*, London: Routledge.

González, F. (1992): 'La Europa que quiere España', *Politica Exterior* 6/30, pp.7–20.

Granell, F. (1990): 'Aims and Outcome of the Spanish Presidency of the Council of the EC', *Revista CIDOB d'Afers Internacionals* 18, pp.105–12.

Granell, F. (1978): 'Long Road to the EEC', *The Banker*, April, pp.65–70.

Granell, F. (1988): 'Spain and the Enlargement of the EC', in I. Greilsammer and J. H. Weiler (eds.), *Europe and Israel: Troubled Neighbours*, Berlin: De Gruyter for the European University Institute, Florence.

Granell, F. (1995): 'The European Union's Enlargement Negotiations with Austria, Finland, Norway and Sweden', *Journal of Common Market Studies* 33/1, pp.117–41.

Matutes, A. (1996): 'España en Europa', *Politica Exterior* 10/52, pp.95-105.

Ministerio de Asuntos Exteriores (1998): *España y la Negociación del Tratado de Amsterdam*, Madrid: Estudios de Política Exterior.

Ministerio de la Presidencia (1999): *España en la UE: Diez años desde la firma del Tratado de Adhesión*, Madrid.

Muns, J. (ed.) (1997): *Espanya i l'EURO: riscos i oportunitats*, Barcelona: La Caixa.

Roy, J. and A. Kanner (1999): *Spain and Portugal*, working paper, Iberian Studies Institute, University of Miami.

Tovias, A. (1990): *Foreign Economic Relations of the European Community: The Impact of Spain and Portugal,* Boulder, CO: Lynne Rienner.

Tovias, A. (1998): 'Spain's Input in Shaping the EU's Mediterranean Policies (1986–1996), *Mediterranean Historical Review* 13/1–2, pp.216–34.

Westendorp, C. (1995): 'Progress Report from the Chairman of the Reflection Group on the 1996 Intergovernmental Conference', *Agence Europe* 27, Sept.

The Enlargement of the European Union: Opportunities and Concerns for Spain

ANGEL VIÑAS

The most important challenge for the European Union is enlargement. How does Spain view it? This article provides a historical summary of the Spanish experience in the European Union in a number of areas. It argues that Spain has always been favourable to enlargement both for political and strategic reasons and that economic and commercial concerns have been exaggerated. The most significant Spanish preoccupations have already been taken care of. However, there are some specific concerns which must be addressed in the negotiations. In a completely new European Union, Spain will be required to make some painful adjustments.

On 13 October 1999 the new European Commission, which had taken office just a month before under the leadership of Professor Romano Prodi, proposed that accession negotiations should be opened with all countries that were candidates for membership of the European Union but had been left behind under previous decisions. This new proposal was addressed to Bulgaria, Latvia, Lithuania, Malta, Romania and Slovakia. These negotiations should in future follow a 'differentiated' approach (according to the 'regatta principle'), based on the primordial need to benchmark each candidate's progress in meeting the political and economic criteria set by the Union (that is, the 'Copenhagen criteria'). The Commission proposed that Turkey should be considered as a candidate as well, although there was no question of opening negotiations. Instead, the Commission suggested a number of concrete actions as a means to encourage in-depth reforms in Turkey and to enable it to respect the established political criteria [European Commission, 1999b].

These proposals represented a far-reaching vision of the enlargement process. If followed, within a few years the Union will embrace up to 28 countries, although the integration process is unlikely to stop there: what about the countries that have emerged out of the break-up of former Yugoslavia? In the not-too-distant future, a Union of more than 30 members will loom as a definite possibility.

The author wishes to express heartfelt thanks to Alfonso Díez Torres, Ministry of Foreign Affairs, and to Luis Javier Gil Catalina, Spanish Permanent Representation to the European Union, for sharing their views with him. The opinions expressed in the study, however, are his alone.

The Helsinki European Council meeting of December 1999 followed the Commission's recommendations and in February 2000 the Union commenced accession negotiations with the six remaining candidate countries. Furthermore, the European Council agreed to convene an intergovernmental conference (IGC), which also started in February 2000, to negotiate the necessary treaty amendments by the end of the year. In this particular respect, the European Council did not follow the Commission's recommendations, believing that the IGC needed only to address a few, albeit critical, amendments to put the Union in a position to face the challenge of enlargement.

The Spanish Experience

For many years, the repercussions of Community membership remained at the forefront of the Spanish political agenda. They were compounded because of long transition periods for sectors such as Mediterranean agriculture, where Spain was highly competitive, and relatively short periods for others (industry) where Community competitiveness was much higher. One of the primary goals for Spanish policy-makers was therefore to minimize the cost/benefit ratio of the original terms of accession. That goal was achieved through the shortening of transition periods, the dismantling of tariff barriers, the integration of the Canary Islands into the Community and a number of other modifications made in the first few years following accession [Elorza Cavengt, 1997].

The economic burden was eased because Spain benefited from considerable net financial transfers from Brussels. The Spanish government was particularly active in the negotiations that led to the 1987–92 financial perspectives, when structural funds were doubled. Spanish engagement was even more pronounced in the negotiation of the 1993–99 financial package. The government argued that the question of cohesion was absolutely crucial for Spain and that unless there was a satisfactory outcome on this particular issue, negotiations on other matters would be blocked. The Spanish prime minister, Felipe González, brought the Edinburgh European Council meeting of December 1992 almost to the point of collapse and made progress on all other issues conditional upon obtaining satisfaction on cohesion, the latter seen as a solidarity mechanism designed to ease the adjustment process and to reduce wealth differences. As a result, among the less developed members of the Union, Spain remained the largest beneficiary of structural and cohesion funds, receiving 27 per cent of these funds, against the 11.7 per cent that went to each of Greece and Portugal and the five per cent allocated to Ireland, for the 1994–99 period [Fernández Martínez, 1997].

Difficulties were overcome thanks to strong domestic leadership and because, in the political field, Spain and Europe embarked on a 'love marriage'. Through membership, Spain attained a qualitatively new phase in its political and social development. In particular, it reconnected with the European mainstream after the experience of isolation, separateness and humiliation that had flourished under the heavy mantle of the Franco regime, still the major historical reference framework for many Spaniards.

Well aware of this qualitatively new phase, Spain's policy-makers consistently tried to inject specific Spanish interests into the common definition of an evolving European interest. For Spain, Union membership was about sharing, rather than losing, sovereignty, a very different approach to those of the British and Danish. The major instrumental aim was to contribute to achieving a more equal Union, based on a stronger sense of solidarity, through political and economic measures destined to give substance to the rhetorical commitment to an ever closer union among the peoples of Europe. In so doing, the openly-avowed aim was to place Spain among the countries that would shape the future of Europe. This meant compromising, to a degree, on some previously held national positions, while supporting an enlargement and expansion of Union competencies. In the Treaty on European Union (the Maastricht Treaty), the greatest Spanish achievement was to enshrine economic and social cohesion as one of the major objectives of the Union. Another Spanish idea was the introduction of the principle of common Union citizenship [Gil Ibáñez 1992: 106–7]. And, last but not least, it was thanks to Spanish efforts that the major hurdles on the way to economic and monetary union were overcome in the mid-1990s. Even following the launch of the euro, public opinion in Spain remained among the most supportive of EMU: opinion polls showed it ranking as the fourth most favourable national opinion after those of Italy, the Netherlands and Luxembourg [Chislett, 1999].

Spanish tactics in spearheading the struggle to gain economic and financial advantage have often been decried. This is somewhat puzzling since the sort of horse-trading employed by Spain is deeply inscribed in the Union decision-making process. Critics also conveniently forget to mention that Spain contributed decisively to the deepening of Union competencies and the encouragement of new common policies. That this had little to do with a purely tactical stance is shown, for example, by the enthusiasm with which the Spanish government reacted to the crumbling of the Berlin Wall and to the incipient process of German unification within the Community framework. This compares more than favourably with the confused, and occasionally confusing, noises that emanated from many other partners in the immediate aftermath of the dismantling of the Wall.

Spanish membership also had a positive impact on the Union's rather limited *acquis* in external relations during the late 1980s. This was felt particularly in policy towards the Mediterranean and Latin America. In the former case, Spain was clearly driven by geography. The outlook of a Spaniard living in sunny Cartagena cannot be the same as that of a Scot enduring long winters in Inverness. For Spain the strategic goal was to link North African and Middle Eastern countries to the EU more intimately than previously and to make the latter contribute in a meaningful way to stabilization and development in the southern Mediterranean. In 1990 the Community introduced, thanks in part to Spanish prodding (a Spaniard, Abel Matutes, was the commissioner in charge), the New Mediterranean Policy. Later, the Barcelona Declaration of November 1995 opened the way for the progressive establishment of a free trade area in goods and for the gradual opening up of trade in services within the framework of the Euro-Mediterranean Partnership. Another Spanish commissioner, Manuel Marín, was in charge of this operation.

In Latin America, it was more difficult for Spain to secure an upgrading of EU policy. Obviously, given the finite resources available for strengthening the external projection of the Union, there was a degree of competition between aims which could not easily be made to converge. Should the developing countries outside Latin America have to bear the costs of Spanish aspirations for the Western Hemisphere? Spain always tried, in co-operation with other member states, to achieve a certain re-balancing. This was achieved, with the two Spanish commissioners previously mentioned pushing for the enrichment of policy towards Latin America.

Furthermore, Spain made great efforts to participate actively in the groupings that have been in the lead as far as new developments are concerned. In 1989, it entered the European Monetary System and the exchange rate mechanism and remained there in spite of all the turbulence and even devaluations it had to endure. A founding member of EMU, Spain also positioned itself among the vanguard pushing for a European defence and security policy. It is significant that a Spaniard, Javier Solana, was put in charge of overseeing the strengthening of this policy, as secretary general of the Council and the first ever High Representative for the CFSP.

To sum up, progress on the EU's internal and international agendas has been attained with the active participation of Spain, in a shifting game of alliance building and interest convergence. It can be safely asserted that Spain has been one of the countries that has contributed productively to the internal and external enrichment of the integration process. The result, as summarized by a British journalist, is that

> Spain is renowned among European diplomats as the one country that is even more stubborn than France in defending its perceived national interests. There are not many issues that Spain feels passionately about, but once it identifies a 'nationally vital' issue, Spain digs in its heels and it almost always wins. Its behaviour inspires awed

admiration rather than bad blood and resentment among its European partners [Kaletsky, 1999].

This background should put Spain in a comfortable position to meet the challenges of enlargement. So, how does Madrid see these challenges?

The Political Opportunities of Enlargement

There is no doubt that integration into the Union is a mechanism of fundamental importance for enhancing stability and democratization in the candidate countries. The Copenhagen criteria have made the principles of liberty, democracy, respect for human rights and fundamental freedoms, and the rule of law explicit conditions for membership. They have been constitutionalized within the Treaty (article 6) and are the political cornerstone of the Union *acquis*. In this respect, the prospect of membership has already encouraged an improvement in relations among the candidate countries themselves, as well as between the latter and individual EU states (the improvement in Slovakian–Hungarian, Hungarian–Romanian and Polish–German relations has been particularly notable). Enlargement will go a very long way towards exorcizing the spectre and the risk of conflict. What Jean Monnet set out to achieve in western Europe back in the 1950s will be realized in an enlarged Union at the dawn of the twenty-first century.

Such prospects are in the interests not only of the candidate countries but also of the current members. They are wholeheartedly shared by Spain, which for the same reasons also actively supported the enlargement of NATO. Moreover, in the run-up to the Helsinki meeting, Spain highlighted time and again its strong desire for the opening of accession negotiations to be extended to Romania and Bulgaria, while recognizing that the economic conditions prevailing in these two countries would preclude their joining the Union in the near future. Political and strategic considerations have also underpinned the Spanish policy of embracing Turkey as a candidate for membership. Spain was in favour of a positive response to Turkish aspirations during the preparations of the Luxembourg European Council meeting of December 1997. This turned out to be impossible, given the uncompromising attitude of other partners. Subsequently, Spain took a number of individual measures to strengthen its own bilateral links with Turkey [Sánchez Mateos, 1999]. The misgivings over Turkey's candidacy which emerged in countries such as Germany (especially within the ranks of the Christian Democrats) had no counterpart in Spain. This said, it seems obvious to many Spaniards that Turkey still has a long way to go before it meets the political criteria for membership. A thorough process of democratization must take place, including, in particular, a removal of the political overseer role of the Turkish armed forces.

Official positions were supported by Spanish public opinion. According to the most recent published polls at the time of writing, in 1999 Spaniards ranked fifth among existing EU members in the strength of their support for enlargement [European Commission, 1999a: 72–5]. Just over half of the Spanish population supported enlargement, this level of support ranking behind only Denmark (62 per cent in favour), Greece (58 per cent), Sweden (56 per cent) and the Netherlands (55 per cent). Interestingly, Spaniards differentiated between accession candidates less than any other EU population: the spread between the country whose accession was most favoured to that least favoured was 18 per cent in Spain, by far the lowest figure in the Union (the second lowest being Portugal with a spread of 26 per cent). Particularly in Greece, Finland, Denmark, Austria and Germany, some of the candidates were strongly preferred to others. Such discrimination was not evident in Spain. Public opinion in Spain was the opinion most strongly in favour of Turkey's accession, with a 45 per cent level of support, compared to the 13 per cent of Greeks in favour of Turkey joining (the EU's lowest figure). This welcome given to enlargement was borne out by the fact that Spaniards were just below the Union average when asked about the importance they attached to the established enlargement criteria: on this issue, Spain ranked eighth but it was third when assessed by the spread between the lowest and the highest percentages in terms of the importance that public opinion gave to the various different criteria.

Spanish attitudes undoubtedly have something to do with a deeply felt sense of solidarity. If Union membership was good for a country like Spain in helping to leave behind a dictatorial past, it must be good too for countries that have been emerging to full freedom from the shadows of oppressive Communist dictatorships. No wonder therefore that official positions have consistently highlighted Spain's positive attitude towards enlargement. The present writer has not found a single authoritative statement that might point in the opposite direction. Just after the Helsinki meeting, Spanish prime minister José María Aznar was adamant in stating that enlargement was an opportunity, and not a problem, for Spain (*El Pais*, 12 Dec. 1999).

Nevertheless, the impression has arisen that Spain, while paying lip-service to enlargement, has in fact harboured great reticence because of fears about the economic and commercial opportunities linked to it. Such an impression has been nurtured by many who would like to take advantage of enlargement to impose, as far as possible, a distribution of costs and benefits biased towards their own interests. This involves transferring to others a substantial part of the economic burden of the initial impact of enlargement.

The discussion has become cloudy because the attitude of member states to enlargement cannot be dissociated from the very different notions that governments hold about the desirable future for the Union. The Spanish government has long believed that the working of the single currency is likely to require more rather than less Europe. This has been hotly contested by other governments with regard to a wide range of potential developments which the combined effect of the single market and the single currency have made appear distinctly possible, namely, the further co-ordination and possibly eventual harmonization of policy on taxation, state aids, social security, the environment and consumer protection, among other matters.

Undoubtedly, enlargement contains economic opportunities for Spain. They may not be so immediate as for Germany, Austria or Italy, but they clearly exist. The fact that they have been recognized to exist explains Spain's support for enlargement, provided the negotiations are conducted in a technically sound and responsible manner with due attention paid to all interests concerned.

The Economic Opportunities of Enlargement

Statistical analyses have underlined the upward trend in Spanish exports to the central European markets, where a catching-up process by Spanish business seems to be developing, albeit at a considerable distance from the Union average [López Moreno, 1999]. Since membership involves a very high level of integration of product and factor markets, and also includes the adoption of the *acquis* in areas such as anti-dumping policy, state aids and, critically, competition policy, it has become evident that the future member states represent a golden opportunity for boosting exports and direct investment towards a region where Spanish interests traditionally have been very weak. Obviously the commercial and industrial benefits of enlargement will be quite unevenly distributed across sectors and current members, depending on their geographic proximity, competitiveness and economic ties to the candidates.

From the Spanish point of view, these considerations do not constitute a case for delaying the accession negotiations. They point, rather, to the need to take that asymmetric distribution on board and to do something about rectifying it. Therefore Spain is carrying out a wide range of measures intended to stimulate exports towards the future members and, more importantly perhaps, to encourage foreign investment in their markets, as this is likely to determine the trade flows of the future. This is, of course, easier said than done. The most impressive example of the internationalization undergone by Spanish investment outside of the current Union has basically been directed towards the Latin American markets. In contrast, Spanish direct investment in the five candidate countries with which accession negotiations were ongoing before the Helsinki European Council meeting accounts for less than one per cent of all Spanish extra-EU investment flows, compared with a Union average of almost eight per cent

[Martín and Turrión, 1999].

In this respect, one cannot but deplore the fact that Spanish business let pass the many opportunities to invest in the candidate countries when they opened themselves to investment inflows from the outside and started an enormously enticing privatization process. In future Spanish business must operate in a vastly expanded single European market. If history is any guide, one could hypothesize that Spanish business will learn how to navigate in this new environment. Since accession to the European Union, Spanish exports have increased more rapidly than world exports, expanding Spain's share of the world market. Spanish exports accounted for only 1.4 per cent of world exports in 1986, increasing to two per cent by 1998. Meanwhile, if in 1985, prior to accession, Spanish exports to the Community represented 52 per cent, by 1998 Spain was selling 71.5 per cent of its total exports to the EU [Novella, 1999]. This would not have been possible without a certain degree of aggressiveness by Spanish business and the increased competitiveness of Spanish products.

Finally, one should not forget that in the immediate future Spain's opportunities are likely to be greater than the new risks it might face. Industrial exports from most of the candidate countries to the EU market have been liberalized since 1 January 1998, when the last quantitative restrictions on textiles were removed. Given that the association agreements with the Union foresee an asymmetric effort in terms of commercial liberalization, the burden now lies with the candidate countries. Their efforts should lubricate the negotiation process in the years to come [Carderera, 1999].

In any case, the Spanish government is among those that have been opposed to fixing deadlines for starting the actual enlargement, as was suggested by the Commission. This is consistent with the position in favour of the 'regatta principle'. For Spain, the importance of a technically sound management of the accession negotiations, on the basis of clearly defined benchmarks, has been paramount. Such a position is based on the notion that there are important hurdles to overcome in the process of enlargement which are linked both to the candidates' interests as well as to the often contradictory interests of the current members. If the negotiation process is carried out in such a way that fundamental Spanish interests are damaged, then Madrid's position has been that negotiations would have to continue until a more acceptable balance was reached. Nevertheless, the Spanish position on a minimal agenda for the 2000 intergovernmental conference will work in favour of a relatively early date for beginning the actual enlargement. From Spain's point of view, the broader agenda suggested by the Commission might delay the adoption of the amendments to the Treaty and thus enlargement itself.

The intergovernmental conference is, in fact, a prerequisite for enlargement. Basically, it will examine the size and composition of the Commission, the weighting of votes and the extension of qualified majority voting in the Council. It will also negotiate on the amendments arising as regards the European institutions in connection with the above issues and in implementing the Amsterdam Treaty. As far as the first three issues are concerned, Spain has long held strong opinions. Spain is strongly interested in achieving the kind of institutional reform that would allow the members with larger populations to have a stronger presence in the Council, be it directly through the re-weighting of votes or indirectly through the establishment of a 'double majority' mechanism. This higher representation is a *conditio sine qua non* for Spain to reduce its number of commissioners from two to one. Needless to say, Spain is not isolated on these issues because it has common interests here with other large partners.

In Spain, as in other current member states, concerns have been expressed about the costs of the enlargement. In the Spanish case, these concerns mostly have to do with fears about the reduction of structural and cohesion funds. These apprehensions have shown that Union enlargement cannot be considered a foreign policy operation only, but rather a process whose consequences do impinge on critical dimensions of the domestic agenda. The Berlin European Council meeting of March 1999 allayed many of these fears, while also establishing the economic and financial basis of enlargement. Without consensus on the basic parameters of the Agenda 2000 proposals tabled by the Commission, the squabbling among Union members would have precluded any further advance. Agreement was attained on the basis of stabilizing Union expenditure in real terms, particularly on agriculture. Economic and social cohesion was kept, thanks to the spirited defence put up by the beneficiary countries, with Spain in the vanguard [Campanella, 1999]. It was also agreed that, for the period 2000 to 2006, the annual breakdown of appropriations for structural and cohesion policy would be degressive. In 1999, the upper limit was reached (Council Regulation 1260/1999, 21 June 1999). All the resources necessary to carry out structural and cohesion policies have been identified until 2006.

In the run-up to Berlin, Spain insisted that it would be difficult to accommodate the automatic extension of the *acquis* in this area, given the budget's upper limit of 1.27 per cent of the combined GDP of the EU [Viguera Rubio, 1999]. The Spanish position ought to send a strong signal to the candidate countries. Spain wanted the Union to uphold the current effort in terms of structural and cohesion policies, against the will of other members that were keen on engineering drastic reductions as soon as possible. Once the newcomers are in, it is unlikely that they will be easily convinced to drop one of the major objectives of the Union enshrined in the Treaty.

A rather interesting matter, which has not been sufficiently highlighted, is that if the current *acquis* were to be applied to the candidate countries today, the mobilization of financial resources would be equivalent to 20 per cent of their combined GDP. At the highest end, Lithuania would receive 34 per cent of its GDP, while at the lowest end Slovenia would receive a mere seven per cent. These are enormous percentages compared with current cohesion expenditure: Greece, for instance, receives slightly less than three per cent of its GDP. In practice, such high proportions will not materialize. Part and parcel of the *acquis* is the limitation that total annual receipts of structural and cohesion policies must not exceed four per cent of a member state's GDP.

If, after Berlin, the future of structural and cohesion policies has been ensured until 2006, what then are Spain's more pressing concerns?

Critical Dimensions of the Enlargement Negotiations

Accession to the Union implies the need for the candidates to accept fully the *acquis* without any significant changes. This involves the content, principles and political objectives of the Treaty; the legislation adopted and the case law of the Court of Justice; all the resolutions adopted within the Treaty framework; the EU's international agreements; and the agreements concluded by the member states among themselves relating to Union activities. It is widely acknowledged that accepting all these obligations may give rise to technical adjustments, to temporary derogations and to transitional arrangements to be defined during the negotiations themselves. However, in no way should such derogations and arrangements lead to amendments to Union rules. Negotiations are simply about how the candidate countries will function as new members, with the same rights and obligations that pertain to the current member states.

In the view of the Commission, the principle of differentiation for conducting negotiations has already led to a diversified range of situations. Although the same number of chapters was opened in 1998 with the six candidates of what was then considered a 'first wave', the number of chapters provisionally closed varies from country to country. This development is bound to intensify as negotiations move into more difficult areas of the *acquis*. The Union has, of course, always insisted on the global character of the negotiations. This means that nothing is agreed until everything is agreed. None the less, the second of the regular reports from the Commission on each applicant's progress towards accession - which were made public in October 1999 - showed a rather satisfactory situation, although with too many question marks over the reform process in central and eastern Europe.

Concrete progress in the adoption of the *acquis* has varied significantly. Generally speaking, Hungary, Latvia and Bulgaria have maintained a good pace of legislative approximation. Slovenia and Slovakia have stepped up their efforts. Estonia, Lithuania and Romania have a mixed record. But the pace of transposition remains sluggish in Poland and in the Czech Republic, which is inconsistent with their aims of rapid accession. Cyprus still has to transpose a substantial amount of legislation. Malta's progress has been slow.

In all cases it is not only a matter of transposing legislation but, more critically, of demonstrating the ability and capacity effectively to implement it. Here the progress is, not surprisingly, even more limited. For many of the candidates, negotiations will still last a number of years. However, the Commission considers that it would be possible to conclude negotiations with the most advanced candidates in 2002. This is not too far away. The major question marks are political. Will enlargement start with the easy countries only, that is, Slovenia and Hungary? Will Poland, one of the most difficult cases to negotiate given the weight and characteristics of its economy, be left aside in the first round?

For Spain, the most critical dimensions of the enlargement negotiations relate to competition policy and agriculture. In the former, the crucial issue is whether the Union should be willing to tolerate a special regime for state aids which would be less rigorous than the one that current member states are obliged to follow. The candidates are aware of the stakes involved. Poland, for instance, has requested transitional arrangements over 17 years so as to exempt a number of special economic zones from applying certain aspects of Union competition policy. Spain has a particular interest in the way in which the industrial reconversion of a number of declining sectors is going to be facilitated. Will limits on competition be tolerated after accession and, if so, to what extent? Will Union funds be called upon to finance reconversion and, possibly, privatization? How will other partners react? It should not be forgotten that many members, including Spain, have lived through a traumatic experience of reconverting their own coal and steel industries.

These problems, however, pale before the ones that are likely to arise in the agricultural sector. This is a rather technical chapter in which the economic stakes are also extremely high, both for the candidates and current members. In the case of the candidates, the agricultural sector accounts for almost nine per cent of their average GDP (with a spread going from 20 per cent in Romania to five per cent in Slovenia), while in the Union the equivalent share is just 2.4 per cent (in Spain 3.7 per cent). Far more telling are the disparities in the manpower employed. The average among the candidates is 22.5 per cent of the workforce employed in agriculture, as against 5.3 per cent in the Union (in Spain 9.3 per cent). But this is only part of the story. The candidates have inefficient agricultural structures, an inappropriate property regime, price systems that do not reflect real market conditions, an abysmally deteriorated environment and extremely low levels of veterinary and phytosanitary standards, along with many other legacies of the command economies they suffered from for so long. It is not clear how the existing or future financial perspectives will ensure appropriate agricultural funding for the candidates, in particular if the current ceiling on expenditure is maintained. The most likely outcome is an adaptation to the specific conditions of the candidates of the current CAP objectives along suitably transitional arrangements. In this respect Spain has clear interests. The transitional period for Mediterranean products ought to be the shortest possible and with the fewest obstacles to imports. This implies the need to oversee very closely the transposition of the *acquis* so as to prevent the candidates from erecting barriers in response to limits placed on the access of their own exports to current member states [Viguera Rubio, 1999].

Finally, Spain is in favour of reducing, both in number and duration, the transitional arrangements dealing with freedom of movement and establishment. This is held to provide additional opportunities for Spanish business to catch up with other partners in expanding the footholds already gained in the markets of the future members.

None of these, or other, problems is insoluble. In the years to come, an already dense network of bilateral contacts will be expanded further to acquaint the candidates with Spanish positions and suggestions for carrying the negotiations forward. It is more difficult to foresee how the enlargement process is to be steered after 2006 when the current financial perspectives expire. The Spanish government has long thought that the next financial perspectives might have to be increased substantially in order to finance an enlargement beyond two or three of the best-prepared candidates. These financial issues will become even more difficult to resolve as the number of accession negotiations increases.

Of course, enlargement-induced additional growth in the European Union economy might go a long way towards generating the resources that could pay for enlargement. For instance, it has recently been estimated that the overall welfare gains to the German economy are likely to be in the region of almost four per cent of GDP per annum. Eastern enlargement may be largely self-financing and promises considerable welfare gains for the current members even under a narrow self-interested economic calculus [Keuschnigg *et al.*, 1999: 25–6].

If such growth were not to emerge, Spain is likely to argue that primacy ought to be given to article 6, paragraph 4, of the Treaty, accepted at Spain's prodding in the Maastricht negotiations. This paragraph foresees that 'the Union shall provide itself with the means necessary to attain its objectives and carry through its policies'. This overriding principle of sufficiency of means would become of key importance under such circumstances. Whether the future financial package can be negotiated without doing away with the

British rebate or with increased financial resources from existing member states, remains to be seen. Countries such as Poland, another relative heavyweight in the same category as Spain, will possibly come to appreciate the foresight of many of Spain's positions. Brussels money alleviates the economic pain of membership. In a Union based on the principle of solidarity, the newcomers will need all the resources they can obtain as a match for the welfare gains that their membership will generate for existing members.

Navigating in an Enlarged Union

The future Union will, for Spain and other current members, be a completely new environment. It will be far more heterogeneous and far more in need of integrating wider perceptions, backgrounds and interests. It will require adaptations, both in its own machinery and from its members. The adaptations to the Union have been more openly explored so far than the changes needed at the national level, simply because Union institutions have been subject to the magnifying glass of much more analysis. The Commission itself came to the fore on 10 November 1999 with a number of recommendations for the 2000 intergovernmental conference. Beyond highlighting the need for streamlining the decision-making process so that, in general, decisions would be adopted by qualified majority voting, the Commission outlined a number of fundamental amendments which were formally presented to member states at the end of January 2000. They involved limits on the use of unanimity, so that qualified majority voting should be the rule and unanimity the exception. The need to make headway on closer co-operation would increase with enlargement. As a consequence, it would be advisable to establish a minimum number of member states for initiating enlargement. Finally, the Commission suggested that in future the Treaty should allow increased co-operation in the common foreign and security policy [European Commission, 2000].

All these issues, and others, will be hotly debated in an enlarged Union. Governments and public opinion will bring to bear on that debate their own perceptions about the desirable political configuration into which the Union should evolve. Member states, old and new, will enter into ongoing discussion about how best to organize the political and economic relations among the states, nations and peoples of the continent. Governments will partly define their contributions on the basis of domestic political processes. Very little is predetermined or pre-ordained. In Spain, policies towards the European Union have relied on a high degree of consensus among the political forces. Will this attitude remain unchanged? For once, among the major political parties positions have started drifting apart in relation to the future construction of Europe and disagreements over the desirable course of European integration have surfaced. This may be the temporary result of the more effervescent political climate that existed in the run-up to the general elections of March 2000. However, there is no denying that the socialist opposition to the centre-right government had become increasingly critical, for at least three reasons: first, the perception that the government was more interested in intergovernmental co-operation than in enhancing the Community framework as the only means capable of sustaining reinforced redistributive policies at the European level; second, the suspicion that essential Spanish social interests were being neglected; and, finally, the allegation that the government had allowed the capacity for the projection of Spanish influence to deteriorate.

Arguably more important is the fact that, although until now Spanish national politics has remained, in the public perception, a relatively autonomous area, somewhat protected from the political fall-out of the thrust towards transnationalization, this thrust is bound to increase in an enlarged Union. In this Union, the spatial distribution of economic activities will be further modified and structural change will proceed with even greater intensity. Extremely important decisions for the performance of the region's economies will be routinely taken in a Union framework. Regional politics will be seen to be directly affected by Brussels. Will sub-state interests fight back, and how? The arena where this is likely to happen is that of national politics. How to forge sub-state compromises so that the Spanish capacity to interact with Brussels is not impaired will become a new challenge for policy-makers. These challenges will impinge on dimensions of great domestic political relevance: relations with Catalonia or the Basque Country, not to mention Andalucía, Castilla-La Mancha or Extremadura may be exposed to additional strains. This new factor could turn out to be important, particularly in the regions where the political opposition is in charge.

Whether or not the collective rallying around policies towards the Union diminishes in future, Spain's ability to navigate in the new environment will also depend critically on forging alliances with the old and the new members on subjects of common interest. Little can be said with certainty about alliance-making within the new environment. In the past, Spain has been close to the Franco-German axis and active in strengthening bilateral relations with France and Germany but also with Italy and Portugal. It is likely that in the enlarged Union, Spain may play more forcefully the card of a southern grouping, trying to do this without weakening its links with Germany too much. Should significant differences emerge between Germany and France, Spain might be tempted to reinforce the southern orientation.

What about the future member states? In a number of policy areas, Spanish interests are likely to enjoy a high degree of convergence with the newcomers. Some officials consider that Poland or Hungary, for instance, will be close to Spanish positions in fields such as the single market, the environment and social policy. In other cases, the demand for 'more' rather than 'less' Europe could also be supported by the newcomers [Carderera, 1999]. The Commission itself acknowledged such a possibility in its Agenda 2000 analysis. In the political sphere, however, the horizon may not be so rosy. The future member states have left behind years of political oppression and repressed national aspirations. Within the CFSP pillar, they may have difficulties in gravitating towards enhanced co-operation. If this were the case, the trend towards intergovernmentalism would be strengthened, although this might not worry a government more active in the second than in the first pillar.

At least two other conditions must be met for a successful navigation under the rougher and more heterogeneous conditions that will prevail in the larger Union. The first one is the need to create and develop the foundations upon which the capacity for penetrating the enlarged single market depends. This has to do with a range of economic and social policies broader than the ones that traditionally have been part and parcel of the domestic policy agenda. The transnationalized area of Spanish policy-making will include human resource qualification and involve fields such as education and the promotion of innovation and entrepreneurship. A trickle-down process into other domestic policy areas will be unavoidable. How Spain will deal with this remains to be seen.

The second condition relates to the need for enhanced political and diplomatic interpenetration with the newcomers. Spain will require more intimate knowledge of how to pull the political strings in and with the future member states. This will not be easy, because the deployment of Spain's political and diplomatic assets has traditionally followed a very different geographical pattern. The human and financial resources at the disposal of the Ministry of Foreign Affairs were not substantially increased in the early heyday of Union membership. It will become useful to do so in the years to come. However, expanding budgets is a necessary but not sufficient condition. More important, perhaps, is the need to increase and redeploy personnel both at home and abroad. Administrative reforms are notoriously slow in Spain (it took years and years, for instance, to whip up the political will to put together the two major elite *corps* in charge of macro-economic policy-making). Whether enlargement will galvanize the sectors of the civil service dealing with foreign political and economic matters remains to be seen.

Finally, working in an enlarged Union will give rise to uncomfortable dilemmas. In contrast with some of the current members, Spain is unlikely to put all its foreign policy eggs in the Union basket. The substantial *rapprochement* achieved with Latin America must be sustained in future. The inroads made in Asia and Africa must be strengthened. Even the

Mediterranean dimension of Spanish foreign policy will require more attention than in the past, simply because the number of actors impinging upon it is bound to increase. Indeed, if there is a strategic dimension to Spanish foreign policy that is likely to be strongly reinforced by enlargement, it is the Mediterranean one. With the prospects of Bulgaria, Cyprus, Malta, Romania and particularly Turkey joining the EU, even an enlarged Union whose centre of gravity will have moved eastwards would find it difficult to underestimate the importance of its southern shores, with their myriad opportunities and challenges.

In this enlarged Union, a wider range of Spanish external policies will become internalized. The distinction between domestic and foreign will become fuzzier with the passing of time. Ultimately, it will be the resilience of the Spanish political and economic system that will determine the way in which the opportunities of enlargement are grasped. For a country like Spain, after 40 years of relative isolation under conditions of dictatorship and 25 years of inebriating involvement in European and world affairs under conditions of democracy, the years immediately following the EU's imminent enlargement are likely to bring the most serious challenges of all.

REFERENCES

Campanella, T. (pseud.) (1999): 'Los desafíos de la UE en el umbral del siglo XXI', *Política Exterior* 69, May–June.
Carderera, F. (1999): 'La futura ampliación de la UE: marco general de la adhesión y perspectivas para los países de la Europa Central y Oriental', *Información Comercial Española* 776, Feb.
Chislett, W. (1999): 'Simulations to Stimulate Currency Awareness', in 'Spain: Banking and Investment', *Financial Times*, 19 Oct., p.VI.
Elorza Cavengt, F.J. (1997): 'Reflexiones y balance de diez años en la Unión Europea', *Información Comercial Española* 766, Oct.–Nov.
European Commission (1999a): *Eurobarometer* 51, Brussels.
European Commission (1999b): *Regular Reports on Progress towards Accession by Each of the Candidate Countries*, Brussels, Oct.
European Commission (2000): *Adapting the Institutions to Make a Success of Enlargement*, Brussels, Jan.
Fernández Martínez, P. (1997): 'Los fondos estructurales europeos y el desarrollo regional. Balance de una década desde la perspectiva española', *Información Comercial Española* 766, Oct.–Nov.
Gil Ibáñez, A. (1992): 'Spain and European Political Union', in F. Laursen and S. Vanhoonacker (eds.), *The Intergovernmental Conference on Political Union*, Maastricht: European Institute of Public Administration.
Kaletsky, A. (1999): 'A Rough Guide to Europe', *The Times*, 2 Dec.
Keuschnigg, C. *et al.* (1999): *Eastern Enlargement to the EU: Economic Costs and Benefits for the EU Present Member States? Germany*, Brussels: European Commission, Sept.
López Moreno, L. (1999): 'La ampliación de la UE. Consideraciones para la política comercial común y de España', *Información Comercial Española* 776, February.
Marks, M. P. (1997): *The Formation of European Policy in Post-Franco Spain: The Role of Ideas, Interests and Knowledge*, Aldershot: Avebury.
Martín, C. and Turrión, J. (1999): 'La ampliación de la Unión Europea hacia el Este:

Oportunidades y desafíos para la economía española', *Cuadernos de Información Económica* 146, May.

Novella, J. (1999): 'El sector exterior de la economía española en 1998', *Anuario Internacional CIDOB 1998*, Barcelona: Centre d'Informació i Documentació Internacionals a Barcelona.

Sánchez Mateos, E. (1999): 'La política exterior española en 1998', *Anuario Internacional CIDOB 1998*, Barcelona: Centre d'Informació i Documentació Internacionals a Barcelona.

Viguera Rubio, E. (1999): 'Las negociaciones para la ampliación: la posición española', *Boletín Económico de Información Comercial Española* 2629, 27 Sept.–3 Oct.

Domestic Actors and Spanish European Policy

ANTONIO ALAMINOS

The national context in which the conservative government conducted its European policy in the period 1996–2000 witnessed changes as well as continuities. Among the changes, different public opinion strategies were adopted to present the government's European policy to Spanish society. Partly as a result of the demands of agricultural interests, a greater emphasis was placed on the defence of 'national interests'. Among the continuities, there was political pressure by regional governments – including those headed by the PP – to be granted a more direct role in European institutions and organizations. Overall, both the conservatives and the preceding socialist government derived a considerable margin for manoeuvre within the EU from a strongly pro-European public opinion. None the less, public opinion, influenced by the mass media, political élites and organized economic interests, did evolve during the 1990s, and towards the end of the decade public expectations raised by a more nationalist official discourse had become a more significant constraint upon Spanish options in Europe.

A government's foreign policy is affected by a range of domestic and international factors. Among the domestic factors, there are important economic, political and social actors, who aspire to influence or modify foreign policy goals. It is necessary to analyse the positions maintained by these actors in order to help explain the Spanish conservative government's policy in the international arena. This study will assess the changes and continuities in these internal variables between the PSOE and PP governments – that is to say, in the period up to and since the general election of March 1996. Such an approach implies evaluating domestic factors in relation to both European policy and Spain's own national foreign policy objectives. From the state's perspective, the social, economic and political actors that participate in the policy-making dynamics of creating foreign policy are quite diverse. Of special relevance are: public opinion; the mass media; NGOs (see Aguirre and Rey, this volume); political parties; and economic actors. Together these press for a diverse set of interests and objectives.

Public Opinion and the Mass Media

In all democratic political systems, public opinion is supposed to influence government activity. This study will evaluate public opinion surveys dealing with national and international affairs. This facet of public opinion interacts closely with the role of the mass media, especially in the Spanish case, for the mass media select which events to cover and at the same time offer their interpretation of these events. In this sense, society's outlook is largely conditioned by the subjective views and particular interests of the different media organizations. It is precisely this mobilization of public opinion by the mass media that is one of the principal features of Spain's recent political history, embracing the replacement of the socialist government headed by Felipe González by the conservative government of PP leader José María Aznar. Both public opinion and the mass media have become established as increasingly important features of political activity in Spain.

The general idea of Europe is a notion that Spanish public opinion strongly supports. In general terms, public opinion backs any activity undertaken by the Spanish government to further integrate or strengthen national membership of the European Union. This fact underpinned the foreign policy developed by Felipe González. The governments headed by the Socialists were based on the idea of 'more Europe', evident in their policy of seeking to incorporate Spain into the single currency and the Schengen area. At the same time, the deepening bond with Europe provided specific benefits such as the structural and cohesion funds allocated to Spain.

The nature of Spanish public opinion facilitated the strengthening of this European dynamic as one of the most important foundations of foreign policy, and it accepted the challenging changes which this implied, seen as necessary steps towards European objectives. This broad support for Europe enabled the Socialist government to introduce product standardization for labelling and manufacturing procedures, for instance, without significant adverse public reaction. The whole logic of the 'Europeanization of Spain' was implicitly strengthened. González was able to use a pro-European discourse without creating internal political tension at home. The strategy of presenting European integration was not based on the particular benefits obtained by Spain, but rather on the general need for 'more Europe' and the broader range of benefits this would generate.

The arrival of José María Aznar's government in 1996 produced a new orientation in public opinion strategy. This resulted partly from the PP opposition campaign developed against the González government. It should be kept in mind that González's image as a respected European leader with a high international profile was one of the political characteristics that positively differentiated the socialist leader from Aznar. Therefore, the PSOE's European policy had to be attacked by the PP opposition as a means of trying to improve its own standing with Spanish public opinion. This strategy was developed by the PP in the period 1992–96. The party's tactical plan was conceived while the PP was a minority party and it seemed a reasonable proposition in the context of the severe economic recession of the early 1990s. However, by weakening the image of González as a European leader, the PP conditioned its own future European policy. As was foreseeable in a situation where public opinion was clearly favourable towards Europe, the PP's strategy did not oppose the notion of 'more Europe' (as the British Conservatives did), but rather focused on a more critical consideration of the 'national interest'. This national interest was defined by the PP as including both 'drawbacks and benefits of belonging to Europe'. Once the PP was in office, the tactical plan became consolidated as the strategic manner of presenting the new administration's achievements to Spanish society. Simultaneously, however, this 'national interest' focus limited the government's room for political manoeuvre within the EU.

So far, we have contrasted the two pivotal notions informing the influence that public opinion has had over European policy: on the one hand, support for the idea of 'more Europe', and, on the other hand, the 'national interest', defined in terms of the specific balance between the economic benefits and drawbacks of belonging to the EU. We will now assess public support for each of these notions.

Spanish public opinion in general is a priori favourable towards 'more Europe', whether judged in qualitative (deeper integration) or quantitative (more countries) terms. This support has been relatively stable over time. Data from the Centro de Investigaciones Sociológicas (CIS) indicates that support for the EU was 67 per cent in 1999 and tending to rise. The variations in the level of support that there have been are largely explained by the dynamics of Spanish domestic politics and the voters' evolving ideological positioning. Overall, support for the EU has been very high, although it declined temporarily in 1992–93, owing to short-term domestic political factors rather than any genuine increase in Euro-scepticism. In opposition, the PP made their critique of the PSOE's European policy an important element of their electoral strategy, based on the argument that the Socialist were not adequately defending Spanish interests in Europe. Accordingly, part of the pro-PP electorate shifted its position on Europe by adopting a more critical attitude towards the EU. When the PP won the general election in 1996, however, it successfully realigned the pro-PP electorate with Euro-optimism, thus achieving a recovery of the level of public support for the EU. Indeed, one can say that, in the period 1992-96, the domestic political environment became more intertwined with Spanish public opinion towards the EU.

In qualitative terms, support for a deepening of European integration has been very strong. This was the case even in the period when the PP electorate became concerned over the PSOE's European policy. The CIS database keeps a record of responses over time to the question, 'In general, are you in favour of or against working for deeper European integration?' This shows a very high level of support for deeper integration, even at the time of domestic political crisis and economic recession at the beginning of the 1990s. Hence, the PP government, like its Socialist predecessor, faces no significant public opinion constraints on the principle of committing Spain to deeper integration.

This desire to deepen EU integration is coupled with support for enlargement of the EU. EU enlargement is essentially a non-topic for Spanish public opinion. Here, one must question the suggestion made in *Eurobarometer Report* EB48 that a 'sense of anxiety among Spaniards about the prospects of enlargement, which could lead to a redistribution of funds among the poorer nations, may explain why Spain (40 per cent) is the only Mediterranean country where less than half the people believe the EU will play a more important role in their daily lives'. This is a dubious affirmation, for it may be that people consider that the EU is unlikely to become more important because it is already so central to their daily lives. The fact is that there is no significant anxiety among Spaniards over enlargement, if only because there has been little debate about it. When asked if individual eastern European countries' applications were supported, Spaniards have expressed a higher than average level of support for all candidates [Eurobarometer, 47–50]. Spanish public opinion expresses a stable and high level of support in the case of all applicant countries. It gives the highest level of support in the EU to Turkey's candidature. Thus far, this support has been a largely emotional response and how it develops in the future will depend on the way in which the mass media address the question.

There is a an apparent mismatch between the political decisions taken in Berlin in June 1999, in relation to preparing the EU budget for eastern enlargement, and public opinion on this issue. In 1997, Europeans were asked about financial decisions in several areas: aid to less developed regions, agriculture, aid to small and medium-sized companies, aid to regions suffering unemployment and industrial decline, improvements to transport networks, research and development of new technologies, aid to urban areas facing problems, the fight against violence, terrorism and drug trafficking, and education and training. The question was whether it would be preferable to increase the EU budget to help finance enlargement. In all these areas, EU citizens in general supported increasing the budget.

There were variations in the responses to this question in the different member states. In the Spanish case, budget cuts were opposed most strongly in relation to the fight against violence, terrorism and drug trafficking, education and training, and aid to regions in difficulty (all of these areas with a 74 per cent level of support for increasing the budget). These areas were followed by aid to less developed regions and agriculture. Evidently, these areas are of great interest to Spanish public opinion: Spain has the fourth largest agricultural sector in the EU, after Greece, Ireland and Portugal – although on this issue the nature of the information presented by the mass media has also been very important.

The other key notion in the public debate on European policy is that of the 'national interest'. Converting European policy into one of building opposition to Felipe González became the starting point of the PP government's subsequent strategy. While the conservative government maintained the need not to 'miss the European train', it placed greater emphasis on the notion of the national interest. In this sense, conflicts over reform of the CAP and the structural and cohesion funds become priority concerns. The conservative government shifted the focus of public attention to what used to be presented as the secondary benefits of deeper EU integration. Accordingly, while the socialist government enjoyed relative autonomy in its negotiations with the EU, the PP was constrained by the expectations it had itself raised and the commitments it had made to the public. Any compromises in European negotiations required greater justification or explanation in terms of some external cause (North–South confrontation, the country that occupies the presidency being biased against Spain, etc.). This required a different public opinion strategy, facilitated by the relatively low level of EU awareness among Spaniards and their consequently emotionally-driven perspective on European integration. The Spanish do not actively look for factual information about what is happening in the EU, but rather are highly dependent on what is offered by the mass media.

In general terms, Spanish public opinion is able to identify the mass media's ideological or pro-governmental postures. When, in different surveys, people are asked to classify newspapers, television and radio stations in terms of being ideologically to the left or to the right, Spaniards are able to answer the question without difficulty. Public television, at both the national and regional levels, is generally identified with the governing party. People learnt to identify the ideological orientations of the media during the transition to democracy, when there was an obvious dichotomy of 'pro-dictatorship media versus democratic media'. This left its mark on journalism as well as on Spanish public opinion. Both the news items that were selected to be covered and the way in which they were handled frequently reflected ideological positions seeking to cultivate a particular current within public opinion. Given this background, Spanish public opinion is sceptical about mass media objectivity. One indication of this is the association between Spaniards' ideological positioning and which television station news they watch. In 1993–96, the PSOE voter was more likely to watch state television or the private channel *Antena 3*, while *Tele 5*, which was very critical of the government, was chosen by the Conservative voter. After the PP won the 1996 elections, they reformed the ownership structure of the television media. As a result, voters placing themselves on the left came more often to watch *Tele 5* news (which was not explicitly pro-governmental), while the Conservative voter shifted to the state channel and *Antena 3* (now clearly pro-governmental).

It is in this context that we must consider the relationship between public opinion and the performance of the PP government in European politics. The information given about European challenges and the government's performance in EU negotiations varies according to the medium that communicates it. In this sense, the pressure exercised by public opinion upon the government's European policy is partly a matter of feedback, reflecting the mass media's own political strategies.

In Spain, as in other EU countries, the perceived benefit of belonging to the EU has to do mainly with the expectation of economic gains at the national level and the public presentation of European negotiations by the Spanish government. In the case of the PP government, relations with the EU have been defined more tightly in terms of a cost-benefit analysis. The concept of 'defending the national interest' has been central to the public opinion strategy of the PP. In the first year of Spain's EC membership (1986), nearly 65 per cent of the population felt their country had not benefited. This proportion then began to decrease. The proportion of people thinking that Spain was benefiting from European membership reached a maximum in 1989–90 and declined between 1992 and 1995. After 1996, this proportion increased once again. The decline between 1992 and 1995 was caused by the internal political situation and the economic crisis. The PP argued in this period that the PSOE's European policy was not benefiting Spain. As soon as the PP won power, it emphasized the need to defend the 'national interest' in almost all negotiations, in particular in agricultural policy.

One of the consequences of the PP's electoral use of European policy was that attitudes towards specific EU policies and levels of general support for the EU became closely associated with whether voters were broadly for or against the national government. For example, in 1999, opinions on the benefits of EU membership in terms of prices, salaries and jobs varied according to political party preferences. By 1999, those who voted for the PP had a more positive opinion of these benefits than did PSOE voters, the latter now associating such issues with PP government policy. In short, public opinion on European policy became more ideologically oriented. Some 41 per cent of the PP electorate considered that being in the EU made it easier to get a job, while only 28 per cent of left-wing voters thought this. In the case of policies such as agriculture, fishing and industry – presented by the PP government as being difficult issues within the EU – 32 per cent of PP voters considered that membership of the EU benefited these sectors, compared with an overall figure of only 15 per cent.

As suggested above, the scarce amount of information about Europe created some apparent contradictions in public opinion. Spanish society both supported greater involvement with the general European idea and adopted some more defensive positions during the period of the first PP administration. This, in part, reflected the impact of the Conservatives' European policy, which defined the relationship with the European Commission in terms of a fight over interests in a range of different sectors: olive oil, milk, fishing and structural and cohesion funds. Indeed, such was the level of this rhetoric that one Spanish minister was eventually obliged to clarify that the government was not accusing the European Commission of being instinctively biased against Spain. The impact of this defensive policy was reflected in Spanish opinion towards the European Parliament: in 1999, 81 per cent of Spaniards felt that an MEP's job was to fight for national interests, rather than to represent transnational ideological groupings.

This view, encouraged by the presentation of government policy through the mass media, that the European institutions are essentially sites where Spanish foreign policy objectives are fought for, seemed to sit uneasily alongside the fact that Spanish public opinion showed a very high level of support for joint EU decision-making in many policy areas. That means it is disposed to give more power to the EU. In 1998, 63 per cent of Spaniards wanted more centralized decision-making at the European level, this being well above the average EU figure [Eurobarometer, 50, 1998]. However, when one examines different sectors, there is a resistance to EU decision making in some areas. The explanation suggested by the *Eurobarometer Report* is phrased in terms of subsidiarity:

> the point to make here is that the (data) above shows that people's opinions towards EU decision-making appear to be based on the subsidiarity principle. People make a distinction between areas, which are more likely to affect them directly, and areas that are more removed from their daily lives. As usual, highest support for EU joint decision-making goes to areas which are less likely to affect people directly or which transcend national borders, such as the fight against drugs, foreign policy, research and humanitarian aid. On the other hand, the majority of Europeans want the national governments to decide in areas that concern them more directly, such as health and social welfare, education, cultural policy and broadcasting rules for the media [Eurobarometer, 50, 1998].

In fact, there are two different factors: subsidiarity and degree of importance. Subsidiarity has to do with levels of administration, while importance is a question of definition. Spanish public opinion follows the EU line except in a preference (48 per cent) for national government competence over agriculture and fishing policy: precisely the areas where it has been suggested to Spanish public opinion by the mass media that the crucial issues of immediate national interest lie.

None the less, there were signs that the PP government was conscious of the self-imposed constraints of their public opinion strategy. Towards the end of its first term, the government began to argue, as seen in some public declarations, that belonging to the lead group of EU countries was an objective hardly compatible with the vehement defence of existing structural and cohesion fund benefits, given that these evidently implied an inferior status. That is, there was a realignment of the way in which the government presented European issues to public opinion, with the aim of giving ministers greater negotiating freedom and deflecting possible domestic criticism by discouraging people from judging European policy exclusively in monetary terms.

The Political Parties

Political parties are among the principal actors in the elaboration of Spanish European policy. The Spanish party system has been dominated by the two largest parties, the PP and PSOE, and a third minority force, the United Left (*Izquierda Unida*), which also has a presence at the national level. Of the regional level parties, the Basque Nationalist Party (PNV) in the Basque Country, and Convergence and Union (CiU) in Catalonia have had greatest prominence, with the Canary Islands Coalition (CC) and the Galician Nationalist Bloc (BNG) playing smaller but increasingly important roles. Here, analysis will be limited to the three national parties, after which some consideration will be given to the possibility of independent action by regional governments through their representation in the EU.

The first question to evaluate is the degree of continuity and change between the first PP government and its Socialist predecessors. As already observed, there was substantial continuity in the underlying objectives of European policy between the two governments, but with the PP stressing a number of different specific sectoral issues to a greater extent. Within this context, three stages can be defined in terms of the evolution of relations between the two main parties on European issues. The first stage ran from when the PP took power in 1996 up to the Amsterdam Treaty; the second stage comprised the period from the signing of the treaty up to the Berlin summit of 1999, which concluded the negotiations on EU financing; and the third stage corresponded to the post-Berlin period.

The first stage was characterized by continuity and support for completing the unfinished policy objectives of the PSOE. This involved defending the structural and cohesion funds and the CAP (both in terms of its general provisions and the different sectoral arrangements within it). Although there was some dissent, the PSOE's criticisms of the government during this period were nuanced rather than substantial. There was explicit agreement over such continuity between the PSOE, foreign minister Abel Matutes, finance minister Rodrigo Rato and high-ranking officials within their two key ministries. The aim was to maintain Spain's benefits during future negotiations on the structural and cohesion funds. Both parties saw the EU's enlargement process as the crucial issue and agreed on the priority of minimizing the potential risks associated with it. As indicated, the PSOE's opposition was essentially a matter of nuances, accusing the PP of orientating policy excessively towards local Spanish interests and therefore endangering Spain's pro-European image. There were more fundamental differences over foreign policy beyond the EU, with the PSOE opposing the PP's new hard line position on Cuba and criticizing its lack of attention to Mediterranean policy. The PP replied that the PSOE itself was guilty of having hindered better trade access for non-EU Mediterranean products.

The second stage witnessed greater divergence between the two main parties, with the PSOE more forcibly criticizing the way in which the PP was handling relations with other EU members. There was growing dissent over the PP's negotiating capacity, although there continued to be a joint effort to obtain certain key objectives. PSOE criticism was directed particularly at the PP's failure to negotiate agreements and establish alliances on EU financing issues. The Socialists adopted a defensive attitude by supporting the idea of closing institutional and financing reforms before initiating accession negotiations. The PP accepted the fact that in practice these issues would not be definitively resolved prior to accession negotiations. The PSOE questioned the PP's leadership and negotiating capacity in accepting this open-ended arrangement on EU reforms, which, the Socialists argued, failed to adequately defend Spain from the economic (reduction of transfers from the EU) and political (reduced weight within EU decision-making) risks of EU enlargement.

The third stage of relations between the parties started after the European Council in Berlin, which reached agreement on the Agenda 2000 (enlargement-preparation) reforms. The new financial framework for the period 2000–6 adopted at Berlin was criticized by the PSOE as insufficient to enable the Union to meet the main challenges of enlargement; the core of the financial framework was basically about ensuring budgetary discipline. Many aspects of the problem of financing were, in fact, left unresolved. The PP supported a minimal institutional reform, at this stage limited to revising the number of commissioners and decision-making procedures (including, in particular, a re-weighting of votes in favour of the larger states, including Spain). The PSOE urged a more comprehensive reform of European institutions – including a more radical expansion of majority voting – before new members were incorporated. In this third stage, the PP and PSOE disagreed not only on how negotiating should be carried out, but also on important questions involving the way in which the EU should develop in the near future. This conflict soon became part of the electoral contest of 1999 to choose Spain's representatives in the European Parliament.

The positions of the United Left (IU) on foreign and European policy have long been radically different from those of the larger national parties. IU has opposed the current European Union model in almost every dimension. They are opposed to the liberal economic model underpinning European integration and also to the current institutional model. IU advocates giving greater power to the European Parliament and the establishment of a European Constitution. Consequently, IU influence upon the PP's European policy has been minimal, just as it was in relation to PSOE policy. Indeed, the significant electoral decline suffered by IU in 1999–2000, along with the retirement of its staunchly communist leader Julio Anguita, has made a modification of their views likely.

Regional Governments

The role of regions within the EU developed significantly during the 1990s. The Treaty of Maastricht (art.146) and later the Treaty of Amsterdam (art. 203) permitted member states to be represented in EU negotiations by regional ministers. This possibility has been repeatedly claimed by different regional governments in Spain since 1993, especially those of Catalonia, the Basque Country and more recently Galicia. The PP government, like its PSOE predecessors, was reluctant to allow regions to take advantage of this provision. In 1998, the political party groupings in the Spanish parliament reached an outline agreement to regulate regional representation in the Council of Ministers. According to this agreement, principal representation would always correspond to the central administration; the presence of the regions would be limited to those subjects in which the autonomous regions have exclusive competence. The finalizing of the agreement has been delayed by the problem of identifying and ratifying a list of those competences recognized as being exclusive to regional government, taking into account the different statutes of regional autonomy and the jurisprudence of the Constitutional Court.

Another divisive issue is the regions' demand to be present in the more than 300 committees that manage daily activity in Brussels. The PP accepted their presence in 55 of these committees. This representation of regional interests in the EU is additional and complementary to their presence in the Committee of the Regions. Other regional initiatives also emerged, such as the proposal by the Valencian regional government to create a forum at the heart of the EU in which the 58 European regions whose per capita income is less than 75 per cent of the EU mean would participate. The future is likely to witness increasing tensions between regional and state representation in the EU.

Although pressure around such demands is felt from all regional parties, it has been more pronounced in the case of the CiU in Catalonia, for whom the issue of EU representation has long been an important cause of tension with the central administration. Further evidence of the trend has been the addition of the PP leader in Galicia, Manuel Fraga, to the list of those calling for greater regional representation at the European level – a curious addition given Fraga's history as a former Francoist minister. The central thrust of these demands is that regions with legislative capacity should be represented wherever EU norms pertinent to their areas of responsibility are debated. The Committee of the Regions lacks the operative capacity that the nationalist parties demand, because it has to combine the different regional models of the 15 member states (the closest models to Spain being those of Belgium and Germany). In its resistance to greater regional representation in the EU, the PP was supported by the PSOE. The two parties argued, and continue to maintain, that regional representation in the Council of Ministers would make possible a situation where one region's interests were promoted at the cost of the interests of Spain as a whole. The European Union provides an opportunity for the regional parties to develop their own international presence and policies, but also represents an avenue for the pursuit of their conflictive relations with the Spanish state.

Economic Actors

A final word is in order on the role of trade union organizations in European policy. The relative weakness of union organizations in Spain has meant that their capacity for influencing Spain's European policy has been limited. An exception has been the influential role played by various agricultural organizations, whose members are affected by the CAP. Indeed, it was the PP's emphasis on the defence of Spanish interests in this sector that conceded an influential space in the mass media to these organizations. At times there has been tension between government efforts to placate this lobby and diplomatic activities to reassure North African countries, in some cases agricultural trade rivals of Spain, that their interests lie in economic interdependence and partnership with Europe.

In other sectors, the policy of liberalization and privatization has produced conflicts expressed at the European level, as in the case of TV decodifiers. Here, the economic policy of the PP government was in tune with that developed elsewhere in Europe as a consequence of globalization.

Conclusion

The influence of different social, economic and political actors on the European policy of the PP government has been conditioned by the strategies developed by the PP itself while in opposition. While in opposition, the PP shifted discussion from the broad, mutual benefits of co-operation among EU states to an emphasis on immediate national interests. As a consequence, there were changes in the presentation of European policy to Spanish society. The success of this declared policy would be measured quantitatively in terms of the defence of the structural and cohesion funds and in the result of negotiations over the Common Agricultural Policy. This created new constraints upon Spanish European policy, and their future impact remains uncertain. Declarations made by government ministers towards the end of the first Aznar administration suggested that in its second term of office, the PP would seek to shift policy back to strategic alliance-building and, to some degree, away from narrow calculations of sectoral interests. But the legacy from the first term of office is not one that facilitates either ambitious European policies or strong Spanish leadership in the EU. Despite the absolute parliamentary majority obtained in March 2000, the announced shift was likely to face opposition from some of the actors associated with the PP.

REFERENCES

Aguirre, M. (1999): 'La arquitectura de la seguridad europea. Actores y escenarios' in Aguirre *et al.* [1999].
Aguirre, M. *et al.* (eds.) (1999): *Europa en la encrucijada*, Zaragoza: Centro Pignatelli.
Anguita, J. (1999): 'Situación sociopolítica en la UE tras las elecciones europeas', *Utopías* 2/180, pp.15–24.
Centro de Investigaciones Sociologicas (1997): *La opinión pública ante el proceso de integración europea*, Estudio 2246, Madrid: CIS.
Centro de Investigaciones Sociologicas (1999): *Barómetro de Mayo sobre la Unión Europea*, Estudio 2339, Madrid: CIS.
Cortes Generales (1996–2000): *Diario de Sesiones de las Cortes Generales*, Comisión Mixta para la Unión Europea, VI legislatura, Madrid: Cortes Generales.
Eurobarometer: *Eurobarometer Report*, published every six months, Brussels: Commission of the European Communities.
Gillespie, R., Rodrigo, F. and J. Story (eds.) (1995): *Las relaciones exteriores de la España democrática*, Madrid: Alianza.
Gillespie, R. (1999): *Spain and the Mediterranean*, Basingstoke: Macmillan Press.
Tortosa, J. M. (1999): 'La Unión Europea: el difícil juego de tres nacionalismos', in Aguirre *et al.* [1999: 159–76].

Spain and the Wider World

Spain, Latin America and Europe:
The Complex Interaction of Regionalism
and Cultural Identification

RICHARD YOUNGS

Spain's commercial, diplomatic and developmental ties with Latin America strengthened considerably during the 1990s. While policy towards the region was one of Spain's most notable success stories, in some areas it was still subject to significant limitations. Conversely, in other areas it might be argued that the focus on Latin America was disproportionate and optimal neither for Spain's own substantive interests nor in terms of Madrid's relations with other EU member states. The relationship between Spain's European and Latin American policies was increasingly complex, neither completely mutually reinforcing nor entirely zero-sum, but subject to different dynamics in different areas of policy. Balancing the forces of regionalization within Europe with the culturally driven orientation towards Latin America constituted an acute challenge for Spanish foreign policy: a challenge which was met with considerable, but not unqualified, success.

Relations between Spain and Latin America experienced a widely-acknowledged resurgence during the early 1990s, after a decade during which Madrid was focused to an overwhelming degree on establishing itself as a mainstream player within European fora. This study analyses the evolution of this revival as the 1990s progressed, paying particular attention to the elements of change and continuity following the PP's entry into government in 1996. A critical perspective is offered, contrasting the increasingly-felt drawbacks of Spain's disproportionate focus on Latin American with the persisting pressure from all areas of Spanish society for an even more marked prioritization of the region within Spain's external relations. An analysis of Spain's relations with Latin America is of broader interest in so far as it is able to shed light on the relationship between the dynamics of regionalism and culture-based 'civilizationalism'. These are two of the most prominent competing frameworks seeking to explain the post-cold war international system. While many analysts have highlighted the division of the international order into increasingly cohesive regional blocs, others have suggested that the ideological allegiances of the cold war

The author is grateful to Richard Gillespie, Benny Pollack and Roberto Russell for comments on an earlier version of the paper and to the latter for allowing him to use the facilities of the Instituto del Servicio Exterior de la Nación (ISEN) in Buenos Aires.

are being replaced by a regrouping of states into distinctive cultural groupings or 'civilizations' [Huntington, 1996].

As a state embedded within the world's most deeply-integrated regional grouping, while simultaneously laying claim to identification with a separate culturally-inspired community of nations, Spain offers an interesting case study of the interplay of these two organizing forces. Crucial to this question is an understanding of the impact of Spain's involvement in the process of European integration on its Latin American policy. Spanish policy-makers have tended to see these two areas of policy as mutually reinforcing: the stronger Spain's 'embeddedness' in the incrementally accumulating dynamics of the EU, the stronger would be the force of its own political and economic presence in Latin America, a presence which would, in turn, strengthen its own weight within the EU. This study argues that this standard claim is an increasingly misleading lens through which to analyse Spain's relations with Latin America. It was some of the limits to European regionalism that were key to accounting for Spain's Latin American policies, while, conversely, the latter were far from being entirely beneficial for Spain's prestige and influence inside European fora.

Economic Relations

The scale and rapidity of Spain's economic expansion in Latin America during the 1990s was widely admired as a truly spectacular success story. It appeared to accord a degree of concrete underpinning to Madrid's claim to influence in the region which had been lacking during the entire twentieth century. The increase in Spanish direct investment to Latin America as the 1990s progressed was, indeed, phenomenal. Between 1991 and 1993, 60 per cent of Spanish foreign investment went to the EU and only 12 per cent to Latin America. By 1994–96, Latin America had overtaken the EU as the main recipient, accounting for 40 per cent of Spanish investment compared with the 33 per cent going to Europe [BID-Irela, 1998: 111]. This trend continued, such that by 1998 over one-half of Spanish FDI was going to Latin America. In absolute terms, Spanish FDI to Latin America increased fivefold between 1995 and 1997 [European Commission, 1999: 7]. By 1998, Spain had overtaken the UK as the second largest provider of new investment and, by 1999, was predicted to overtake the US as the largest investor in the region. Significantly, many investments were facilitated by tax incentives and credit facilities granted within the scope of bilateral friendship agreements [Schumacher, 1995: 131].

These investment patterns undoubtedly gave real economic substance to Spain's presence in, and pretensions of influence over, Latin America. There were, however, a number of reasons for doubting the degree to which these trends constituted an unqualified success for Spanish policy. First, Spain's economic presence in the region looks far less impressive when trade flows are examined. In 1997, only 6.4 per cent of Spain's exports went to Latin America, with 4.3 per cent of its imports coming from the region, proportions which had not grown since the late 1980s [European Commission, 1999: 9]. While these shares were above the EU average for trade with Latin America, they were only marginally so. Spain's trading patterns continued to shift towards Europe. By 1997, Spain was conducting almost twice as much trade with Portugal as with the whole of Latin America and was importing more from Switzerland than from Argentina, Brazil or Mexico. It was running an increasingly large trade surplus with Latin America: consistently one of the largest surpluses in the region of all EU states over the 1990s, this had reached nearly $1,500 million in 1997 [IMF, 1998: 220–21].

The Asian devaluations of 1996–97 encouraged Spanish importers to switch their supply sources from Latin America to Asia, further aggravating Latin American trade deficits. Spain did continue to press for upgraded EU trade preferences for Latin America, in notable contrast to its more tempered enthusiasm for liberalization (and, in some cases, straight protectionism) in trade negotiations with other areas of the world. However, even in negotiations with Latin America, Spain was often ambivalent and in some cases resolutely unwilling to compromise when faced with its own sectoral problems. Madrid's position on CAP reform was strongly criticized by Spanish NGOs working in Latin America. To Central America's considerable chagrin, Spain sided with the UK and France in opposing a scaling down of the EU's tariff-quota banana regime, prioritizing the interests of producers in the Canaries. It also fought hard in EU fishing negotiations with Argentina (although it did not hold co-operation to ransom in the same way it had done with Canada). Spain was also one of the states most reluctant to countenance fundamental reform to the Multilateral Fibre Agreement. In this sense, Spain must take its share of responsibility for the growing perception among Latin American elites that trade liberalization could most productively be pursued either intra-regionally or with Washington.

Even with regard to direct investment, there were still significant limitations to the nature and scale of Spain's presence. In 1997, for the first time in contemporary Spain, investment outflows exceeded inflows. While undoubtedly this was a noteworthy development, Spain was, after 1997, still an extremely small net provider of FDI and seen in Latin America as a competitor for funds from northern European states as much as itself a source of investment. Moreover, Spanish investment in Latin America was motivated as much by 'negative' as by 'positive' factors. It was widely recognized that the explanation for the rise in Spanish investment to Latin America lay in developments within Europe. The single market had opened the floodgates to EU investment to come pouring into Spain. In order to survive, Spanish companies were obliged to begin looking for new markets. Few companies in Spain were competitive enough to prosper in other parts of the EU, needing easier markets elsewhere [CEPAL, 1997: 92].

This was a more robust explanation of Spanish FDI trends than those predicated on cultural factors. While frequently alluded to, the role played by cultural and linguistic commonalities was difficult to quantify and was seen by most Latin American policy-makers as deliberately overplayed by Madrid [Russell, 1999: 24]. If they did not themselves provide the incentive for the explosion in Spanish FDI, cultural factors did, however, help Latin America become the natural focus for Spanish companies seeking for the first time to establish a significant international presence. This was compounded by the tendency for Spanish companies, tentative in their first excursions abroad, to 'cluster' in areas where other Spanish firms had already established a presence: this helps explain the concentration of investment in a small number of sectors and countries within Latin America – up to 1996, over 60 per cent of Spanish investment in Latin America was concentrated in two countries, Argentina and Peru [BID-Irela, 1998: 111).

The pressures on Spanish companies to internationalize also fortuitously coincided with the launch of privatization processes in a number of Latin American countries. It was, however, the relative disinterest in Latin America on the part of other European countries that played a major part in facilitating Spain's success in the region. Spanish companies invariably took the vast majority of funds available under Commission programmes aimed at enhancing investment flows to Latin America (such as Al-Invest and ECIP) (*Agence Europe*, 25 Feb. 1999, p.8). At the same time they benefited from the lack of a comprehensive Europeanization of investment promotion – still primarily a national competence – which would have levelled out the more generous incentives provided by the Spanish government relative to those on offer to other European companies. Indeed, the private sector was worried that the government's efforts to awaken greater European interest in Latin America might work to Spain's disadvantage, given the extent to which the latter's success was due to the lack of effort from other European investors (interview, CEOE, Madrid, Sept. 1999).

It would be difficult not to conclude that the inverse also applied: that is, that Spain's success in Latin America implied an inability on the part of Spanish investors to take advantage of possibly more profitable opportunities elsewhere. Spain's presence in Asia, for example, was extremely limited. No other European country's investments were so concentrated in one region. No other European state's investors were attracted to Latin America by this logic of displacement, but rather as an addition to already well established investment projects both within the EU itself and regions such as North America and East Asia.

The Latin American reaction to Spanish investment was mixed, and increasingly prickly as the 1990s progressed. Talk of a backlash against the Spanish presence was increasingly common. Some lamented the fact that Spain did not seem willing to provide the same conditions of access to receive incipient Latin American investment that it had insisted on for its own investment into the region [Terragno, 1999]. Iberia's unhappy experiences in Latin America were particularly damaging to Spain's image. The airline dumped most of its interests in Latin America in order to meet Commission requirements for Iberia to be eligible for subsidies to finance its European operations.

This provided a high-profile case of an apparently direct conflict between Spain's European and Latin American policies – to the clear disadvantage of the latter. Latin Americans argued that Iberia had, if anything, generated a 'reverse' transfer of technology. Some companies, such as Telefónica, used their increasingly dominant positions within local Latin American markets to frustrate governments' plans to open up service provision to greater internal competition. Price hikes implemented by Spanish companies in a number of basic utility sectors provoked tension and in some cases strikes (for example, in Peru and Chile). In several countries, such actions led directly to the tightening up of anti-trust legislation. In Argentina, even business sectors proposed a New Labour-style windfall tax to hit Spanish companies, arguing that the wave of privatizations had contributed to the deepening of social inequalities (*El País Negocios*, 22 Aug. 1999, p.12).

The increasing competition between Spanish companies themselves for shares of the Latin American market engendered a wave of frequently shifting and destabilizing alliances and demergers. Key civil society groups – both in Latin America and Spain – argued strongly that the conditions through which Spanish investment had flooded the Latin American market had contributed to, rather than tempered, the problems of corruption and bad governance (interview with the president of Transparency International Latin America, Buenos Aires, August 1999).

Spanish companies were a convenient target for populist Latin American politicians. There was increasing concern among Spanish businesses, which began to undertake polling to assess their image amongst local populations. Significantly, they also began to pursue more of their plans through joint ventures, working with local counterparts, to mitigate accusations that their presence had invariably brought with it a heavy-handed displacement of local capacity (interview, CEOE, Madrid, September 1999). By the end of the 1990s, in a direct reversal of previous positions, the PSOE was now criticizing the PP for allowing the actions of Spanish companies to affect Spain's overall image in Latin America prejudicially (*El País Digital*, 30 Nov. 1999).

Some of these more problematic elements of Spain's economic presence did register with the PP administration and conditioned the nature of policy over the latter part of the 1990s. By 1999, Rodrigo Rato was suggesting that Spanish companies did need to begin to diversify, especially into the Asian market (*El Clarín Económico*, 11 July 1999, pp.10–11). Another priority was to increase the presence of smaller firms in Latin America and to encourage both sectoral and geographic diversification of Spanish investment patterns within the region, with the need to correct Spain's still limited presence in Brazil a particular concern. In practice, there were no signs that Spanish investors were at all likely to diversify their interests beyond Latin America, although the PP's efforts with regard to small and medium sized business did seem to be generating some response (interviews, Spanish Foreign Ministry and CEOE, Madrid, Sept. 1999).

The PP also acquiesced to the principle of a voluntary Code of Conduct aimed at ensuring Spanish companies' compliance with basic labour standards, a significant even if primarily symbolic move to reverse the deteriorating image of Spanish business practice in the region. At the same time, the government sought to distance itself from high-profile investment projects. There was much criticism under the PSOE of the extent to which large-scale investments appeared to be arranged at the political level: for example, a reputedly reluctant Iberia took over Aerolíneas Argentinas after a deal had been struck between González and President Menem. This political element became increasingly controversial in Latin America and was increasingly resented by other EU states. It sat uneasily with Spain's own strictures on the need for more transparent government in Latin America. The PP went to great lengths to present itself as not seeking to influence decisions taken by the private sector. In practice, the political element still continued to be notable, with, for example, King Juan Carlos lobbying energetically on behalf of Repsol's bid for the Argentinian petroleum giant YPF.

Shared Democratic Values: European and Latin American Perspectives

As the 1990s progressed, Spain put increasing emphasis on the promotion of shared, democratic values as the overarching rationale of its diplomatic initiatives in the region. To the extent that Latin America's progress in consolidating democracy and the rule of law explained Madrid's intensified efforts in the region, this contrasted with the security concerns that drove Spain's engagement in the Mediterranean. As both Spain and Latin America moved away from authoritarianism over the 1970s and 1980s, the way was opened up for a new partnership predicated on the strengthening of modern, democratic political values. Franco's cultural expansionism was replaced by the concept of Spanish–Latin American relations being based on the shared experience of poorly developed economies emerging from dictatorship [Grugel, 1995: 144]. The promotion of the shared objectives of political modernization constituted the essential basis upon which Spain's notion of a 'Community of Ibero-American Nations' was to be constructed. This objective was reflected in the fact that by 1997 Spain was spending a higher proportion of its aid on democratization and institution-building than all other EU states except Denmark and Sweden [OECD, 1999; European Commission, 1999: 18].

An impressive breadth and density of dialogue developed on corruption, human rights, electoral transparency and political party reform. The very concept of 'community' ensured that Spain pursued an overwhelmingly and uniquely co-operative diplomacy towards Latin America, with the principles of sovereignty and non-intervention prominent in the declarations of the Ibero-American summits. The PSOE government opted unequivocally to encourage the deepening of democratic norms and human rights protection through a policy of positive engagement and political support. While Madrid did suspend aid to Peru following President Fujimori's 1992 auto-coup, it was slower to do so than was the US, imposed a narrower range of sanctions than Washington and was quicker to restore relations to normality than most other states. Spain expressly eschewed the kind of criticism put forward by other EU governments and NGOs in relation to human rights abuses, particularly in Colombia and Mexico.

The PP's criticism of González's policy of positive engagement seemed to indicate that this would be an area of policy that would change after Aznar took office in 1996. In reality, the degree of continuity was more striking. The PP government increased the focus on co-operation in the field of democracy promotion, committing itself to doubling – from six per cent to 12 per cent – the proportion of ODA devoted to this objective by 2002 [MAE, 1999: 303]. It also pushed for greater emphasis on this issue at the European level, given that EU funding correlated to democratic progress would favour Latin America over other developing regions [Montobbio, 1998: 22]. The PSOE's basic orientation was retained, the PP government generally pushing for less 'coercive' or 'critical' EU positions and initiatives. Official positions stressed that Spain would only seek to help embed 'shared' democratic values where Latin American governments were themselves actively seeking assistance to this end [MAE, 1999: 303].

In response to pressure from a number of EU states to increase pressure on human rights issues through the EU–Rio Group dialogue, secretary of state Ramón de Miguel argued that he saw 'no grounds' for criticizing Latin American governments' human rights performance (*Agence Europe*, 10 April 1997, p.7).

Policy towards Cuba was the obvious, high-profile exception to this, but what was significant in this case was the extent to which the PP retracted from its initial hard-line stance towards Havana. By 1998, Spain was urging other EU states to upgrade co-operation with Havana and accept the principle of Cuba's accession into Lomé without political preconditions (*El País Digital*, 22 Nov. 1999). No other EU state was as keen on such commitments prior to at least some movement on human rights issues. Within two years of taking office, the PP's Cuba policy could not in any significant way be distinguished from that of González, based on the promotion of investment and commercial links, with such economic engagement being justified as the best means of promoting political change. Events at the November 1999 Ibero-American summit in Havana attracted differing assessments. Many in Spain lamented what they interpreted as a new hardening of Aznar's policy, manifest in the prime minister's refusal to sanction an official visit to Cuba by the King, his insistence on meeting dissidents in Havana prior to the summit and the securing of a Human Rights Commission within the new Ibero-American Secretariat (this having been urged primarily by Cuban dissidents). Others judged that the very holding of the summit in Cuba, combined with the traditional conviviality between Ibero-American leaders, had provided succour to Castro's regime. Significantly, most EU member states, already carrying out more systematic dialogue with dissidents, tended toward the latter view, continuing to be concerned over the potential of Ibero-American summits to undermine supposedly common European positions.

While press, academic and NGO attention in Spain focused heavily on Cuba, similarly nuanced divergence between Spanish and other EU states' positions could also be detected in relation to a range of other issues. The enthusiasm shown by most EU states over the prospect of General Pinochet being put on trial was not shared by Madrid, the latter searching for a politically negotiated means of overturning Judge Garzón's extradition request and smoothing relations with Chile. When northern EU states advocated a tighter form of conditionality in relation to good governance in Latin America, Spain was the state most adamantly opposed to this (interview, European Commission, Brussels, May 1999). In the protracted negotiations with Mexico over the EU's 'democracy clause', Spain was the state most willing to acquiesce to Mexico's demand for diluted wording that would reduce European influence over the country's internal affairs (and Spanish MEPs were those most instrumental in the European Parliament eventually consenting to a trade mandate, while the situation in Chiapas was still worsening).

In Venezuela, the PP government reacted to Hugo Chávez's piecemeal dismantling of the country's liberal democratic institutions over the course of 1999 in an expressly non-critical fashion, with Spain again holding back some EU states keener to adopt a more critical stance (interview, Spanish Foreign Ministry, Madrid, Sept. 1999). Conditionality was operated in only a modest fashion through an anti-corruption clause introduced into the conditions for soft loans, thus bringing to bear some, albeit limited, pressure on good governance issues.

Such policy developments, in particular Spain's frequent departure from the outlook of many – and invariably, most – EU states on Latin American issues, might be interpreted as giving weight to the long-standing contention that a distinctive Latin or Hispanic political and economic culture exists. A number of analysts have argued that such specificity continued to be of great significance into the 1990s, with many of those values and customs prominent in Latin America being shared by Spain to a greater extent than by other European states: the importance attached to social dialogue and support for neo-corporatism; the preservation of traditional community links; the prevalence of personal loyalties over meritocracy; the reliance on quasi-constitutional organic laws delineating the rights and duties of different groups within civil and political society [Véliz, 1994; Wiarda, 1996: 79–81]. The deepening of Spanish–Latin American relations was often advocated as a means of strengthening a pole within the international system uniquely committed to combining individual liberty and communal solidarity [Hochleitner, 1998].

Even discounting the more excessive hyperbole on this point, the basic claim to an underlying sociological and philosophical commonality between Spain and Latin America, nebulous at the best of times, seemed deeply out of tune with events inside the EU over the latter part of the 1990s. It would be difficult not to conclude that many of the values of a supposedly distinctive Hispanic political and economic culture were precisely those that Madrid was having to reassess owing to the increasing intrusion of European integration into Spanish domestic affairs.

With Spain increasingly obliged to adapt its regulatory structures to the requirements of the single market and EMU, its scope for deviating from European 'best practice' was, whether desired or not, ever more curtailed. A safer explanation of the nature of Spanish policy is that, for the furtherance of its own interests and presence in the region, Spain was increasingly sensitive to charges of neo-colonialism in Latin America and keen to meet the region's insistence that the Community of Ibero-American Nations be a 'community of equals'. Spain's historical baggage caused it to tread slightly more carefully than some EU states in the region (this mirroring French positions in Francophone Africa, slightly less so UK policies in the Commonwealth).

Spain's own corruption problems of the mid-1990s also put Madrid on to the back foot in terms of promoting the Spanish transition as a model for Latin America. In 1999, the head of the Spanish International Co-operation Agency (AECI), responsible for managing anti-corruption programmes in Latin America, was himself forced to resign on corruption charges! The desire to avoid problems for Spanish investors was the most important factor, the extent of Spanish FDI in the region compounding the difference in perspective with many other European states. Significantly, critical pressure was applied by the PP government only on the issue of judicial capacity and independence – precisely the area of good governance of concern to Spanish investors (interview, CEOE, Madrid, Sept. 1999).

Moreover, despite Spain's heightened caution over any form of coercive interference in Latin America, the region's governments themselves still reacted with significant ambivalence to the concept of supposedly 'shared values'. While some Latin American élites appeared to hold to the notion of a distinctive Hispanic political culture as an alternative to Anglo-Saxon institutional and regulatory approaches, and saw Spain as a welcome conveyer of such values, others were increasingly keen to converge with US policy-making styles. This gave Washington a firmer foothold in its efforts to encourage the uptake of US regulatory structures, a development of increasing concern to Spain and some other European states (interview, European Commission, Brussels, May 1999).

In practice, Spain found relatively limited space available to co-operate in any meaningful way in the propagation of the much-vaunted 'community of shared values'. Latin American governments' insistence on being treated as equals – particularly resolute in the case of the region's more prickly states, such as Mexico – diluted the focus on civil society and governance issues at the Ibero-American summits (interview, Spanish Foreign Ministry, Madrid, Sept. 1999). A number of areas of democratic reform for which Spain offered finance in Central America were rejected (interview, Instituto de Cooperación Iberoamericana, Madrid, Sept. 1999), and there was even talk of the Democratic Governance programme in the region being dropped. Upon taking office, Andrés Pastrana specifically rejected the Spanish democratic model as a solution to Colombia's ills (El País, 28 June 1998, p.6). Most Latin American states still perceived the Inter-American Development Bank to be the main player in the region, the bank operating a more limited, apolitical concept of good governance.

If Latin Americans were ambivalent towards Spain's concept of promoting 'shared political values', so also was Spanish domestic opinion. The PP government was subject to increasingly vocal opposition from civil society groups on human rights issues. Key NGOs, such as Abogados Democráticos, pushed increasingly hard for the government to take a firmer line on human rights in Colombia and in Chiapas [Alvarez, 1997: 46].

Considerable controversy was caused by the claim of NGOs that they had not been defended by the Spanish government when restricted in their operations in Chiapas by the Mexican authorities. The cases against Pinochet and former officials of the Argentine dictatorship were driven forward by civil society groups involving Latin American exiles resident in Spain, with family links playing a prominent role in generating momentum behind the issue of impunity.

Conversely, beyond their advocacy of stronger criticism of egregious human rights abuses, Spanish NGOs expressed their concern that development funds were being deployed in too heavy-handed a fashion to promote a 'Spanish model' of democracy. These NGOs pressed the government to divert democracy promotion funds to poverty reduction projects and basic service provision. They also suggested that where funds were dedicated to civil society strengthening, the government was guilty of focusing on state level, often business-oriented, organizations, and under-funding grass-roots groups. NGOs rejected the principle of conditionality (although a minority did favour its more limited, 'positive' form). While this opposition was broadly in line with the PP's policy, it did add extra weight to pressures on the government to retract from its initial hard-line policy towards Cuba (interview, Coordinadora de Organismos No Gubernamentales para el Desarrollo (ONGD), Madrid, Sept. 1999).

The nature of general public opinion was also found to belie the popular conception of Spaniards being uniquely interested in, and identifying themselves with, Latin America: the Spanish population was significantly – and increasingly – more concerned with, and aware of, European than Latin American affairs, and they expressed greater admiration for the United States, Japan, Germany and even the UK than for any Latin American country [Del Campo, 1998: 29, 33, 51]. Spaniards were keen for additional assistance to be given to Latin America, but this seemed increasingly to derive from sympathy for the region's plight than from a normative belief in a distinctive value-based political community.

The Community of Ibero-American Nations and Spain's International Projection

The existence of shared internal values and a genuine 'Community of Ibero-American Nations' were seen as the foundations upon which a common Hispanic identity in international politics could be developed. Senior policy-makers involved in Ibero-American relations during the 1990s claimed that the summits had succeeded in elevating the Hispanic community to a status where it enjoyed a separate and distinctive presence in international affairs, reflecting the common interests of its constituent members [Fraga, 1998]. This was an aspect that the Aznar government has been keen to develop further: that is, a conscious objective after 1996 was to accelerate the move away from perceived cultural paternalism towards the concept of a community of nations co-operating on the world stage, this conceived as a means of strengthening Spain's own presence in international affairs [Mallo, 1997: 103]. Aznar defined Spain's promotion of the Ibero-American Community as 'an essential *strategic* option' (*El País*, 10 Nov. 1997, p.3, emphasis added).

In practice, this external dimension was the area where Madrid's rhetoric most obviously continued to exceed reality. It was difficult to identify international issues where the Ibero-American Community acted in concert as a distinctive foreign policy actor. There was no attempt to spell out the values upon which the supposed distinctiveness in international relations would be predicated. By the end of the 1990s, the Ibero-American Community had not developed anywhere near as substantive an international protagonism as, for example, the Commonwealth, the latter increasingly undertaking its own autonomous concrete operations in fields such as election monitoring. It was widely felt that on foreign policy issues the Ibero-American summits were extremely vague and lacklustre. The international dimension of the summits' follow-up work programmes was particularly weak, with even modest concrete manifestations of Ibero-American protagonism conspicuously failing to emerge [Mallo, 1997: 108].

Debates on a range of issues indicated how far Madrid was from securing an alliance with Latin American countries on broad global issues. A number of Latin American countries opposed western operations in the Balkans and Iraq. Attempts to delineate guidelines within the United Nations for a post-cold war 'new interventionism' were not welcomed by most Latin American states. On these issues, Madrid had increasingly aligned itself with the main EU actors, the difference in perspective with Latin America actually widening over the latter part of the 1990s. Madrid's proposal for the creation of an Ibero-American Peacekeeping Force, presented in 1998, met with considerable scepticism on the part of Latin American states and, by the turn of the century, did not appear close to being realized.

On reform of international financial structures, Ibero-American summit declarations did incorporate the demands of Latin American states for more restrictive controls on cross-border capital flows and, at the 1999 EU–Latin America summit in Rio, Spain did garner EU support for an undertaking to investigate how global financial instability might be tempered. However, from the Latin American perspective, Spain had become as aggressive a perpetrator of this feature of globalization as other developed countries and, in effect, Madrid eschewed any firm commitments that would curtail its own international financial interests as firmly as did London or Bonn. At the 1999

Ibero-American summit, Latin American leaders' calls for restrictions on capital mobility contrasted with Aznar's emphasis on the need for states to undertake 'necessary internal adjustments' (*Clarín Digital*, 17 Nov. 1999).

On the issue of international terrorism, tensions continued to be engendered by Madrid's difficulty in securing as fluid a co-operation as it desired from Latin America on the extradition of ETA members. This was an issue on which Aznar expressly pressured with greater force, in particular by urging tighter co-operation between Spanish and Latin American police forces, which engendered considerable unease on the part of many of the region's governments. On the issue of counter-narcotics strategy, Latin American states were themselves divided, several closer to Washington's predilection for building-up military capacity than to the European focus on the social roots of drugs problems. Common Ibero-American approaches to such issues did not appear to be imminent by the end of the 1990s.

In the wake of the 1994 Summit of the Americas in Miami, there was a *rapprochement* on many issues between Latin and North America, this increasingly rivalling – if not, eclipsing – Spain's Ibero-American pretensions. Important examples of this trend were to be found in Mexico's participation in NAFTA, leading it to seek an alignment with North America on a broad range of issues, Chile's application to join NAFTA and Argentina's prioritization of 'carnal relations' with Washington. It was in preparation for negotiations on the prospective Free Trade Area of the Americas where Latin American governments most eagerly sought unity in their external projection: precisely the issue on which Madrid's claim to leadership over an Ibero-American space appeared most incongruous.

It would be difficult to rebut the contention that the more significant impact on the international system derived from an incipient hemispheric, rather than the Ibero-American, logic. Latin American states resisted an institutionalization of the Ibero-American Community similar to that which they had warmly supported in connection with the Summits of the Americas follow-up work programme. The permanent, Madrid-based Ibero-American Secretariat which was finally agreed in 1999 was a notable development, but was given significantly more modest responsibilities – limited to a co-ordination of different national projects rather than the instigation of new common competences – than the Spanish government had desired. The keenest rivalry to US hegemony in Latin America came, of course, from Brazil's long-standing and increasingly felt pretensions to regional leadership. Brazil, however, was in this sense as suspicious of Spanish as of US designs: both Cardoso and Aznar acknowledged the political element of Spain's relations with Brazil to be negligible (*El País*, 21 April 1998, p.6).

Moreover, it was not clear how Ibero-american international projection, if realized, would combine with CFSP's development. Given that Spain was both a keen advocate of CFSP's institutional deepening and an increasingly prominent and valued contributor to its practical implementation, it seemed unlikely that Madrid would, in practice, opt to align itself with an Ibero-American voice should this differ from European positions. In practice, Spain moulded itself far more to the nascent European external identity than to Ibero-American interests. In reaction to Argentina's 1999 petition to join NATO, for example, Madrid was less categorically dismissive of the idea than other EU states, but readily aligned itself to a common EU rejection of Buenos Aires' somewhat audacious initiative.

Assuming there was no intention actively to cut across CFSP procedures, Spain's position appeared to acknowledge the impossibility or even undesirability of a CFSP with truly global coverage. The Ibero-American Peacekeeping Force idea was proposed by Madrid at the very moment when internal EU debate on the development of autonomous European capacity for 'soft security' operations began to move forward. The implication that Madrid doubted the EU's capability or willingness to deploy such capacity in areas where peacekeeping work was desired by Latin American states was not seen as helpful by other EU member states.

In the run-up to the 1996-97 IGC's conclusion, the French and Italian foreign ministers warned that some member states' prioritization of historical links was undermining the coherence of CFSP priorities (*Le Monde*, 12 Oct. 1996, p.15). This IGC witnessed a significant evolution of French positions, with Paris coming to support far tighter constraints on national diplomatic manoeuvrability for the sake of inducing more efficient European action. If the balance between CFSP minimalists and maximalists was shifting in favour of the latter, in Madrid this began to force consideration of the precise relationship between the government's Ibero-American and European diplomacy. If the international component of the Ibero-American Community was hard to detect during the 1990s, the gathering momentum of CFSP dynamics over the latter part of the decade rendered its future prospects even more doubtful.

Financial Assistance and Development Co-operation

The extent to which Spanish development policy was oriented towards Latin America demonstrated the disproportionate importance attached to the latter in relation to other developing regions. The new International Development Co-operation Law, agreed in 1998, ring-fenced a minimum of 40 per cent of Spanish aid for Latin America, in effect tightening a provision dating from 1987 which determined that Latin America should be the principal recipient of Spanish funds. The actual proportion of aid allocated to Latin America came down from nearly two-thirds during the late 1980s, but then stayed relatively constant at over 40 per cent during the 1990s, including after 1996 [OECD, 1999]. This gave Spain a unique development co-operation profile. The United States donated under one-fifth of its aid budget to its 'back yard' (although both the US and Japan still donated three times more to the region than Spain). Portugal channelled virtually all its aid (over 99 per cent) to its ex-colonies in Africa [OECD, 1999], indicating a distinct lack of enthusiasm for the Ibero-American solidarity espoused by its neighbour. The disproportionately high share of aid allocated to Latin America ensured that, despite its relatively limited total aid budget, Spain was in absolute terms the second largest EU donor to the region during the 1990s, behind Germany – although displaced to third place by the Netherlands in the closing years of the decade.

Spain's advocacy of Latin American interests within international donor organizations continued unabated under the PP administration. In negotiations for the EU's 1999–2003 budget, the Spanish government fought hard to block the desire of all other EU states to divert development funds away from Latin America to poorer African and Asian states. The PP government also pushed for the new Highly Indebted Poor Countries debt write-off package to include the maximum possible coverage for the most overburdened Latin American states. During the 1998 international financial crisis, Spain not only provided one of the most generous assistance packages to Latin America itself, but also galvanized the IMF into agreeing a special initiative to shore up the region's economies: Rodrigo Rato acknowledged that Spain was uniquely motivated in seeking to prevent the spilling over of the Asian and Russian crises due to the disproportionate presence of Spanish companies with interests in Latin America (*El País*, 25 Sept. 1998, p.69).

Spanish generosity to Latin America was, however, subject to significant limitations. Overall Spanish aid amounts declined from 0.28 per cent of GDP in 1993 to 0.23 per cent in 1997, one of the lowest in the OECD Development Assistance Committee – by 1997, only Japan, Italy and the United States were less generous. Per capita, Spanish aid amounts were four times lower than the French and three times lower than the German development budgets – that is, a far greater difference than the gap in per capita wealth (only Italy, Portugal and the US were lower per capita donors) [OECD, 1999]. By the turn of the century, the PP had not fulfilled its commitment to significantly increase these shares; the modest increases that it did agree to were forced on it by the action of civil society groups. The debt relief offered to Latin America by Spain was also proportionately less than that arranged by other EU member states: when Hurricane Mitch struck, for example, Spain was still Central America's largest creditor

[MAE, 1999: 373]. In fact, Spain was still a net receiver of funds, with EU cohesion fund receipts amounting to 1.3 per cent of Spain's GDP (*El País*, 17 June 1998, p.3).

This fact did not escape the attention of Latin Americans. The very existence of the cohesion funds was seen by Latin American politicians and NGOs as emblematic of the inward-looking nature of the EU and an indication of how much more successful Spain had been in protecting its own interests within Europe than in promoting Latin American interests beyond the EU's borders. The structure of Spanish aid also attracted growing criticism, with the OECD pressing Spain to move away from its uniquely heavy use of soft, tied loans – in 1996 Spain was the only DAC member with a 100 per cent 'tied aid status' – channelled through the Development Aid Funds, or FADs. The criteria for the granting of these funds focused on financial liquidity and credit rating and thus went overwhelmingly to middle income countries – this explaining the fact that Argentina was the largest recipient of Spanish aid. As these tied loans were gradually reduced, overall aid amounts dropped by about one-half between 1993 and 1997 [OECD, 1998a]. Interestingly, the issue of the FADs, one of the clearest examples of outside influence on Spanish external policy, involved a convergence to OECD norms, rather than reflecting a specifically 'Europeanizing' dynamic.

Indeed, the fact that Spain was able to orient its aid so disproportionately towards Latin America again relied on the lack of a fully Europeanized policy. In fact, Spain's prioritization of Latin America was perceived by many member states to be one of the principal obstacles to a co-ordination of national aid strategies around a tighter focus on the poorest parts of the developing world. Due to its heavy bias towards Latin America, Spanish aid was considerably less directed at extreme poverty than that of other EU member states. Over the early 1990s, Spain was giving only a little over ten per cent of its aid to sub-Saharan Africa, by some margin the priority of other European states.

By the late 1990s, the proportion of Spain's development budget going to sub-Saharan Africa had increased to over 20 per cent, but at the cost of the share to North Africa and the Middle East, not Latin America. Even within Latin America, other EU states oriented their aid far more towards the poorer countries of Central America than Spain, with its relatively greater flows to the Southern Cone. None of this helped Spain's image within the EU development policy community. Other member states were increasingly exasperated at Madrid's apparently greater concern with shoring up its own commercial and foreign policy interests than with elaborating a more coherent ordering of developmental priorities – such exasperation sitting uneasily with the more usual view of Spain's representation of Latin American interests according it added prestige and respect within the EU. Neither was it clear that the pattern of Spain's aid priorities was entirely compatible with its enthusiastic advocacy of more 'Europeanized' development policies: the overwhelming majority of member states would insist on a single European development policy shifting funds away from Latin America.

Whether Latin America has obtained significant advantage from Spain's sponsorship within the EU is debatable. It was undoubtedly the case that Spanish pressure secured a more generous share of Commission-managed development funds for Latin America than would otherwise have been forthcoming. Most notably, the PSOE government acquiesced in the principle of eastern enlargement only after securing an agreement that new aid transfers to eastern Europe would be accompanied by similar increases to Latin America. Spain succeeded in ensuring that, at a juncture when the EU was initiating a whole new policy in eastern Europe and enhancing its focus on the southern Mediterranean, Latin America's share of Commission aid actually increased, with the region receiving far more in per capita terms than poorer Asian states.

Spain, in fact, pushed for a dismantling of the regionalization of EU external relations, judging this to have relegated Latin America to a low ranking of priority [Montobbbio, 1998: 22]. The evolution of Commission aid suggests that such an objective was misplaced: it was precisely the regionalization of EU policy that enabled Madrid to insist on upgraded policies to Latin America in return for consenting to other member states' initiatives elsewhere in the developing world. However, the evolution of bilateral aid indicates that Spain was increasingly hoist on its own petard. Spain focused its development resources in Latin America believing the latter to be insufficiently attended to by other member states and then used its lead role in the region to strengthen its own weight and prestige within the EU. In turn, however, it was precisely this claim to such a lead role that, by the latter half of the 1990s, was encouraging a majority of member states to reduce their aid budgets to Latin America, seeing this as an area for which Madrid was happy to assume responsibility. In this sense, something of a 'reverse Europeanization' could be detected: if the original intention was for Spain to get EU resources behind its own Latin American priorities, other member states had now come to expect Spain to take a disproportionate share of European responsibilities in the region. Arguably, Latin America had become Spain's 'burden', as much as an opportunity for raising its profile within the EU.

The cultural underpinnings of Spanish assistance were reflected in the high proportion of aid given to education, training, audio-visual co-operation, historical heritage and the restoration of colonial buildings

[Gracia, 1998: 74–7]. This cultural and linguistic focus was significantly more pronounced than in British or French development assistance in their respective ex-colonies. The PP increased the emphasis on education, seeing this not only as an area of comparative advantage for Spanish development projects but also one particularly necessary for strengthening the understanding of democratic norms and responsibilities (interview, Instituto de Cooperación Iberoamericana, Madrid, Sept. 1999). These were, in general, not priority areas for Latin America governments, who pushed for such funds to be used for infrastructure and basic service programmes. The PP administration also sought to develop co-operation through 'mixed funds', getting more advanced Latin American states to contribute to projects in the region's poorer states. There was also a greater insistence on matched funding from local governments for many projects. This too met with some resistance, with Latin American governments concerned that they were being asked to contribute to Spain's underlying foreign policy objective of raising its own influence in the region.

Interestingly, there was no apparent questioning of Latin America's dominance in Spain's development funding from within Spanish society. No political party advocated a fundamental restructuring of aid priorities and business was happy to see development funds backing up its own orientation towards Latin America. Aid managed by the Spanish regions (12 per cent of the total by the late 1990s) was even more markedly biased towards Latin America than was central government aid [Freres et al., 1998: 179]. Public opinion felt that Latin America was the area where an upgrading of Spanish policy was actually most urgent [Del Campo, 1998: 63].

This was reflected in the fact that NGO work and campaigns centring on Latin America received over half of private donations in Spain [Freres et al., 1998: 165]. Even those Spanish NGOs urging a more poverty-focused aid profile advocated only a reorientation to poorer states within Latin America and not any transfer of assistance from the latter to sub-Saharan Africa [Intermon, 1999; interview, Coordinadora de ONGD, Madrid, Sept. 1999]. Indeed, all such NGOs opposed the prospect of any decline in the proportion of EC funds allocated to Latin America. An alliance between NGOs and opposition political parties pushing for more generous provisions within the new International Development Co-operation Law was a noticeable case of successful civil society pressure, which did produce concessions from the PP government [Hughes, 1998]. However, this alliance focused on the managerial quality of the implementation of aid projects, the transparency of allocation and the need further to reduce FADs. It was notable that within the debate on the new law, no one advocated a shift of funds away from Latin America to poorer regions of the world.

The operations of Spanish NGOs were themselves heavily concentrated in Latin America: in 1997, 60 per cent of NGO projects were in Latin America, this proportion not having declined since 1993 [Coordinadora de ONGD, 1998: 37; 1994: 233]. As with investment, the international projection of Spanish NGOs was a relatively new phenomenon and development organizations were attracted initially to the area of the world within which they felt most comfortable. This was compounded by the tendency of Spanish NGOs to operate through personal contacts. The PP modified the nature of NGO funding within Latin America, with Catholic organizations and business-related work being more heavily favoured [Hughes, 1998: 186], but did not encourage any significant diversification of NGO work away from the region.

Spanish NGO activity was not Europeanized to any significant extent. European networks of European NGOs mushroomed in the latter half of the 1990s, but the relatively little attention given by these networks to Latin America encouraged Spanish NGOs to retain their priority bilateral links with Latin America and resist any European-level restrictions on their scope for prioritizing Latin America. At the European level, Spanish NGOs focused their lobbying activities almost exclusively on Spanish MEPs, rather than seeking to develop a Europe-wide strategy for raising awareness of Latin American issues. These NGOs placed more effort on lobbying preparations for the Ibero-American summits than on the plethora of EU meetings. NGOs' complaints continued to centre not on the degree of priority attached to Latin America, but rather on the extent to which development work continued to be coloured by commercial interests – NGOs argued that the PP had actually increased the share of tied aid – and on the fact that the backlash against Spain in the region was beginning to affect their own operations (interview, Coordinadora de ONGD, Madrid, Sept. 1999).

Conclusions

The foregoing account outlines the ways in which Spain's relations with Latin America were conditioned by the interplay of global constraints, transnational dynamics, domestic political considerations and the intersubjective preferences of political elites. Notwithstanding the importance of these levels of analysis, it was the role played by the European dimension that emerged as the pivotal determinant of the nature of Spanish policy in Latin America, the intervening variable influencing the impact of other variables. Crucially, this role was an increasingly complex one, resisting parsimonious generalization. The relationship between the European and Latin American dimensions of Spain's external relations was neither one of purely zero-sum conflict nor entirely mutually reinforcing.

The complex nature of European integration ensured that its influence was felt in different ways in different areas of policy. If the harshness of its impact on Spain provided an incentive for the latter to strengthen its links with Latin America, in a number of arenas it was rather the weakness of EU norms that facilitated the persisting distinctiveness of Madrid's international profile, while in still others the convergent dynamics of the EU ensured a lack of substance to Spain's pretensions in the region. The standard view was that Spain pushed for as strong a possible EU framework for the region, expecting that it would be in the best position to take advantage of the consequent opportunities [Grugel, 1996: 80]. It was also argued that Spain was held back by the EU, but that Madrid pushed other EU states into slightly more committed policies, with greater overall benefit to Latin America than a maximized Spanish policy combined with more modest EU commitment would have offered [March, 1996: 171]. Both these claims fail to capture the multifarious impact of the European dimension. In several areas, Spain gained from the absence of common EU competence and was only held back in terms of trade policy, an area where its own generosity to Latin America was anyway severely restricted. In the area of foreign policy, there were elements of both convergence and divergence. While EU states continued to see Spain's privileged access to the region as broadly facilitating the conveyance of common European policy goals, this was on occasions off-set by internal CFSP tensions caused by Spain's stated desire to develop an international profile for the Ibero-American Community, as well as by what was perceived by some other states to be Madrid's excessive indulgence of the region's political elite. The next challenge presented by the accumulation of EU competence is likely be in the area of migration: here, domestic pressures have thus far been dominant – with, for example, the PP actually increasing the number of permits for Latin Americans after strong union and opposition party pressure [Watts, 1999: 142–6] and Abel Matutes expressly seeking preferential treatment for Latin American immigrants in the 1999 Immigration Bill. The Amsterdam agreement to move towards a Europeanization of immigration policy, which is likely to converge around the tightest prevailing national rules, will pose new problems for Spain in combining its European commitments and its privileged provisions for Latin America.

The modest changes introduced by the PP administration aimed to accelerate the trend away from the more excessive and nebulous claims of a 'civilizational' justification for the priority attached to Latin America, towards a more concrete focus on underpinning commercial interests (interview, Ministry of Foreign Affairs, Madrid, Sept. 1999). Alongside its increasing neglect of Mediterranean policy, the PP's retention of the PSOE's prioritization of Latin America did suggest that the combination of economic interest with cultural identification was still capable of outweighing the influence of dispassionate realist-type calculations of immediate strategic and security interest. In terms of Huntington's schema, Spain might be seen as a 'torn country', bridging but also divided between two different civilizations [Huntington, 1996: 139]. Quite clearly, in many areas of policy Spain was not so much torn as comfortably at home within two non-confrontational civilizations. Significantly, however, the *nature* of Spain's relationship with each region changed. If, during the early 1990s, it was accepted that the Spanish perspective could be described as, 'Europe in the mind, Latin America in the heart' [Gillespie and Pollack, 1993], there were good grounds for arguing that by the end of the decade this was fast reversing. All strata of Spanish society by then claimed to identify themselves fully with Europe, perceiving a commonality of values and interests with Europe, rather than Latin America, but with the latter seen to be important as an area of preferential commercial advantage for Spanish firms (*El País*, 8 Nov. 1997, p.4).

José Saramago once famously used the metaphor of the Iberian peninsula breaking off from Europe and drifting towards the New World as a means of hinting at a reconstitution of the values of communality and instinct, seen to be more imminently latent in Iberia and Latin America than in the western powers standing guard over the international system. In practice, Spanish policies towards Latin America were either increasingly constrained by Spain's embeddedness within the new European order or, where not so shackled, driven by more prosaic concerns. Either way, they were more constitutive of, than challenging to, the prevailing regional distribution of international power.

REFERENCES

Alvarez, J.R. (1997): 'Aproximación a las relaciones España-Colombia durante los años noventa', in *Síntesis* 27–28, special edition entitled 'España y América Latina: relaciones y cooperación en el cambio de siglo', pp.37–58.
BID-Irela (1998): *Inversión extranjera directa en América Latina: la perspectiva de los principales inversores*, Madrid: Instituto de Relaciones entre Europa y América Latina.
CEPAL (1997): *La inversión extranjera en América Latina y el Caribe*, Santiago de Chile: United Nations, Comisión Económica para América Latina y el Caribe.
Commission of the European Communities (1999): *Las relaciones de los estados miembros de la Unión Europea con América Latina y el Caribe: España*, Brussels: European Commission.
Coordinadora de ONGD (1994): *Directorio ONGD 1994*, Madrid: Coordinadora de Organismos No Gubernamentales para el Desarrollo.
Coordinadora de ONGD (1998): *Directorio ONGD 1998*, Madrid: Coordinadora de Organismos No Gubernamentales para el Desarrollo.
Del Campo, S. (1998): *La opinión pública española y la política exterior*, Madrid: Informe Incipe.
Fraga, C. (1998): 'Las cumbres iberoamericanas', *Política Exterior* 64/12, pp.151–63.
Freres, C. (ed.) (1997): *La cooperación al desarrollo bilateral de la Unión Europea en América*

Latina, Madrid: Agencia de Investigación y Estudios de Temas Iberoamericanos (AIETI).

Freres, C. *et al.* (1998): 'España', in Freres (ed.), *La cooperación de las sociedades civiles de la Unión Europea con América Latina*, Madrid: Agencia de Investigación y Estudios de Temas Iberoamericanos (AIETI).

Gillespie, R. and B. Pollack (1993): 'La política exterior de España en 1992: Latinoamérica en el corazón pero Europa en la mente?', *Anuario Internacional CIDOB 1992*, Barcelona: Fundació CIDOB, pp.5–31.

Gracia, J. (1998): 'La cooperación española en Iberoamerica', *Revista Española de Desarrollo y Cooperación* 2, pp.71–9.

Grugel, J. (1995): 'Spain and Latin America', in R. Gillespie, F. Rodrigo and J. Story (eds.), *Democratic Spain: Reshaping External Relations in a Changing World*, London: Routledge.

Grugel, J. (1996): 'Spain: Latin America as an Ambiguous Topic', in F. Algieri and E. Regelsberger (eds.), *Synergy at Work: Spain and Portugal in European Foreign Policy*, Bonn: Europa Union Verlag.

Hochleitner, D. (1998): 'España y América Latina ante el siglo XXI', *El País*, 10 June.

Hughes, N. (1998): 'The International Development Co-operation Law: The Impact of the Development Community on the Spanish Legislative Process', *International Journal of Iberian Studies* 11/3, pp.178–88.

Huntington, S. (1996): *The Clash of Civilisations and the Remaking of World Order*, London: Simon & Schuster.

Iglesias-Caruncho, M. and M.P. Ramos (1997): 'La relación hispano-cubano en el centenario del 98', *Síntesis* 27-28, special edition entitled *España y América Latina: relaciones y cooperación en el cambio de siglo*, pp.37–58.

IMF (1998): *Direction of Trade Statistics 1998*, Washington, DC: International Monetary Fund.

Intermon (1999): *La realidad de la ayuda 1998–9*, Barcelona: Intermon.

MAE (1999): *Estrategia para la cooperación española*, Madrid: Ministerio de Asuntos Exteriores.

Mallo, T. (1997): 'De las cumbres iberoamericanas a la articulación de una Comunidad Iberoamericana de Naciones', *Sintesis* 27–28, special edition on *España y América Latina: relaciones y cooperación en el cambio de siglo*.

March, J. A. (1996): 'España y América Latina', *Política Exterior* 52/10, pp.160–76.

Montobbio, M. (1998): 'La política exterior española y las relaciones Unión Europea-América Latina', *Revista Española de Desarrollo y Cooperación* 3, pp.17–31.

OECD (1998a): *Spain: Development Policy Review*, Paris: Organization for Economic Co-operation and Development.

OECD (1998b): *Tendances des Migrations Internationales*; Paris: Organization for Economic Co-operation and Development.

OECD (1999): *Development Co-operation Efforts and Policies of the Members of the Development Assistance Committee: 1998 Report*, Paris: Organization for Economic Co-operation and Development.

Russell, R. (1999): *Las relaciones Argentina-Unión Europea en los años noventa: adelantos y perspectivas,* Madrid: Instituto de Relaciones entre Europa y América Latina.

Saramago, J. (1989): *The Stone Raft*, London: Harvill Press.

Schumacher, E. (1995): 'Spain and Latin America: The Resurgence of a Special Relationship', in S.K. Purcell and F. Simon (eds.), *Europe and Latin America in the World Economy*, Boulder, CO: Lynne Rienner.

Terragno, R. (1999): 'España como socio', *Noticias*, 24 July.

Véliz, C. (1994): *The New World of the Gothic Fox*, Berkeley: University of California Press.

Wiarda, H. (1996): *Iberia and Latin America: New Democracies, New Policies, New Models*, Maryland, MD: Rowman & Littlefield.

Watts, J. (1999): 'Italian and Spanish Labour Leaders' Unconventional Immigration Policy Preferences', in M. Baldwin-Edwards and J. Arango (eds.), *Immigrants and the Informal Economy in Southern Europe*, London and Portland, OR: Frank Cass.s

The Mediterranean: A Firm Priority of Spanish Foreign Policy?

JESÚS A. NÚÑEZ VILLAVERDE

Spanish foreign policy pays special attention to the Mediterranean, basing itself on a model established in the mid-1980s. The model is focused excessively on the Maghreb. While the period that led to the Euro-Mediterranean Conference at Barcelona in 1995 was characterized by creative activism in both the bilateral and the multilateral sphere, the period since then has seen the Mediterranean lose prominence on Spain's foreign policy agenda. The challenges to be found in the area, most importantly underdevelopment, Islam and emigration, require a change of attitudes and instruments from those currently involved in Madrid's policy.

Once Spain had put an end to its secular isolation, one area where it attempted to create room for manoeuvre internationally was the Mediterranean.[1] This new policy interest has been shaped by a concurrence of complementary interests and visions. On the one hand, Spain has attempted to be seen not only as a useful bridge between Europe and North Africa but also as a country that seeks solutions to all the region's problems. It has attempted to utilize both its knowledge stemming from geographical, historical and cultural associations[2] and the traditional (although not always adequately developed) relations that have involved regular friendship and dialogue with all the countries bordering the Mediterranean, including Israel since 1986. After joining the principal international bodies (the Atlantic Alliance and the European Community), Spain was required to play a new international role and Latin America and the *Mare Nostrum* became the main areas where it felt it could assume a role of some importance.

On the other hand, geographical proximity also made Spain the European country that was most exposed to any destabilizing development. This bred preoccupation over the evolution of the Mediterranean, with Spain conscious of its own limitations when facing the various challenges to be found there. Spain has been anxious to obtain a more active response from its new European and Atlantic partners in order to put an end to the growing instability that characterizes both the Maghreb and the Middle East.

The combination of these different sensibilities has provided the basis of Spain's Mediterranean policy, at least since the beginning of the 1980s. It

---

Translated by Stephen MacKey.

was then that a Socialist government came to power in Madrid and introduced a strategic about-turn in the focus of Spanish relations with the area, which has remained practically unaltered ever since. This was a shift from a view based on apparently inevitable confrontation, stemming from conflicting Hispano-Moroccan interests over Western Sahara, Ceuta and Melilla, to another that believes that these interests are better defended through dialogue and co-operation. The latter approach would create a 'bedrock of mutual interests' which would avoid any type of confrontation.

The Bases of Spain's Global Mediterranean Policy

The recent period has seen policy based on a consciously designed model of relations that has been characterized as 'global'. The objective was in part to avoid the blackmailing tactics used by Morocco and Algeria in response to Spain's earlier 'policy of equilibrium', applied up to the early 1980s, and in part to develop a genuinely Mediterranean policy out of one that hitherto had been exclusively centred on the Maghreb [Gillespie, 1995]. This global concept thus implied a shift in Spain's territorial pretensions in that Madrid now recognized the need to open up to the eastern Mediterranean. It also affected the content of policy by recognizing the need to address not only commercial relations but also political, economic-financial, social and cultural ones.

These new presuppositions led to Spain aspiring to two fundamental aims: the defence of its own interests and the conversion of the area into a zone of economic prosperity and political and social stability. It may even be said that the latter is no more than the means of achieving the former, if it can really be assumed that the 'safeguard of Spanish interests in the region will depend directly on the degree of development of our neighbours' [Moratinos, 1991a]. In any case, the achievement of these aims immediately came up against three difficulties: a broadening of the range of interests to be defended, the growing risks emerging from negative events in the region and the limitation of Spain's own capacity, which left it unable to respond adequately to the challenges on its own.

Interests

Spain's list of interests to be defended is headed by those of a territorial nature: Ceuta, Melilla, the Chafarinas Islands, the Rock of Alhucemas and the Rock of Vélez de la Gomera. The defence of these territories against the desire of Morocco to exercise sovereignty over them completely overshadowed Spanish policy towards the Maghreb up to the 1980s, while the current global policy has not totally achieved its aim of 'encapsulating' the problem. Spain has rejected all Moroccan attempts to establish a dialogue on their future, let alone negotiations. This stance has been maintained up to the present day. Spain has not recognized the Averroes Committee[3] as a framework in which the 'think tank' proposed by Hassan II in 1987 could be developed. With the military option for the recovery of this territory publicly discarded, Morocco maintains its claims in the hope that the rhythm of history will grant their recognition eventually. Meanwhile, the demographic evolution of Ceuta and Melilla (around 72,000 and 60,000 inhabitants respectively) suggests that in the near future the population of Spanish origin will be in the minority. Nobody knows how, short of public initiative, economic development will establish a viable future for the two towns.

Geo-strategic interests possess the same level of importance, given that the stability of the western Mediterranean is vital to the maintenance of living standards in Spain as the country attempts to reach the levels of its EU partners. Not only does the area around the Strait of Gibraltar continue to be an important guarantee of the peninsula's security, but it also plays a fundamental role in the defence of the Canary Islands. Every year more than 70,000 boats sail through its waters, making it one of the principal nerve centres of world maritime traffic and for Spain a valuable sea channel. But increasingly, the Mediterranean also represents an important source of Spain's energy supply, providing 72 per cent of its gas and 17 per cent of its oil. The relationship with the Maghreb involves a mix of strategic and economic interests, with 80 per cent of the phosphates that Spain requires coming from Morocco, while from a socio-economic perspective Moroccan, Saharan and Mauritanian fish stocks are highly valued by Spanish fishermen.

In the field of economics, there are growing trade exchanges, which are at the same level of those with Latin America; in these Spain enjoys a growing, although hardly significant, surplus overall, although with Algeria and Libya there is a deficit. Similarly, Spain's business and investment presence in the area is growing, mainly in Morocco where it is now the second trading partner and second foreign investor. Although neither of these variables is really significant when the level is compared with the potential of an economy the size of Spain's (Spanish investment in the Maghreb does not exceed one per cent of Spain's total foreign investment), there is optimism about the future. If by the year 2010 a free trade area has been established by the EU and its Mediterranean partners,[4] as envisaged by the Euro-Mediterranean Partnership, it is calculated that there will be promising commercial prospects for those who entered the market early and hold advantageous positions through satisfying the needs of a population that will rise from 230 million in the mid-1990s to more than 300 million by 2010.

There are over two million Spanish speakers in the Maghreb, another factor that features in Madrid's hopes of achieving its aims within the region. The advance of the Spanish language, demonstrated by the growing demand to participate in the activities of the Instituto Cervantes in the Maghreb, offers a fresh opportunity to replace the negative stereotypes that, even today, exist among the civil societies of both the northern and southern Mediterranean countries.

It can be seen immediately that practically all of Spain's specific interests in the Mediterranean are concentrated in its western part. However, recent years have seen an increase in attention to the Middle East, fundamentally in terms of Spain's relations with Turkey and the Palestinian Territories. With the former, Spain's basic interest is financial (for example, Expotecnia 99, held in Istanbul[5] or the negotiations over the sale of military material), with the aim of further increasing its already considerable trade surplus.[6] However, in the Palestinian case Spain's motives are political, in that it is attempting to participate, at the same level as other EU countries, in the efforts to solve the principal security problem of the whole Mediterranean region.

Risk Analysis

The second aspect of Spanish policy to be considered here is Madrid's fear of regional destabilization, arising from a series of regional and local problems. At the heart of this is the conviction that only through the resolution of the Arab–Israeli problem can the current climate of mistrust disappear and give way, eventually, to the creation of a Mediterranean space of peace and security, in accordance with the aims of the EMP's political co-operation and security chapter. Channels for resolving the conflict are seen as promising a new scenario in which it will be difficult for the region's leaders to go on justifying either authoritarian attitudes and behaviour or the repeated failures of economic management.

Although in general terms it is assumed that the southern Mediterranean countries present no threats to European security and that the principal risks are not of a fundamentally military nature, the latter type have not disappeared from the periodical reports that the EU foreign ministries draw up. The most serious of these risks is the proliferation of weapons of mass destruction, for the area has a level of arms build-up that surpasses the world's other regions [Brom, 2000]. There is a general acceptance of the forecast that within ten years, this type of weapon will be deployed in the eastern and southern Mediterranean countries and will have the capacity to reach the European continent [Núñez, 1999]. For Spain this possibility is seen in recent Algerian and Libyan attempts to possess this technology. In the final analysis, however, the real risk lies not so much in the manufacture of weapons of this type in the medium term but rather in their acquisition on the international market. Thus, efforts to avoid this need to be concentrated not only in the countries where arms proliferation is occurring, but also on the supply side by imposing controls that put an end to the desire of the main arms manufacturers to export at a global level. There is hardly any other way of making progress in this field, as demonstrated by the Libyan attempt in 1999 to obtain North Korean parts and technology, which fortunately was foiled in London.

The lack of legitimacy which nearly all the countries of the region suffer in varying degrees is another factor to consider as it has a destabilizing effect. In essence, this is no more than the consequence of a series of negative factors, the most important of which include: (a) the failure of economic development models, which promised the populations of North Africa future welfare standards comparable with those of the northern Mediterranean countries; (b) some limiting political models based on paternalism and authoritarianism which deny the immense majority the chance to exercise their rights; (c) the foreign debt crisis, which has obliged countries (with the exception of Libya) to implement structural cost-cutting programmes which are both costly in social terms and economically counter-productive; (d) demographic growth in excess of the limited capacity of these economies to attend to the basic needs of the population (food, health, education and housing) and to integrate it properly into the respective labour markets; (e) the rise of radical Islamic movements, critical of inefficient and corrupt governments and determined to mobilize the large sectors of the population excluded from the system through promising an efficient model that attends to basic needs; (f) the danger of exclusion from the international stage at a time when the EU seems to be absorbed with the eastern European countries and to be closing its entry points to the migratory flows generated by the southern Mediterranean countries' deficiencies.

The worst of all possible scenarios, in the calculations of all the Mediterranean EU foreign ministries, is of an Islamist group taking power in any country of the region. In this case, it is clear that the new regime would be destabilizing and anti-Western while simultaneously provoking a massive exit of citizens in the direction of the northern Mediterranean. Avoiding this prospect, seen by Spain as the most dangerous regional scenario, is the principal motivation behind the current strategy of Euro-Maghreb relations.

In Search of Help

These considerations help us to understand Spanish foreign policy in the region. Spain attempts to avoid any action that might adversely affect its own interests and it does all it can to try to maintain regional stability. However, the old tactic of playing North African countries off against one other has been dropped. Instead of trying to avoid risks by encouraging weakness and permanent misunderstanding between the Mediterranean countries (particularly those of the Maghreb), today 'Spain supports a politically stable, economically prosperous and socially developed Maghreb' [Moratinos, 1991b: 9]. Here we should note that the fixation with the Maghreb rather than the Mediterranean as a whole is maintained.

Once it is understood that there are no threats to Spanish interests of an eminently military nature and that the existing risks have a basically socio-political and economic character, a preventive strategy needs to be articulated. Here the available resources never seem to be enough. Spain cannot attend to this task alone and this explains its interest in drawing the attention of its EU and Atlantic partners. This is how Madrid's attempts to avoid the exclusion of the Mediterranean from the EU agenda should be interpreted, it having been a former Spanish foreign minister who portrayed the situation in North Africa in the early 1990s as 'a time-bomb, which Europe can deactivate' [Ministerio de Asuntos Exteriores, 1992: 8]. It is not forgotten that, from the security viewpoint, it is equally necessary to maintain a deterrent of unquestionable credibility in the face of any possible scenario. Once again, the conviction that its own forces are insufficient to fulfil this role on their own has led Spain to propose initiatives within the defence and security organizations which it joined during the 1980s.

Bilateral Efforts

In the bilateral sphere, the instruments with which Spain attempts to carry out its Mediterranean policy are centred basically on developing a regular political dialogue at different levels with all the region's countries. They are also based on undertaking a policy of co-operation which attempts to institute and develop joint projects, not only in the traditional social, cultural, economic, scientific and technical fields but also more recently in the fields of security and defence. It is not surprising that most of this activity continues to be, even today, directed at the Maghreb, leaving the rest of the Mediterranean somewhat neglected.

Spain and the Maghreb

Despite the attempts to pursue Spain's relations with the Maghreb in a 'global' fashion, in practice we must acknowledge the reality of an 'uneven regional policy' [Gillespie, 1995: 218], in which Morocco receives most attention. This country remains a priority for Madrid, as was demonstrated by the fact that the destination of the first visits abroad by two successive incoming Spanish heads of government, González and Aznar, was Rabat. In other words, more than 15 years after this new global framework was devised, the groundwork has still not been built upon through the signing of similar accords to those that exist with Morocco, despite the intention being repeatedly declared [Núñez and Larramendi, 1996]. On the contrary, even by 1994, at the time of the killing of a number of Spanish tourists in Marrakesh, it was being affirmed that, 'in the best of cases, the policy of democratic Spain towards North Africa has been defensive. The essential aims appear to have been to avoid any tension in the dispute over Ceuta and Melilla and guarantee the supply of Algerian gas' (*El País*, 29 Aug. 1994).

Morocco remains the basic reference point when analysing the evolution of Spanish policy and evaluating attempts to realize its aims. A series of agreements exist between Spain and Morocco covering all the relevant aspects of policy. This gives the impression that the work to create a 'bedrock of mutual interests' has been done. The agreements suggest the existence of common interests and seem to promise that any possible crises in Hispano-Moroccan relations will be resolved through dialogue. Their centrepiece is the Treaty of Friendship, Good Neighbourliness and Co-operation, signed in Rabat on 4 July 1991, which signifies a qualitative leap from an immediate past that was full of suspicion and misunderstanding. Now there are regular political relations and co-operation in the economic and financial spheres, and in those of defence, cultural, legal and consular affairs. Since then, however, only one other similar treaty has been signed by Spain and a North African country: that with Tunisia (26 October 1995). It remains Madrid's intention to sign similar treaties with Mauritania, Libya and Algeria when circumstances permit.

The so-called global policy has developed three priority lines of action: political dialogue, security and defence co-operation and development co-operation. The first of these assumes that the aim is not the disappearance of occasional crises nor the elimination of problems, which are inevitable between neighbouring countries with different interests. Rather, the idea is to institute mechanisms that will allow bilateral communication to be maintained at all times, even during crises. The policy also aims to make some joint interests so solid that it will never be profitable to provoke a crisis owing to the significant losses that this would occasion. To this end, a system of regular bilateral summits has been sought with all countries of the region, although so far this has only been successful in the cases of Morocco since 1989 and Tunisia since 1997.

Secondly, the development of this policy approach has permitted security and defence relationships to become very different to those that existed in the recent past. As recently as 1984, at the time of the signing of the (short-lived) agreement on union between Morocco and Libya, the Spanish reaction was one of obvious concern, and in some circles it was seen as an immediate threat to the country's interests. This view has since given way to another, which viewed the signing of the Treaty of Marrakesh, constituting the Arab Maghreb Union (13 February 1989), as a sign of regional stability. Spain has tried to encourage not only regional integration but also co-operation in matters of defence. Agreements in this field have been signed with Tunisia (14 December 1987), Mauritania (7 February 1989) and Morocco (27 September 1989). The new spirit has been perceived since the issuing of the first National Defence Directive following the cold war, when it was declared that there was no threat to security from the South and that 'there should continue to be support for initiatives that promote stability and security in the Mediterranean and consolidate bilateral relations with the countries along the southern shore' [Ministerio de Defensa, 1993]. During the 1990s, however, it did not prove possible to do so by signing comparable accords with Libya and Algeria.

With respect to economic and financial co-operation, attempts have been made to follow a course parallel to that above, through the creation of closer commercial ties (which have increased substantially since the opening of the Maghreb–Europe gas pipeline in 1996), greater investment on the part of private enterprise[7] and the opening of some beneficial credit lines. In regard to the latter, protocols for financial co-operation with Morocco were renewed in 1996, providing $1,000 million up to the end of 2001. Tunisia and Mauritania have also benefited from such agreements, as has Algeria, which in 1996 was granted credit worth $900 million to finance the purchase of Spanish assets and services and to carry out projects of joint interest. Meanwhile, bilateral development aid to the region continues to flow at its usual levels, well below the 30 per cent of the total envisaged in the outline of Spanish development co-operation policy agreed by Parliament back in 1992. A significant recent development has been a degree of experimentation with debt-for-equity swaps, in the cases of Morocco and Mauritania, under which a proportion of foreign debt has been converted into investment in agreed projects.

In short, Spain's preference remains one of close engagement with these countries as the best means of guaranteeing its interests. Closer relations can only bring advantages that will strengthen Spain in its attempt to play the role of defender of the Maghreb cause in Brussels and to serve as a corridor, above all for Morocco, providing access to EU markets.[8] On the other hand, Spain's cultivation of relations in the field of defence allows it, simultaneously, to reduce regional tension and become an important supplier of arms to the armed forces of the Maghreb (with Morocco once again at the head). Moreover, it allows Spain to maintain a strategic advantage in case of any negative evolution of the situation, both through the control of supply lines and through knowledge of the characteristics of the arms deployed in the region.

This exercise, which combines very different resources and agendas, cannot be considered as completed at any moment, even if only because of the permanent demands of the continuous historical process of evolution. This is why it is worrying to see what has happened since 1996, the year when bilateral policy towards the Maghreb seemed to enter a slower phase and the region even suffered from exclusion because of other priorities on the foreign policy agenda (fundamentally the entry of Spain into the Economic and Monetary Union). During the 1996–2000 legislature, no initiative to perfect or modify the model inherited from the previous Socialist administration was developed, apart from the aforementioned debt conversion operations. Nor has the administrative reorganization of the Ministry of Foreign Affairs, in which the Mediterranean was downgraded, helped to address the sense of relative abandonment.[9] To a great extent, an unprofitable arrangement has resulted, with Spain losing the role of proponent that it acquired in the period leading up to the Barcelona Conference of 1995. This role was immediately taken on by others, while Spain adopted a complacent attitude towards the deterioration of the region, trusting that the most acute phase of the crisis had passed. Thus, there was a lack of proposals or initiatives connected with Algeria and Libya, and a reaffirming of the low profile adopted since 1975 in the search for solutions for Western Sahara.

It is doubtful whether Spain's best interests in North Africa are served by a strategy of convincing itself that the 'time-bomb' does not exist or that enough has been done to avoid the events that could adversely affect the Maghreb. It seems clear that the gulf between the two shores continues to broaden in every respect and that internal instability (not only in Algeria) could result in a regional crisis with obvious consequences for Spain. The argument that the socio-political and economic development of these countries is the best means of guaranteeing the stability of the western Mediterranean is one that needs to be strengthened if it is to prevail at the policy level. Spain still has much work to do in order to complete the first stage of creating that 'bedrock of interests', particularly with countries like Algeria and Libya which appear to be further removed than ever from the European vision of North Africa's future.

Spain and the Middle East

While with the Maghreb we can talk, regardless of the results obtained, of an independent model of action with defined policy profiles from the mid-1980s, the same cannot be said of Spain's relations with the countries of the Middle East. In fact, it was not until the presentation in 1990 of the Hispano-Italian proposal for a Conference on Security and Co-operation in the Mediterranean,[10] that Spanish diplomacy perceived the need to become more involved in the Mediterranean through adopting a wider perspective [Fernández Ordóñez, 1990]. The need to convince other partners, with as different outlooks as those of the United States and the northern states of the EU, of the expediency of devoting part of collective efforts to the resolution of the problems of the area gave an impulse to this volte-face. However, no scheme for global action has yet been formulated. In practice, Spanish activity in the area thus far has been subordinated to policy directed towards the Maghreb, so the development of relations with Middle Eastern states remains a fundamental precondition for the development of a truly global policy, besides which they are also valued in terms of an economic and commercial interest in gaining greater market shares.

In the political field, the number of meetings at different levels has increased since the late 1980s. This has been part of an attempt to give substance to the recurring image of a traditional friendship with the Arab people which was usually limited in practice to occasional, usually unproductive contacts, almost all for reasons of protocol. It is enough to recall that the visit made by the Spanish Foreign Minister to Lebanon on 7 April 1994 was the first for 22 years. However, it should be recognized that in recent years, above all since the Barcelona Conference of 1995, there has been a considerable increase in the number of top-level visits. These include those made by Spain's head of state to Israel (November 1993), Jordan and Saudi Arabia (November 1994) and Egypt (second visit, February 1997).[11] For his part, Spain's prime minister has undertaken two tours in a short space of time to Egypt, Israel and the Palestinian Territories (June 1998) and to the latter two again, as well as to Syria and Lebanon, at the end of July 1999.

With respect to commercial relations,[12] Spain enjoys an overall trade surplus with the Middle East. The volume of trade is low, with the exception of hydrocarbons and the growing Spanish attention being given to the Turkish market (see Table 1). Nor is the flow of investment strong, again with the exception of Turkey. Overall, this confirms the impression that Spain, the world's tenth economic power, does not maximize its potential in the area, nor does it benefit from the theoretical advantage that might result from its image as a traditional 'friend of the Arab world'.

The Turkish case deserves a special mention owing to the dynamic character that bilateral Hispano-Turkish relations have acquired, above all in the commercial and investment fields. While there are no political disputes between the two countries and Madrid has supported Ankara's attempts to become a member of the EU, economic relations have intensified to the point that Turkey is currently Spain's eleventh most important customer. Trading relations, in which Spain has a clear surplus, have increased in a sustained manner, with annual growth of between 45 and 60 per cent since the start of the customs union between Ankara and the EU in 1996.[13] Although by the end of the decade no more than a dozen Spanish companies were present in Turkey, new opportunities were opening

TABLE 1
TRADE RELATIONS BETWEEN SPAIN AND THE MIDDLE EAST (1997)
(IN MILLION DOLLARS)

	Egypt	Israel	Pal.Terr.	Syria	Lebanon	Jordan	Turkey
Exports from Spain	333.0	75.3	11.8	95.6	157.2	57.6	1,228.2
Imports into Spain	156.0	370.6	0.0	265.2	6.9	10.0	555.4
Spanish investments		0.0	0.0	0.0	0.0	0.0	1,283.0
Invested in Spain		790.0	0.0	0.0	13.0	65.0	0.0

Note: It has not been possible to obtain data for Egypt, but in any case the figures here are very small.

Source: Compiled by the author using data obtained from the Secretaría del Estado de Comercio, Turismo y Pequeñas y Medianas Empresas, Madrid.

up to participate in international tenders for the creation and improvement of basic infrastructure. In this sense, the existence of an Agreement on Economic and Financial Co-operation, signed in January 1998, is of importance. Under this, Turkey was granted a credit package worth $410 million for use in the period 1998–2000.[14] Turkey is also the only country in the eastern Mediterranean with which a level of political contacts similar to that with Morocco has been established. An action plan provides for annual bilateral summits and permanent consultation mechanisms. This is therefore the most comparable example with those of the Maghreb and it may be used as an example of what could be achieved with other Middle Eastern countries, with which Spain would like to see a similar framework of relations.

If in the field of trade Turkey is a country to be highlighted, in that of politics and development co-operation the Palestinian Territories acquire a similarly special character. The choice of Spain as the venue for the Madrid Peace Conference of 1991, owing to the country's 'credibility, neutrality and balance', served to reward the enthusiastic efforts made to bring the Mediterranean on to both the EU and NATO agendas. Moreover, it gave Spain the possibility of playing an important role in contributing from the outside to the resolution of the Arab–Israeli conflict. Without renouncing its traditional support for the Palestinian cause, which was clearly reflected in declarations made on 17 January 1986 and 27 June 1989,[15] Spain has been able to establish full relations with Israel without adversely affecting its relations with the Arab world.

In an initial stage, which ended with the holding of the Barcelona Conference, it was possible to acquire a discrete protagonism both in the political field and in that of co-operation. In the former case, Spain produced new proposals. These included the holding of a conference that urged all parties to the conflict to debate possible development initiatives in cultural and educational matters in an attempt to remove the negative stereotypes that affect a section of public opinion in the respective countries. Spain also offered, again without success, to host the signing of any accords that were achieved. As an actor interested in reducing the economic problems of the Palestinians, its activity has been more notable. In 1993 Spain was the third biggest donor to the Palestinian Territories, behind France and Italy. An active member of the group of contributors ever since the first donors' conference, held in Washington in October 1993, Spain is currently the 'shepherd' of agriculture and tourism in the Working Group on Regional Development that forms part of the multilateral dimension of the peace process initiated in Madrid.

This interest in playing a major part in the search for a solution to the Palestinian drama is clearly demonstrated by the fact that Spain was the first country in the world to sign a Memorandum of Co-operation with the Palestinian Authority (29 November 1993). The constant growth of Spanish financial support for the Palestinians, amounting to $50 million for the period 1997–99, has made the Palestinian Territories the most important destination for Spanish bilateral development aid in the region, although this does not exceed four per cent of total Spanish aid.[16]

The four years of the first Aznar government did not see the completion of a global framework of Mediterranean relations. The situation has not always allowed previous positions to be built upon, as was demonstrated by the negative reaction to the prime minister's offer to host another peace conference, similar to that of 1991, during a visit to Madrid by the Israeli prime minister in March 1998, and by the criticisms made of the inopportune timing of Aznar's return visit the following June.[17] The only positive elements in this period can be summarized as: the appointment of a Spanish diplomat, Miguel A. Moratinos, as the EU's Special Envoy for the Peace Process, in October 1996; the decision adopted in 1998 to condone one-third of Jordan's bilateral debt (out of a total of $104 million); and the UN request, initially responded to in favourable terms, to assign Spanish soldiers to a multinational unit to be deployed in the south of Lebanon, in the case of the new Israeli government complying with its commitment to withdraw.

Multilateral Efforts

As in the case of bilateral activity towards the Maghreb and the Middle East, there has been a considerable decline in the level of multilateral effort focused on the Mediterranean since 1996. Following a period of frenetic activity in all the forums that Spain had joined during the 1980s, aimed at placing the Mediterranean on their respective agendas, the election of the Aznar government ushered in a period of hibernation. Clearly, one must acknowledge here that the behaviour of some of the countries with which Spain was   hoping to improve relations and the evolution of the international system during this period have not facilitated *rapprochement* and have even hindered progress. But this does not explain the change of governmental attitude towards the area, which continues to be one of Spain's few possibilities for enjoying a degree of international protagonism. Moreover, it is not as if the level of Spain's exposure to regional instability has been reduced, or that the risks have disappeared.

Little remains now of the initial Spanish impulse developed in the Atlantic Alliance, European Union and Western European Union (WEU) to push multilateral proposals in the field of security or economic co-operation. In the first case, it should be recalled that it was in Seville on 29 September 1994, at an informal meeting of NATO defence ministers, that the agreement was reached that gave rise to NATO's Mediterranean Dialogue, launched the following February.[18] This was the culmination of an attempt to bring the regional reality closer to a defence organization which seemed to need to identify a new adversary with which to justify its very existence. What Spain sought to do, with the agreement of the other Mediterranean members of the Alliance, was to avoid the exclusion of the South at a time of growing NATO interest in eastern Europe. Spain did not want the Mediterranean to be seen erroneously as the source of a principally military threat. The dialogue was proposed, moreover, with the intention of broadening the channels of communication between the northern and southern shores and of improving NATO's negative image in the region [Moya, 1995]. Evidently, the initiative was nothing more than a concession by the United States and most of the northern members in exchange for the support of countries like Spain and Italy for eastern European expansion. The fact that the Mediterranean has never been a high priority for the Alliance helps explain why its achievements have been so limited thus far [Bin, 1998].

Despite these antecedents, there continues to be scope (although Spain seems to have decided not to explore it) for giving this instrument of co-operation some substance. Perhaps the lack of ideas in Madrid explains why, even in an area where its has a particular interest and potential influence, Spain chose to resort to an American assessment as the basis of proposals regarding the future development of the NATO Initiative,[19] just as Italy did two years earlier. Meanwhile, the possibility of reproducing in the region something similar to the Stability Pact or the Partnership for Peace, concerning the eastern European countries, remains a remote possibility. Nobody seems interested in extending new invitations to the rest of the Mediterranean countries or in pursuing more ambitious co-operation initiatives that might be of interest to Spain's southern neighbours. The same can be said of the parallel dialogue that the WEU has been developing since 1992 with Algeria, Morocco and Tunisia and more recently with Egypt and Israel, of which Spain once again was one of the main proponents. This dialogue has suffered from the same lack of definition of the aims and the instruments that need to be utilized in order to achieve a peaceful and stable Mediterranean.

Even in a more reduced multilateral framework–limited to France, Italy and Spain–the achievements correspond to an earlier period. Back in 1988 the three countries, who share a similar Mediterranean sensibility and a greater level of exposure to the problems of the area than that of other EU member states, were already seeking to identify joint responses at the level of defence. The conclusions they reached included proposals to acquire four Airborne Warning and Control Systems (AWACs), to carry out joint naval patrols in the western Mediterranean and to build an observation satellite to cover the same area. Although the first two ideas did not come to fruition owing to budgetary problems, July 1994 finally saw the launching of the Helios satellite, later complemented by a second satellite from December 1999.[20]

Little more has been achieved through the EU, the principal avenue for economic co-operation with the region. Following a successful stage, stretching from the first Spanish presidency in 1989 to the holding of the Euro-Mediterranean Conference in Barcelona in 1995, there has been no Spanish initiative of note in relation to the area, despite all the blockages and patchiness that have marked the progress of the Euro-Mediterranean Partnership [Núñez, 1996]. While it is true that during this period the EU itself has concentrated almost exclusively on deepening its own integration, this argument does not seem sufficient to explain the practical disappearance of Spanish protagonism. This implies not only an inability to profit positively from the Barcelona process, but also the absence of consistent projects for an area that is so important for Spanish interests. It all seems to boil down to relying upon what was done previously, before 1996, and the expectation that new steps will be determined by other states. The failure of the most pessimistic predictions from the late 1980s to materialize has provoked a dangerous sense of relief that the instruments employed up to now are sufficient to manage regional problems.

Provisional Evaluation and Future Prospects

A review of the state of the Mediterranean is unsettling owing to the many events and, above all, trends that point to increasing instability. As such, it is difficult to find cause for optimism. Internal problems have increased in most of the countries of the region and there are continual delays in the adoption of urgent measures to prevent a generalized crisis.

Both the European Union and NATO, with Spain among the most active proponents, have tried to define new frameworks of relations that combine dialogue with deterrence. These opt for a combination of direct defence of their interests with a generic principle of contributing to the stability and development of the region. However, this approach raises two problems which arise from the fact that the security frameworks remain marked by the legacy of the cold war and have found it difficult to adapt to new international challenges. Firstly, they regard the defence of their interests as requiring the identification of an adversary who could endanger them and the drawing up of a defensive strategy. This explains why the proposals from Brussels have been generated within these organizations, and at best some Mediterranean countries have been invited to sign up subsequently. There has been no attempt to initiate a process giving rise to a joint strategy involving joint aims and channels for common action. On the contrary, given the European belief that we possess the truth, we tend to exaggerate our capacity to solve our neighbours' problems and to influence their behaviour according to our own values.

Instead of embarking upon a joint project, which could only materialize in the long-term on the basis of a dialogue among equals, the legacy of bipolar confrontation continues to prevail, according to which stability is understood exclusively in terms of maintaining the status quo. According to this perspective, preference is given to sustaining unlawful regimes; so long as they continue to guarantee regional 'stability', there is no real will in Brussels to promote the essential political and economic reforms that these countries need. The only condition required of the regimes is that they do not question the rules of the game at a regional level and do not disturb peaceful maritime traffic in the vital sea-lanes of the Mediterranean. The permanence of authoritarian regimes in power, however, can only delay social explosions both in the political and the socio-economic spheres. The unfinished task for Spain and its partners is to come to terms with the fact that true stability can only be achieved by replacing the current regimes in most countries of the southern and eastern Mediterranean. Given their character as closed societies controlled by the authorities, this process will involve periods of unstable transition before new political actors, which inevitably will include Islamic groups, are able to participate in the decision-making process in each country.

On the other hand, the European contribution to the development of these countries has been very limited thus far. The bilateral programmes and the frameworks designed by Brussels (from the Global Mediterranean Policy of 1972 to the current EMP) have failed to mobilize sufficient resources to fulfil their theoretical aims. It still seems that policy-makers do not understand that development promotion is the best instrument to achieve the stability that they so desire. Inadequate policy responses to the serious economic and social problems encountered by the vast majority of the Mediterranean countries simply fan the flames of radicalism and conflict. Correcting this tendency would involve much more than simply increasing substantially the resources devoted to development aid or the funding of the MEDA programme. It would imply, among other things, contributing decisively to the development of those productive sectors that are labour-intensive (such as textiles, agriculture and tourism), reducing the burden of foreign debt (60 per cent of which is owed to EU countries), applying a regime of free trade to Mediterranean agricultural exports and establishing a less restrictive immigration policy.

In Spain, this latter point best illustrates the discrepancies in existing criteria. On the eve of the general election of March 2000, José María Aznar's People's Party administration promised to repeal a new, more progressive, immigration law which had come into force on 1 February 2000, owing to an initiative from other political parties. Meanwhile, new physical barriers were being erected around Ceuta and Melilla and there were plans also to shield the Strait of Gibraltar from the pressure of migrants trying to enter Spain from Morocco. The approach of the Spanish authorities, in which policing criteria predominate, does not seem the best way of dealing with a phenomenon that will be unstoppable so long as underdevelopment persists in the South and inequalities continue to increase between the countries along the two shores of the Mediterranean. The forecasts of demographic trends envisage a scenario for Spain of accelerated ageing which, according to estimates by the UN Population Division, will create a need to attract 240,000 immigrants each year up to 2050 in order to maintain the existing labour force and the social security system.

In view of such projections, the Spanish government will have to adopt a multidirectional strategy that takes into account factors such as: (a) the conviction that it is necessary to open the doors to a migratory inflow that will increase substantially the number of foreigners residing in Spain, from the figure of 800,000 (1.3 per cent of the population) at the present time; (b) the need to prepare the Spanish population for this influx, by establishing programmes that will publicize the various advantages arising from it; (c) the progressive integration of immigrants by giving them the same rights and obligations as Spaniards; (d) support for the development of neighbouring countries, by encouraging co-operation in all fields as a mechanism to help improve their standard of living and create activities that generate employment;[21] and (e) the desirability of joint management of migratory flows with the country of origin, not least to halt the proliferation of clandestine networks. Instead of accepting the role of guard of one of the principal ports of entry to the Schengen area established in 1995, Spain should seek to develop the process initiated at the EU Council of Tampere in 1999 by emphasizing policies that concentrate on integration, while explaining both the unstoppable and the beneficial nature of immigration.

Clearly, none of these proposals is without obstacles, but this is the only approach that can facilitate the deactivation of the 'time-bomb'. This opinion is based, not on some supposed but non-existent altruism on the part of the countries of the North, but an intelligent selfishness which realizes that the defence of their own interests makes this attitude necessary.

In recent years Spain, like the rest of the EU countries, has shown no signs of being able to face the existing challenges. The official Spanish attitude continues to fall between mere management of what was created previously, as if this were sufficient to fulfil its aims, and acceptance that the current international groupings are too busy with other matters to seriously address the problems of the Mediterranean. Obviously, the symptoms of decline in the region cannot be blamed entirely on Spain's lack of activity. Moreover, a medium-sized power like Spain will not be able to undertake any new regional initiative on its own. But this does not justify Spain's passivity. Nor does it justify the predominance of commercial and corporate interests, whose discourse is echoed by senior officials responsible for these areas, together with entrepreneurs and agricultural and fishing interests. Spain's best political interests are represented by those who argue in favour of promoting the development of the non-EU Mediterranean countries, but thus far, unfortunately, these people have proved either unwilling or unable to act accordingly.

NOTES

1. Unless otherwise specified in the text, 'Mediterranean' will be used here as a global term that embraces the countries of the southern and eastern shores, including Mauritania, Jordan and Turkey.
2. For analysis of the historical evolution of these relations, see Rein (ed.) [1999].
3. A bilateral committee, created in 1996, in which representatives of public and private institutions are organized in three working groups (history and education, the economy and civil society, the media and culture). It meets twice a year, the first meeting having been held in Seville on 8 March 1997.
4. The partners of the EU involved in the EMP are Morocco, Algeria, Tunisia, Egypt, Israel, the Palestinian Territories, Jordan, Syria, Lebanon, Turkey, Cyprus and Malta. Libya may join this group in the medium term if it manages to consolidate the *rapprochement* with the EU following the lifting of UN sanctions in 1999.
5. This is an annual fair organized by Spain to publicize its products in emerging markets. It took place in the first week of June 1999 with the presence of 281 Spanish companies.
6. In 1998 Spain's exports were worth $1,251 million compared with imports worth only $610 million.
7. By the end of the century, there were over 700 Spanish companies in Morocco while in Tunisia their presence did not reach double figures.
8. The repeated, ill-advised attempts by Spanish agrarian and fishing organizations to block the

transit of Moroccan merchandise en route to Europe in no way serves the real interests of Spain.

9. The former Dirección General del Norte de África was replaced and its functions diluted through the creation of a new Dirección General de Política Exterior para África, Asia y Pacífico, while there was no accompanying increase in human and financial resources. In the Agencia Española de Cooperación Internacional (AECI), something similar happened, with the Instituto de Cooperación con el Mundo Árabe being transformed into the Instituto de Cooperación con el Mundo Árabe, Mediterráneo y Países en Desarrollo, but continuing to suffer from inadequate provision of resources.

10. This proposal was presented at a meeting of the CSCE on the environment, held in Palma de Mallorca in September 1990.

11. During the latter visit, a commitment to sign a new financial protocol was announced. Finally signed in February 1998, Egypt was conceded credit worth $310 million for use by the end of 2000. This is composed of $150m from Spain's Development Fund (FAD), $150m in OECD credit and $10m as a donation to pay for feasibility studies.

12. Analyses of trade with the region can be found in the articles published in the special issue on 'La empresa española en Oriente Próximo', *Economía Exterior*, 5, summer 1998.

13. However, Spain's exports to Turkey remain smaller than those of Germany (seven times greater), Italy (four times) and the United Kingdom (twice as great).

14. The package consisted of $200m in FAD credit, $200m from OECD funds and $10m in donations to finance feasibility studies.

15. The first declaration was motivated by Spain's recognition of Israel and the second, during the European Council of Madrid, served to update the Venice Declaration of 1980. Together they embody the following fundamental points: Israel's right to exist and to security within safe frontiers; the right to self-determination of the Palestinian people and the recognition of the PLO as their legitimate representative; support for UN resolutions 242 and 338 as bases for resolving the conflict; the rejection of terrorism in all its forms; rejection of Israel's settlement policy and the designation of Jerusalem as Israel's capital.

16. Bilateral aid from Spain to the Palestinian territories between the establishment of the Palestine Authority to the end of 1997 reached approximately 10,000 million pesetas (including official development aid, contributions to the UN Relief and Works Agency and FAD credits).

17. In both cases criticisms were centred on the keenness for protagonism which was displayed, with a proposal which only satisfied Netanyahu, wanting to renegotiate questions which had been agreed previously, and the mistaken signal of support for an Israeli leader who was isolated internationally because of his negotiating intransigence.

18. Initially Morocco, Tunisia, Mauritania, Egypt and Israel were invited to participate. Jordan joined later.

19. The Spanish Ministry of Defence commissioned a report from the Rand Corporation, presented in February 1999 on *The Future of NATO's Mediterranean Initiative: Evolution and Next Steps*, compiled by Ian Lesser, Jerrold Green, Stephen Larrabee and Michele Zanini. The report for the Italian ministry, bearing the title *NATO's Mediterranean Initiative: Policy Issues and Dilemmas*, was presented in September 1997.

20. This is an optical recognition satellite in helio-synchronized orbit some 685 km from the Earth. Spain has a seven per cent share and processes the information derived from it at Torrejón de Ardoz, near Madrid.

21. The PAIDAR plan for northern Morocco provides a good model to follow, but unfortunately was suspended in 1996 before reaching the implementation stage.

REFERENCES

Bin, A. (1998): 'Contribución de la OTAN al fortalecimiento de la cooperación en el Mediterráneo', *Revista de la OTAN*, 4, pp.24-27.

Brom, S. (ed.) (2000): *The Middle East Balance 1999-2000*, Tel Aviv: Jafee Centre for Strategic Studies.

Fernández Ordóñez, F. (1990): 'El Mediterráneo en busca de una estructura de seguridad, *Revista de la OTAN*, 5, pp.7–11.

Gillespie, R. (1995): 'España y el Magreb: una vía posible de política regional', in R. Gillespie, F. Rodrigo and J. Story (eds.), *Las relaciones exteriores de la España democrática*, Madrid: Alianza Universidad.

Ministerio de Asuntos Exteriores (1992): *Europa ante el Maghreb*, Madrid: Dirección General de Política Exterior para África y Medio Oriente.

Ministerio de Defensa (1993): *Directiva de Defensa Nacional* 1/92, 27 March 1992, Madrid: Dirección General de Política de Defensa (DIGENPOL).

Moratinos, M. A. (1991a): 'El Magreb, nuestro desafío del Sur', *El País*, 15 March.

Moratinos, M. A. (1991b): *La política exterior y de co-operación en el Magreb*, Madrid: Ministerio de Asuntos Exteriores, Informativo 8.

Moya, P. (1995): *Frameworks for Co-operation in the Mediterranean*, Brussels: North Atlantic Assembly, AM 259 CC/MB (95) 7.

Núñez, J. A. (1996b): 'La Asociación Euro-Mediterránea: ¿una garantía de estabilidad y desarrollo?, *Información Comercial Española*, 759, pp.19–32.

Núñez, J. A. (1999): 'La no-proliferación de armas de destrucción masiva en el Mediterráneo: un reto para la seguridad regional", in *Un estudio sobre la no-proliferación*, Monografías del CESEDEN, Madrid: Ministerio de Defensa.

Núñez, J. and M. Larramendi (1996a): *La política exterior y de cooperación de España en el Magreb (1982–95)*, Madrid: Los Libros de la Catarata.

Rein, R. (ed.) (1999): *Spain and the Mediterranean since 1898*, London and Portland, OR: Frank Cass.

Spain and the United States: Military Primacy

FELIPE SAHAGÚN

Democratization, modernization and consolidation as a medium-to-large sized European power are the three strategic objectives that have guided Spain's internal and external policies since Franco's death. In the process, US–Spanish relations, the main pillar of Spain's foreign policy for nearly half a century, have been transformed. The EU partners have come to overshadow the USA in Spain's political, economic, financial and commercial external relations. Yet, in the military and cultural spheres, although deeply affected by Spain's integration into NATO and the globalization process that permeates everything, the US remains the main partner of Spain. From the Spanish government's perspective, it is a very unequal partnership requiring urgent change.

The following thoughts on US–Spanish relations in the year 2000 are structured in seven parts: a brief introduction to the aims and goals of both countries; a description of the very unequal means that each nation possesses in their efforts to attain these goals; the different perceptions that affect the bilateral relationship; the military contacts, still dominant in spite of the end of the cold war; the multilateral connections, today focused primarily on the so-called Transatlantic Agenda; the economic aspects; and, finally, the cultural challenge.

Officially, the USA, Europe and, as part of Europe, Spain share five post-cold war priorities: to secure peace in the regions of greatest conflict, such as the Balkans and the Middle East; to create a new European security system, which integrates the new eastern European democracies and a democratic Russia; to halt the proliferation of weapons of mass destruction; to protect the environment; and to promote free trade.

To this effect, the Clinton Administration, after initial vacillations, came out in favour of European military, economic, monetary and political integration. 'Of course we're in competition, but the benefits to the US of a strong Europe outweigh the possible disadvantages,' the former ambassador to Spain Richard Gardner has affirmed (*La Vanguardia*, 12 Oct.1996). Yet many US actions seem to imply the opposite: its veto of a European SACEUR (Supreme Allied Commander Europe) in NATO, for instance; or its squabbles with France over the Great Lakes region and the Middle East. Also going against Gardener's words are Washington's version of the concept of 'European integration', its repeated attempts to apply American laws beyond national boundaries, the recurrent disputes in the World Trade Organization and the country's behaviour during the latest Balkan crisis.

A politically and militarily united Europe, with a common army and currency, seem acceptable to Washington only if the US, through bilateral and multilateral agreements, is included in all phases of the integration process (the Euro-Atlantic free trade zone would be one step in that direction).

The US attitude toward monetary union has gradually evolved from outright rejection to unenthusiastic acceptance as a lesser evil rather than as a desirable process. Any astute observer can see that a strong European reserve currency would end up competing with the dollar.

The Spanish–US agreement of 26 September 1953 (particularly the 'automatic activation clause' relating to the military bases and included in a 'secret memo' added to article III of the text) turned Spain into an additional weapon in the American containment arsenal in exchange for decisive political, economic and military support for the Franco regime. Since the end of dictatorship in Spain in the mid-1970s, one of the main objectives of successive democratic Spanish governments has been to recover the sovereignty ceded through that 1953 agreement, repeatedly renewed to this very day, albeit with modifications.

With the cold war over, the US is in the process of defining new foreign policy goals, but it continues to consider its privileged relationship with Spain, including access to Spain's military bases, an important strategic element in providing protection against the new dangers that have cropped up in Europe, Africa and the Middle East.

Now that the Soviet threat has mostly disappeared, Spain (as a part of Europe) and the United States have three common interests – peace, stability and democracy – both within and beyond Europe, but the two differ over the most effective way of defending these interests and the priority placed on each. So long as the Warsaw Pact was a greater threat, these perennial differences were almost always resolved behind closed doors. Without that common threat, the main reason for glossing over differences between the old allies has disappeared.

Since Spain's incorporation into the EU and NATO, the Spanish–US relationship has become an inseparable domain of the larger transatlantic linkage. Consequently, most of the difficulties, misunderstandings and more serious disputes between the US and its European allies have some bearing on the bilateral Spain-US linkage.

Less Unequal

Differences in geography, history, population, wealth and culture make the relationship between Spain and the US a complex, dense and unbalanced network of interests that go back to the origins of the two nations. Political and economic changes over the last 20 years, however, have significantly reduced these differences as common interests have multiplied. Starting from a position of weakness and isolation, Spain has traditionally defended the status quo; the United States, on the other hand, has supported any change or revolution favourable to its strategic interests. Spanish diplomacy has been and continues to be, essentially, passive or reactive, while American diplomacy, since the Second World War, has been among the most active. All major international governing bodies, including the European Community by way of the Marshall Plan and the OECD, can trace their origins back to the United States. Today more than ever, American interests are global interests.

Spain – under and after Franco, under dictatorship and democratic rule – has limited its strategic priorities to four fronts: neighbouring Europe, Latin America, the Mediterranean and the United States. US priorities, like those of the Spanish Empire during the reign of Philip II, know no limits, not even in outer space.

The US has come a long way since its 'no alliances or secret pacts' policy, touted by George Washington two centuries ago. It has gone on, in fact, to become the country with the most bilateral and multilateral alliances in the world. During Franco's time, Spain had only one military alliance: the bilateral agreement with the USA. Since then, the country has made all kinds of efforts to reduce the inequality of that relationship by modifying the US linkage and establishing a whole network of new alliances.

The history of Spanish foreign relations from the late seventeenth century to the 1980s was one of dependence and decline. The history of the United States, since its birth, has been a gradual progression toward hegemony: first on the continent, then in the world. From the late nineteenth century to the 1980s, Spain had been generally excluded from the international relations game. The US, on the other hand, had withdrawn voluntarily during most of the nineteenth century and in the inter-war period, but after the victory over Fascism and the Nazis it renounced isolationism for good.

Spanish isolation came to an end with the advent of democracy, although Spain had already sneaked into the Atlantic Alliance and other international organizations by the back door as early as the 1950s, with the help of the US. Nevertheless, as the late Spanish foreign minister Francisco Fernández Ordóñez pointed out on more than one occasion, in the 1980s Spanish foreign relations experienced a veritable 'big bang'.

For the first time in generations, Spain began to formulate a more coherent and realistic model for the conduct of foreign policy: the means were adapted, although never perfectly, to the desired ends. Three factors made this possible: democracy at home, economic growth over the previous 35 years and the willingness of other democratic governments to admit Spain as a member of the major international 'clubs' from which it had been absent or marginalized during Franco's rule.

Since its consolidation as a superpower, the US has defended its interests by all available means – especially military – in accordance with a geostrategic vision that includes global interests and responsibilities. Spain, due to its military weakness and its lack of strategic vision beyond the Balearic–Straits of Gibraltar–Canary Islands axis, has lacked, even years after the advent of democracy, a minimally coherent security policy and sufficient means to carry it out. As often occurs in weak countries, Spain has tried to hide these deficiencies behind a stereotype-laden rhetoric and propaganda based on the successes of a distant past. It has also tried to compensate for it by forming pacts or alliances with stronger neighbours.

Commerce and culture have broadened Spain's possibilities of foreign involvement, for they are increasingly considered the best instruments for promoting development, democracy and co-operation. That is precisely why it was a heavy blow for the Clinton Administration when the US Congress rejected its so-called Fast Track proposal, which would have allowed the rapid negotiation of trade agreements. The reaction of Congress was symptomatic of the universal fear of globalization, even in the USA. It was also a clear example, above all, of the limits to the American executive branch's ability to carry out a coherent foreign policy.

In Spain, by contrast, the power to conduct foreign policy is far more concentrated in the executive branch – despite the fact that Spain is now, in effect, a nation of highly-autonomous nations, while the US is a federation with a powerful central government, whose expenditure accounts for half the national budget (compared to only 35 per cent of the Spanish budget).

The Spanish parliamentary system gives the 'president of the government', or prime minister, a degree of control over foreign policy that a US president can only dream of when his party enjoys a majority in both the House of Representatives and the Senate. With a Republican majority in both houses on Capitol Hill, Bill Clinton was held hostage by the opposition's most conservative wing, represented in the Senate Committee on Foreign Affairs by the Senator from North Carolina, Jesse Helms.

This explains, in part, the American paralysis in the Balkans over recent years, the embargoes against Cuba, Iran, Iraq and Libya – which have hurt the businesses of US allies, including Spain – and the country's refusal to pay its debt to the UN in membership fees, which has hampered the organization's ability to adapt to new post-cold war challenges. The conservative stranglehold on the White House also helps explain why the US pressed for the use of force against Iraq despite the fact that all the indicators pointed to the ineffectiveness of such means for reaching their two stated objectives: to get rid of Saddam and/or his weapons of mass destruction.

US foreign and domestic policy cannot be understood without taking into account the influence of lobbies and legally organized pressure groups which are constantly fighting for policies most favourable to their own interests. Major decisions tend to come about as the result of pressure from these lobbies, combined with the interests of administrative departments – Defense, Agriculture, Treasury, Commerce, Industry, State – as well as those of local and state governments. It is very difficult to influence the 'output' of US foreign policy making by means of traditional diplomacy if one does not have access to the channels (mainly lobbies) that determine the final decision.

In spite of the growing Hispanic community in the US, today over 30 million strong, only in the last few years has Spain begun to take into account the need for a strong lobby in the US in order to make itself present where the power is, on Capitol Hill, and to better promote Spanish interests.

When the US paid rent each year for using the Spanish bases, the yearly budget debate in Congress forced both the Spanish and American administrations to lobby the greatest possible number of legislators on Capitol Hill. When in 1989 Spain stopped charging for the use of the bases, the need for such lobbying disappeared and, with it, the transparency of public debate.

US politics and society are much more open and transparent than they are in Spain, and both are shaped to a greater extent by the media, especially television. Germany, Italy, Israel, Greece and Great Britain have understood this fact for years – and, more recently, China and Mexico have as well. These countries, therefore, have made an effort to name ambassadors with experience of journalism and to reinforce diplomacy by maintaining intimate contact with non-governmental sectors of American society. Only in the last few years has the Spanish Ministry of Foreign Affairs started to understand the importance of this change.

Today the US has six times the population of Spain (280 million people compared to 40 million projected for the year 2000), but its fertility rate is almost double (2.1 children per woman of child-bearing age, compared to 1.2), and so Spain is ageing much faster [UNDP, 1997]. The GNP of the USA is 13 times that of Spain (almost $7,000 billion compared to $500 billion), but in order to produce this income, the US consumes 20 times more electricity, measured in kilowatts per hour. This explains, in part, the fact that the US pollutes the environment 20 times more than Spain does, if we measure contamination by the emission of greenhouse gases.

The United States is 20 times larger than Spain (9.8 million square kilometres compared to nearly 505,000), but the percentage of irrigable and arable land in the US is much less than that of Spain. Each year America spends 35 times more than Spain does on defence ($280 billion or 3.8 per cent of GNP compared to $8.5 billion or 1.5 per cent of GNP). Since 1985, however, the US has slashed its defence budget from 6.5 to 3.8 per cent, while Spain has cut its budget from 2.4 to 1.5 per cent.

In the late 1990s, the two countries had identical levels of urbanization (78 per cent) and similar inflation and economic growth rates: higher in the US over the last six years, higher in Spain over a period of 15 to 20 years. What most differentiates the two economies are the unemployment rates, the composition of production and the degree of dependence on communication technology, with Spain lagging far behind the US.

Officially, US unemployment does not even reach five per cent while in Spain, as of 1999, the number of people out of work topped 15 per cent. Few believe, however, that the true unemployment rate is that high. Professors Mario Gaviria and Enrique Fuentes Quintana, for instance, estimate that the reality is half that figure [Gaviria, 1996].

Spain's farming sector, measured in percentage of active population, continues to be double the size of that of the US (eight to nine per cent compared to only four per cent, in 1990), whereas the service sector makes up 55 per cent of the Spanish economy, compared to 71 per cent of the American economy.

The number of radios per 1,000 inhabitants is six times higher in the US, the number of televisions almost twice as high, the number of cellular phones nine times higher, the number of Internet users almost 25 times higher and that of PC users four times higher. The relationship between the two countries becomes even more skewed if we take into account military strength, the number of Nobel prize winners, the world-wide influence of the English language and US dominance in the leading economic sectors of the future: computers, the aerospace industry, new materials, genetics, telecommunications, environmental technology, robotics and the film and television industry.

But Spain surpasses the US as far as quality of life is concerned, if we take into account – as the UN does each year in its *Human Development Report* – other social indicators, such as life expectancy, the poverty rate, crime and aid to developing countries. The statistics speak for themselves: 12 out of every 10,000 mothers in the US died during childbirth in 1990, compared to only seven in Spain. Sixty-one out of every 1,000 babies born in the US died before reaching their first birthday in 1995, compared to only six per 1,000 in Spain. This type of inequality, in which Spain comes out the winner, is especially interesting when we consider per capita income: $14,000 in Spain compared to $28,000 in the US: clear proof that, despite everything, Spain is a fairer and more-egalitarian industrialized nation than the United States.

Spain is also more compassionate, with 0.24 per cent of its GNP in 1995 devoted to aid to developing countries, compared to only 0.1 per cent of US GNP in that year. This statistic is even more impressive if we recall that, as recently as the early 1980s, Spain was still a recipient of development aid.

After analysing Spain's status with respect to more than 60 political, economic, social and cultural variables, Gaviria concludes that Spain is 'the seventh world power'. What is more, he adds: 'There has been a poor diagnosis of the Spanish condition regarding not only domestic factors, such as the economy and society, but also Spain's position in the world' [Gaviria, 1996: 21]. In other words, through his 'Spain is doing fine' slogan, José María Aznar did not merely express his personal wishes or a recent reality: he was also stating a fact, backed by statistics on Spain's evolution over the last 35 years.

Image and Reality

Soon after being named US ambassador to Spain, Richard Gardner recognized: 'Our relationship has never been better, but unfortunately, our unprecedented cooperation doesn't reflect a deeper understanding between our two peoples' [Gardner, 1994]. Although Gardner made great efforts to dispel myths, that comprehension gap he alluded to continues to hamper relations between the two countries.

Never before has Spain been so active in world affairs as it is today, and never before have its activities and positions coincided to such an extent with those of the US. Spain participates more actively than ever in NATO, the OSCE, the UN and the OECD. With greater conviction than ever before, it has joined the pursuit of regional security and a freer world marketplace; it has promoted the defence of democracy and human rights; it has fought for the protection of the environment and against terrorism and drug trafficking; and it has participated in peace missions and educational exchange programmes.

Public opinion polls, nevertheless, still show a high level of scepticism – higher than in almost every other European country – on the part of Spanish citizens toward the US, its policies and its values. Today Spaniards are much more interested in Europe and the European Union than they are in the United States. Although to a lesser extent than in the early 1990s, the majority still want to see an end to the US military presence. This opposition has weakened, however, along with the number of those who support withdrawal from NATO.

The poor image of the US is most evident in perceptions of threat. To 77 per cent of Spanish citizens, and 89 per cent of their leaders, there is no country that currently threatens peace in Spain. But as far as world peace is concerned, almost nine per cent of the citizenry, and 2.5 per cent of Spanish leaders, view the US as a major threat, the third hghest figures after Russia and Iraq. The perception of the US as a threat, however, has decreased noticeably since the end of the cold war. Ideology continues to be a factor shaping this opinion, and a marked contrast exists between the opinions of Spanish leaders and the population as a whole [INCIPE, 1995].

Few American citizens, on the other hand, are aware of, or value, Spain's contribution to US history or the democratic achievements of the former dictatorship since the mid-1970s. Many Americans, in fact, still think Spain is located in the Western Hemisphere, and they imagine the country to be a romantic land of beaches, bulls and flamenco. In Spain, meanwhile, the main stereotype of the typical American is a rich, uncultured warmonger worried only about the buck. In the US, the Spanish stereotype since the second half of the twentieth century has been the same as that described in the form of a question by the US Ambassador to Spain, Carlton J. M. Hayes, in the early 1940s:

> Are Spaniards not especially cruel and intolerant? Haven't they treated the Jews, Indians, and Blacks with extraordinary cruelty? And what about those barbaric bullfights, are they not proof of their brutal treatment of animals? Haven't they been extremely intolerant to the Jews and Protestants? Is Spain not ruled by despotism? Do the Spanish masses not live in poverty and underdevelopment? Are Spaniards not lazy? Isn't it true that their infrastructure is sorely lacking? [Hayes, 1952: 41–3].

Many of these stereotypes have been eroded in recent years owing, among many other reasons, to the excellent publicity campaign that Spain waged to boost its image leading up to the 1992 Olympic Games in Barcelona and Expo '92 in Seville. The subsequent rise in US tourism has also helped (the number of American visitors doubled between 1992 and 1996), as has the increase in commercial and cultural exchanges. Peace missions and other joint projects, moreover, have strengthened the contacts between the two countries. We can see evidence of an improved image in the positive accounts of today's Spain in American media, such as the article which appeared in *Time* magazine on 17 November 1997. Much work remains to be done, however.

'Spain's economic presence in the US, despite improvements, is still deficient', Professor Joaquín Roy of the University of Miami has warned.

> Despite the country's democratic advances, Spain's image in the American press continues to be a traditional one, based on folklore. The American public's general ignorance about Spain stands in stark

contrast to the overwhelming amount of information – which never reaches the masses – concentrated in various university departments, especially language, literature, history and to a lesser extent, international relations [Roy, 1986: 175].

The factors that have most shaped the negative attitudes of both nations are as follows:

(1) Overall ignorance of more than 300 years of shared history;
(2) Mutual isolation during the larger part of the nineteenth century;
(3) The Spanish–American War of 1898;
(4) Spanish neutrality during both World Wars;
(5) Franco's ties to Nazi Germany and Fascist Italy;
(6) US ideological, economic and military support for the Franco dictatorship;
(7) Profoundly divergent strategies to meet the major challenges posed by Latin America, at one time based simply on differing political views, but now based on trade and economics as well;
(8) Different perceptions of regional and global threats, and divergent opinions on the use of force to carry out foreign policy;
(9) The fact that European integration has become Spain's number one strategic priority, which could somehow clash with US interests;
(10) The images of Spain and the US depicted in each other's media, especially film and television.

Unfortunately, the 1998 commemoration of 100 years since the Spanish-American War revived many of the worst stereotypes of the Black Legend and Yankee imperialism. Official statements by both countries as to how '98 should serve as the launching pad for a new era of understanding and co-operation – rather than an excuse to rouse negative feelings – were undercut by patriotic television series and the decision by the US Congress to hold a referendum on whether to make Puerto Rico the fifty-first state of the union. Florida Senator Robert Graham was right when he said that 'the best way to commemorate the 100-year anniversary of the Spanish–American War is to ignore it, because it could become a Molotov cocktail that destroys the positive momentum of Spain–US relations' (*La Vanguardia*, 24 July 1997).

This momentum – to call it a honeymoon would be no exaggeration if it were not for differences over Cuba – began during the final years of Socialist Party rule in Spain and has been reinforced since the People's Party victory in 1996. The effects, though, show up more in political and cultural spheres than in commerce.

The Primacy of Military Relations

Over the last decade, the foreign policy and security priorities of both Spain and the United States have been profoundly modified as a result of the ending of the cold war and Spanish membership of NATO and the European Union. Now that Spain has given up its control over trade and monetary policy to the EU – and has yielded a considerable part of its autonomy in military affairs to NATO – the majority of the country's problems regarding Spanish-American relations are multilateral in nature, as indeed are the solutions. Any political, economic, military or cultural problem that arises between the USA and the EU affects Spain, sometimes more directly and with more serious consequences than do strictly bilateral problems, which fortunately are becoming more and more scarce.

At the start of the twenty-first century, the term 'bilateral' confuses more than it clarifies, in fact, when analysing relations between two countries like the US and Spain which are allies in major international organizations. To a growing number of Spanish leaders and citizens, ties with the US have lost importance owing to Spain's membership of the EU and of the Atlantic Alliance. Yet that is not really the case, for various reasons. In the first place, international relations is not a zero-sum game. Secondly, the US plays an integral part in the European economy due to its heavy investment there, as well as its trading relations and its manufacturing activities on the continent. Finally, with respect to security issues, the US continues to exercise hegemony in Europe through its indisputable control of NATO. If there was ever any doubt about that, it was erased by the wars in the Gulf (1991), Bosnia (1993–95) and Kosovo (1998–99). A few hours' walk through the Rota and Morón military bases during the Kosovo war would have been enough to understand the growing and decisive importance of the Spanish bases to US global strategy in the late 1990s and early 2000s.

Far from the Iberian country becoming dispensable, military relations between Spain and the US have intensified as a result of Spanish membership of the Atlantic Alliance. The Spanish–American political relationship has shifted to the back burner while military ties have been strengthened following the temporary mismatch of historical memories when the Hispano-American War of 1898 was revisited. Without a solid institutional fabric – there are no regular bilateral summits, for instance, like the ones that have taken place between Spain and the main European countries since the 1980s – political ties with the US have been eclipsed by a growing number of military, economic and cultural ones. The only regular, periodic meeting is that between the military and defence chiefs of Spain and the United States of America.

Following the 1999 reform of the Ministry of Foreign Affairs, relations with the US and Canada came under the jurisdiction of the Security and Disarmament Department, while European security and defence issues were allocated to the Political Affairs Department, which also has responsibilities relating to the UN and other international organizations. In response to opposition in Parliament criticizing this organizational reshuffle, Secretary of State Ramón de Miguel responded that it had been done this way because, now that Spain's full integration into the new NATO structure was nearly completed, the Security and Disarmament Department had been left with a light workload [MFA, 1999: 18.706]. This was not a very solid reason for such an important decision.

The decision-making process that has dominated US–Spanish relations has changed little in the last 30 years. The intergovernmental relationship continues to be based on the bilateral agreement. The current one went into effect in May 1989 with an initial term of eight years. It has been extended automatically since 1996. At the time of writing (January 2000), the agreement was into its fourth renewal, effective until May 2001.

The Permanent Standing Committee, which oversees fulfilment of the agreement, is located at Ministry of Defence headquarters and is run by a military officer with the support of only one diplomatic liaison official. However, it is not the Committee but rather top officials in the Defence and Foreign ministries who are in charge of decision-making. The Spanish prime minister and his ministers and secretaries of state tend to get involved personally in all important decisions regarding relations with the US. In other words, most decisions are approved, as a senior Defence official has put it, 'at the highest level'.

The US and Spain also collaborate over defence-related industry, technology and commerce. This co-operation should have been the outcome of a separate accord, but such an agreement was never negotiated. Instead co-operation has continued on the basis of complementary agreement number 4 of the Bilateral Agreement of 1982. Under this, an exchange of memos was established between the two countries. This aspect of the relationship has obviously benefited Spain in the past, but today it is rather unbalanced and requires urgent revision.

Regarding the purchase of US military equipment, one must distinguish between arms bought under the so-called Foreign Military Sales (FMS) or governmental programme, and those bought on strictly commercial terms. Since 1954, Spain's commercial acquisitions of US defence material have risen to $1.124 billion. By January 2000, 153 commercial contracts were still in effect, totalling $821 million. Another 5,096 contracts – worth close to $7.9 billion in sales – have been drawn up under the FMS programme, and 407 of them (worth $6.1 billion in sales) were still in effect at the start of 2000.

The main purchases made in the 1990s were: in 1995, FFG frigates for $434.3 million and EF-18 jets for $275.8 million; in 1996, SPARROW missiles for $31.3 million; in 1997, F-100 frigates for $748.5 million; and in 1998, AMRAAM missiles for $45 million and LAMPS helicopters for $219.9 million [Ministerio de Defensa, 1999]. The dominant opinion at the Spanish Ministry of Defence is that the US does not offer Spain any special advantages or privileges beyond those given to any other ally.

Since the cold war threats to Europe disappeared, the periphery, in which Spain is located, has taken on a greater importance for the world-wide strategic interests of the US. The Iberian strategic region (that is, Spain and Portugal) can be defined, according to General Alonso Baquer, as an appendage of Europe, the flank of the Mediterranean, the gateway to Africa and the bridge toward America. Spain's main geo-strategic positions are based on the following principles: peninsular unity, membership of the EU, membership of the Atlantic Alliance, co-operation with the US through the bilateral agreement and an increasingly active participation in peace missions [Pardo de Santayana, 1996: 121–3].

Now that the threat from the East has disappeared and Spain has joined the EU, the country has lost its cold war position as the rearguard of southern Europe. It needs, however, sufficient strength to join its allies in south-western Europe (France, Portugal and Italy) in facing existing and potential new regional and local challenges.

As a European member of the Atlantic Alliance, Spain has widened the so-called transatlantic bridge – which during the cold war was confined to the area between the English Channel and the North Sea – and has extended it to the Cantabric Sea and to the Mediterranean approaches. Previously, the southern flank of NATO was not a priority. Now the value of this region, and with it, the role of Spain, is being reassessed.

The strategic advantages derived from the bilateral pact with the US, which were quite significant when it was Spain's only link to the so-called western world, have been overshadowed by new world developments. Spain's strategic value grows, however, as the number of operations outside NATO's traditional zone – modified during the Washington summit of April 1999 – gain in importance and multiply, as has happened since the summit.

'The Spanish pact with the U.S. creates obligations, but it also increases Spain's ability to influence global strategy beyond Europe by taking advantage of its position as the bridge to the Americas and the gateway to Africa, that is, if we consider Africa in the broad sense, which includes the Arab world', writes retired Lieutenant General José R. Pardo de Santayana [1996: 127].

Two statistics accurately reflect Spain's growing importance to the new US global security strategy: every hour for the last 10 years, a US military aircraft has landed or taken off from a Spanish base; every day for the last decade, a US warship has cast anchor in some Spanish port. According to official data from the Spanish Ministry of Defence, this amounts to 87,798 landings or take-offs and 6,380 flights over Spanish airspace between 1989 and 1999: a yearly average of 8,562. The total number of US warships that docked in Spanish ports during that time is 2,481: an average of 226 conventional ships and eight nuclear propulsion ships a year. Except for Germany, there is no other US ally in which the forces at the disposal of the Pentagon maintain such an active presence.

Along with Sigonella (Sicily), Souda Bay (Crete) and Naples Capodicchino airport, Rota is one of the key stepping stones for the US to send an uninterrupted flow of personnel and *matériel* to ships in the Mediterranean and beyond. Urgent cargo crosses the Atlantic using military or civilian long-range aircraft (C-5s, C-141s, C-17s, C-9Bs, C-130Ts and civilian equivalents). At some point, these passengers and materials must be transferred to smaller aircraft (normally MH-53Ss or C-2Ss), or to logistic combat ships for direct transport to ships at sea. This process is performed at temporary Forward Logistic Support Sites (FLSS) established throughout the Mediterranean on an as-needed basis depending on the locations of Fleet concentrations. These temporary support sites, manned by naval reservists performing active duty overseas, also depend on good relations with their host nation. According to Rear Admiral John Ryan, the four bases are: 'geographically suited to allow this transfer regardless of the location of the fleet. All of them, plus a dynamic mix of FLS sites, are required to support a fast-moving fleet that can quickly move from the west coast of Africa to the Red Sea or the Arabian Gulf if required' [Ryan, 1997: 3].

In addition to airborne re-supply, ports, piers, ammunition supply points and fuel depots, these stations provide the required infrastructure to support the movement of larger, bulk commodities to the fleet. Access to these ports is crucial to US logistic force combat ships, which need to load commodities such as fuel and ammunition, as well as critical repair parts that may be too large or heavy to deliver by air. This network has repeatedly proved its viability. Actions in Bosnia, Liberia, the Central African Republic, Albania, Iraq, Zaire and, most recently, Kosovo demonstrate that US forces can reach any target quickly, any time, with the means to do the job, but only with the help of such an effective system, in which Spain, particularly Rota, plays an important part.

Rota provides a base for land-based operational and support aircraft, as well as command and control facilities from which engagement and mobilization are possible. Its runway has undergone major resurfacing. The aprons were near the end of their useful life and required repair. Spain's re-entry into NATO's infrastructure programme gave the US the opportunity to seek Alliance funds for this work. Family housing on the base has also undergone a phased renovation, completed in 1998. Improvement of the barracks, also begun in the mid-1990s, will be completed by 2005 if all goes according to plan. 'Rota is my best QOL [quality of life] base', Rear-Admiral John Ryan said [1997: 7].

The location of Rota makes it ideally suited to support airlifts to any parts of North or Central Africa, the Balkans and the Middle East (CENTCOM), as was demonstrated in operation Desert Storm. The US Air Force maintains a permanent presence of more than 100 personnel to support day-to-day missions at Rota, but during the late 1990s, the base's increased activity forced the Americans to consider opening bases elsewhere on the Iberian peninsula and to undertake a major expansion at Rota itself, which already has a major airfield (with a 10,000-foot runway), a deep water port, an ammunition supply point and a fuel depot. When Spain re-entered NATO's military structure – in operation from 1 January 1999 – Rota also became a NATO base [Liberal, 1993: 181–2].

For the USA, there has always been a common denominator to its interest in Spain: an exclusively military one, in which Spain enables the US to carry out its role as a world power by permitting the deployment and support of its armies, to paraphrase Admiral Angel Liberal Lucini, Spanish Defence Chief of Staff 1984–86 and chairman of the Spanish military commission that negotiated the renewal of the agreements with the US in 1982.

He adds:

> The US needs to have its armed forces present in critical zones at any given moment, and to that end, Spain's strategic position, then as now, is of extraordinary value in its area of influence, which extends to Europe, the Atlantic Ocean, the Mediterranean Sea and North Africa. The changing conflicts in these areas, as well as the technical issues surrounding the means for confronting each crisis, have altered the degree of US interest, but Spain's strategic importance has continued up to today [Liberal, 1993].

Spain's interests in maintaining close ties to the US have changed substantially over the years: they began by dealing, essentially, with domestic policy (Franco's need to legitimize his dictatorship) and foreign affairs (a means of emerging from isolation). Later other motives emerged, such as the modernization of the armed forces and economic aid. At the dawn of the twenty-first century, Spain's main interest in US ties is to obtain – in exchange for the use of its bases, so critical to the US – political recognition commensurate with Spain's new strategic value. Although the Spanish government has not yet defined what would constitute adequate compensation, it is clear that the terms of the current relationship are tipped in favour of the US and must be adjusted to the new geostrategic global realities.

Spanish leaders have clear views on the general terms of negotiation. Washington has insisted that it wishes to expand the base at Rota to accommodate 16 Galaxy transport aircraft. Spanish foreign and defence ministers responded publicly and privately to the effect that they saw no problem with the plan, and yet final approval has been delayed owing to domestic concerns including public opinion and because Washington has not shown appropriate sensitivity to what Spain considers its more-than-earned rights to higher international recognition.

Spain clearly wants to demilitarize the relationship, to politicize it, broaden it and imbue it with matters that are now handled by non-governmental players. The US – which has held a free and decisive trump card in Spain since 1989 – logically has no interest in changing the *status quo*.

Bilateral and Multilateral Relations

During José María Aznar's first term in office (1996–2000), US–Spanish relations ran the gamut from a high when Madrid was selected to host the NATO summit of July 1997 to a low marked by differences over the US Helms-Burton Act. Of course, for the US government, the restructuring and eastward expansion of NATO is the cornerstone of European security and the main mechanism for continued US involvement in Europe [Gardner, 1997].

In the opinion of former Spanish foreign minister Abel Matutes, coordination between the US and Spain has resulted in a common vision on practically all issues, including the reorganization of NATO's command structure and the development of a European Security and Defence Identity. Both countries, according to Matutes, see NATO's eastward expansion as a historic challenge which requires an immediate response, and they consider expansion to be an evolving process that started in 1999 with three countries but which should be open to more in the future. The US and Spain also agree on giving full support to the recently created Euro-Atlantic Association Council, and they both support co-operative efforts between Russia and NATO, special links to the Ukraine, a strengthening of the Mediterranean Dialogue and the creation of a Mediterranean Co-operation Group [Matutes, 1997].

Aznar's first administration, like its predecessor, considered the Helms-Burton Act a violation of international law. Unlike the Socialist government, however, the People's Party administration felt a need to play a more active role alongside Washington in promoting democracy in Cuba. After publicly criticizing the lack of freedom on the island, Aznar was forced to do without an ambassador in Havana for two years, from 1996 to 1998 – despite the fact that his administration maintained and strengthened the traditional 'special relationship' between Latin America and Spain.

On 13 February 1999, the Spanish cabinet approved a proposal to protect citizens that could be penalized under the American Helms-Burton and D'Amato-Kennedy laws, which prohibit and punish investment – under certain conditions – in Cuba, Libya and Iran. As a result, Spanish citizens who find themselves directly or indirectly affected by these laws are obliged to ignore them, report the situation immediately to the European Commission and not divulge any information to the United States. The regulation provides for financial compensation to those who suffer under the said laws.

Although the Socialist Party made a 180-degree turn in its attitude toward the US and NATO after it came to power in the mid-1980s, there always was some division in Washington as to the sincerity of Felipe González's change of heart over transatlantic relations. Doubts were raised, for instance, by his diplomatic battle to get the 72 F-16 fighter-bombers out of Torrejón during the 1988 negotiation of a new bilateral agreement and by Spanish wavering over NATO membership both before and after the 1986 referendum. The Socialist administration's flirtations with the Sandinistas and Fidel Castro only fuelled American suspicions.

US scepticism was reduced as a result of Spain's support for Washington during the Gulf crisis, and of the success of the Madrid Conference on the Middle East in 1991. Yet even though the US State Department got along well with González, the Pentagon always considered Socialist Spain a second-class ally. In fact, González's main contribution to Spanish-American relations was multilateral, not bilateral, in nature: negotiation of the EU-US Transatlantic Agenda, signed by Bill Clinton, Jacques Santer and Felipe González in Madrid in December 1995, during Spain's turn at the helm of the EU.

The fruits of those efforts included Javier Solana's election as secretary-general of NATO in late 1995, Carlos Westendorp's election in 1997 as High Representative to Bosnia, and Miguel Angel Moratinos' election as EU envoy to the Middle East.

On 12 March 1996, the USA and Spain signed the third supplementary treaty on extradition, which the then foreign minister Westendorp called a 'model' agreement. Then, in December 1997, the US authorities for the first time detained a member of ETA, Ramón Aldasoro, who was finally extradited to Spain in 1999. The new American anti-terrorist policy thus went into effect, after being announced by the State Department early in

October 1997. The policy, among other things, prohibited members of ETA and other groups classified as 'terrorist' from entering the US or raising money there (*El País*, 9 Oct. 1997).

On the eve of his victory in March 1996, PP candidate José María Aznar recognized the profound changes in the strategic environment and committed himself, upon winning the election, to make Spain a fully-integrated member of the Atlantic Alliance, to improve relations with the United States and to carry on the Transatlantic work of González. 'The Transatlantic Declaration', he said, 'provides a good framework for our efforts over the immediate future, both in terms of bilateral relations and work through the EU' [Aznar, 1996].

While the USA was once Francoist Spain's main link to the outside world, by 1996, when the People's Party took office, it had already assumed a secondary – though still important – role in Spanish foreign policy compared to that of the main European powers: France, Germany, Italy and Great Britain.

Five months after becoming the seventh foreign minister since the restoration of democracy, Abel Matutes recognized that Spanish–American relations still suffered from a 'militaristic vision of our relationship' and said it was 'imperative' to overcome 'the currently limited levels of co-operation. The New Transatlantic Agenda with the EU, signed in Madrid, gives us the opportunity to increase relations of all kinds' [Matutes, 1998]. Four years later, relations had multiplied, but the US continued to consider Spain above all a loyal military ally. In 1997, at the inauguration of the Third Spain–US Forum in Washington DC, which was one of the main fruits of the Agenda, Matutes added:

> It is clear that for Spain, as a member of the EU, political and economic convergence in the European integration process is logically the first priority. But that in no way takes care of all its foreign policy options. Today Spain can intervene simultaneously in every international forum or situation where its interests might be at risk. I can state that Spanish foreign policy contains various indispensable objectives, which are not mutually exclusive. Our interests in Europe do not contradict those in Latin America, and even less those in the Mediterranean. Nor is EU convergence irreconcilable with Transatlantic collaboration, which is carried out on two planes: the bilateral plane, in relations with the US, and the multilateral one, mainly through the EU and NATO [Matutes, 1998].

Economic Relations

In the economic sphere, intensified relations with the European Union have reduced the relative weight of US trade and investment in Spain. In 1986, the first year of Spanish membership of the European Community, the United States was still the second largest importer of Spanish goods in the world, behind only France. It was the fourth largest exporter to Spain, behind only Germany, France and the United Kingdom. US imports that year totalled about $2.7 billion (slightly more than nine per cent) and exports to Spain totalled about $2.6 billion (almost ten per cent) [EIU, 1997: 18–19].

Ten years later, in 1996, the value of Spanish-American commercial exchanges surpassed $10 billion and the United States was still Spain's most important trading partner outside the EU, with the balance of trade clearly unfavourable to Spain. In 1998, Spain imported $6.5 billion worth of goods from the US, while exports were worth $3.6 billion. Achieving a more equitable balance of bilateral trade is thus a primary objective for Spain. If one bears in mind the depreciation of the peseta against the dollar, the reality is that, in overall figures, bilateral trade increased only slightly during the 1990s, while seen as a percentage of total Spanish trade it decreased considerably: from approximately ten per cent at the start of the decade to less than five per cent by the end of it [Hidalgo, 1996: 158].

By the mid-1990s, Spanish investment in the US – which in 1997 ranged between $300 and $400 million a year, representing five per cent of Spain's total foreign investment – had already surpassed US direct investment in Spain, so great has been Spain's development progress during the last two decades.

But the economic importance of the US to Spain is much greater than the aforementioned statistics suggest. Every one per cent increase in US GNP leads to a one per cent increase in the EU over a five-year cycle. In the case of Spain, the cumulative effect amounts to an increase of 1.5 per cent. The reason for this discrepancy is that, while growth and contraction of the US economy affect the European economy proportionally, the effect in Spain is amplified [Raymond, 1994: 77]. The least one can say about these figures is that the optimism about US-Spanish commerce usually found in the discourse of politicians and diplomats is quite exaggerated and has nothing to do with the current economic reality. This means also that a good deal has yet to be done, because there is great potential.

The economies of the US and EU are ever more intertwined as a result of direct investment, joint ventures and free trade agreements (reached first through GATT, then the WTO). In the case of Spain and the US, the sectors in which the greatest number of joint enterprises are forming are telecommunications and banking. Telefónica, Bazán, Santander, Banco Bilbao Vizcaya (BBV) and Banco Central Hispano (BCH) are some of the principal examples. The growing presence of all these entities in Latin America is an added incentive for three-way collaboration, the so-called *relación triangular,* more and more sought after by US businesses.

To reduce US complaints, Aznar's first government administration removed the quotas on foreign films in Spain. Although the US audio-visual industry has failed to reciprocate – Spanish film exports continue to be negligible, Almodovar apart – the agricultural industry has made a concession. The US Department of Agriculture has finally authorized the sale of Serrano ham and other Spanish products, so long as they match up to US health regulations.

For Spain, which handles almost all its trade negotiations through the EU, few bilateral issues with the US remain in this regard. One of them relates to the import of bananas from the Canary Islands. In this matter, the WTO has ruled against European, including Spanish, interests.

The Cultural Challenge

In order to manage these growing contacts more efficiently – and without getting bogged down in the inevitable conflicts over the important interests at stake – Spain and the United States have established bilateral forums which complement the Transatlantic Agenda between the European Union and the US. Despite the abundant flow of tourists, students and business people between Spain and the US, many Spaniards and Americans agree that the people of both nations know each other very little, and what they think they do know is often mistaken. In four visits to the US during the early part of his first term of office, Aznar cited the 'image problem' as Spain's primary challenge in that country. The main response has been to organize forums of debate to strengthen non-official ties.

Following the first two forums – in Seville in 1995 and Toledo in 1996 – Vice-President Al Gore made a private visit to Spain, met Aznar and agreed to a series of initiatives that grew out of these forums, as well as the personal efforts of ex-ambassador Gardner. The most important initiatives are as follows:

- a new teacher exchange programme sponsored by the William J. Fulbright Fellowship Program;

- a substantial increase in the number of high school teacher exchange programmes with various American states, aimed at language teachers in both Spain and the US;

- the incorporation of Spanish students into Vice-President Gore's GLOBE programme, which, via Internet, joins together secondary school students from all over the world to participate in environmental education projects;

- additional efforts to promote the study of each other's language and society, such as the Spain-US 2000 Program, which each year sends 26 'future Spanish leaders' to conduct graduate work in the US with grants financed by the private sector;

- the promotion of internship programmes for young Spaniards and Americans in business and professional organizations, as well as parliamentary offices;

- sponsorship of a Publishers' Conference, held in October 1997 in Madrid, which brought together leading representatives of the publishing industries of both countries to study the possibility of collaborating on publishing activities of mutual interest.

The conditions for furthering educational, cultural and scientific co-operation have never been better. Whereas back in the 1920s and 30s there were only two pioneer exchange centres, the National Institute of Physics and Chemistry associated with the Rockefeller Foundation and the Student Residence of Madrid – and a complete void in the 1940s and 50s – there is now a close network of relationships, in which the Fulbright Program has always held an important place.

For 40 years the two countries have sponsored one of the largest two-way exchange programmes in the world. The bi-national Commission on Educational, Scientific and Cultural Exchange distributes $5 million a year to the Fulbright academic exchange programme and provides another $2.5 million towards scientific exchanges. Although both governments continue contributing to these programmes, the majority of the funds – some 140 grants a year to students, lecturers, researchers, journalists, speakers and professionals – now comes from the private sector.

Some 3,500 Spaniards have studied or conducted research in the US with grants from Fulbright. Another 1,500 Americans have studied or taught in Spain under the same programme. Since its origins in 1958, the Fulbright Program has been the primary tool for two-way cultural co-operation. Over the years, the US government has contributed $11.5 million to the programme and the Spanish government $5 million. The Spanish private sector, though joining the project late – the first to participate was the Caixa bank of Barcelona in 1983 – has contributed another $15 million.

Without the support of the hundreds of Hispanic Studies scholars in the US, aided by Fulbright, the recent advances in the study of Spain – the King Carlos I Center for Hispanic Studies at New York University, for example, and the Real Complutense College at Harvard – would have been unthinkable. To all those with scholarships today, one must add more than 5,000 Spanish students who study each year at American universities without government aid, and more than 7,000 American students who study under the same conditions each year in Spain.

According to the Secretaría de Estado de Universidades e Investigación in the Spanish Ministry of Education, the US is the first-choice destination of Spanish researchers who want to further their scientific training abroad. It is the preferred country for post-doctoral studies for 38.5 per cent of Spanish researchers, followed by the UK (20 per cent), France (18.3 per cent), Germany (5.5 per cent) and Italy (3.9 per cent). For Masters or PhD programmes, the percentage is even higher: here the US attracts 46.7 per cent of the students compared to figures of 17.9 per cent for Great Britain, 8.4 per cent for France, 6.8 per cent for Germany and only 6.0 per cent for Italy. As far as academic fields go, 80 per cent of the researchers devote themselves to science and technology, and only 20 per cent to the social sciences and humanities.

With 30 million Hispanic citizens, the US is now the nation with the fifth highest number of Spanish-speakers in the world. Spanish is already the main foreign language taught in American schools. Another Cervantes Institute has just opened in Chicago, adding to the one already operating in New York. Moreover, in April 1997 King Don Juan Carlos and Queen Sofía inaugurated a centre at New York University which bears their name.

Washington Irving, US ambassador to Madrid during the first half of the nineteenth century, and Walt Whitman, a great admirer of Spanish culture one hundred years ago, would have been proud.

Conclusions

Twenty-five years after Franco's death, relations between Spain and the US have undergone important changes, although these are not as radical as those affecting Spain's relations with its main European partners. The military dimension is still dominant and the relationship is very unequal, badly understood by public opinion and, therefore, has much potential for improvement both in quantitative and in qualitative terms. Adding to that potential is the increasing importance of the Spanish language in the US. Democratization in Spain, Spanish integration into the EU and NATO, the end of the cold war and, most important of all, Spain's new economic prosperity have changed the relationship for the better. Yet, many high-level officials in both countries seem to ignore or be ignorant of this new situation. Starting from near total Spanish dependence on the US, both economically and militarily, over the years the military value of Spanish bases has increased instead of diminishing but the economic dimension of the relationship, in proportional terms, has been cut substantially.

REFERENCES

Aznar, J.M. (1996): 'Presente y futuro de España en el mundo', Conferencia pronunciada en la Casa de América, Ensayos INCIPE 8, Madrid: Instituto de Cuestiones Internacionales y Política Exterior.

EIU (1987): *Spain Country Report*, London: Economist Intelligence Unit.

Gardner, R. (1994): 'Spain and America in the Marketplace of Ideas', speech given by the US Ambassador, Madrid: Casa de América, 26 Oct.

Gardner, R. (1997): 'Reflexiones sobre una relación especial: España y los Estados Unidos', Madrid: Casa de América, 18 June.

Gaviria, M. (1996): *La séptima potencia. España en el mundo,* Barcelona: Ediciones B, Grupo Z.

Hayes, C. (1952): *Los Estados Unidos y España*, Madrid: Ediciones y Publicaciones Españolas (EPESA).

Hidalgo, D. (1996): *El futuro de España,* Madrid: Taurus.

INCIPE (1995): *La opinión pública española y la política exterior,* Madrid: Instituto de Cuestiones Internacionales y Política Exterior.

Liberal, A. (1993): 'Cuarenta años después (1953–1993)', *Política Exterior* 7/35.

MAE (1999): *Diario de Sesiones del Congreso de los Diputados*, Comisión de Asuntos Exteriores, VI Legislatura, No. 641, Madrid: Ministerio de Asuntos Exteriores.

Matutes, A. (1997): 'Relaciones entre España y los EE.UU.', III Foro España-Estados Unidos, Washington, DC.

Matutes, A. (1998): 'La política exterior española', Conferencia inaugural del curso académico, Madrid: Escuela Diplomática.

Ministerio de Defensa (1999): Nota informativa interna.

Pardo de Santayana, J. R. (1996): 'Geoestrategia y espacio español', *Política Exterior* 10/49.

Raymond, J.L. (1994): 'Condicionantes externos de la evolución de la economía española', in *El nuevo rumbo de la economía mundial y el estado de bienestar,* Santander: Universidad Internacional Menéndez y Pelayo/Asociación de Periodistas de Información Económica. Documentos de Trabajo 104.

Roy, J. (1986): 'Presencia de España en los Estados Unidos: economía o cultura, una propuesta para el 92', in *Realidades y posibilidades de las relaciones entre España y América en los ochenta,* Madrid: Instituto de Cooperación Iberoamericana.

Ryan, J. (1997): Statement to the Armed Forces Committee, US House of Representatives, 3 April, http://thomas.loc.gov/home/hearing.html

UNDP (1997): *Human Development Report*, New York: United Nations Development Programme.

Spanish Defence Policy: Eurocorps and NATO Reform

CRISPIN COATES

Spain's eagerness to play a major role in Europe's new security architecture has not been marked by complete success. Problems in transforming a large and backward military establishment have been exacerbated by a declining budget and long-term dependence upon imported technology. On the diplomatic front this has been shown by only limited success in extending military protection to Spanish interests in the Mediterranean and only a partial fulfilment of national ambitions at the NATO summit in Madrid in July 1997. However, some satisfaction has been derived from Spanish attempts to achieve a stronger regional emphasis within European security institutions.

> [T]he objective of our defence policy is to provide Spain with an effective instrument of deterrence, readiness and response in order to permanently guarantee its sovereignty and independence, its territorial integrity and its constitutional order, as well as protect lives, peace, liberty and prosperity of Spaniards and national strategic interests wherever they are to be found (Directiva de Defensa Nacional, January 1996).[1]

As Spain reached the end of the twentieth century, it could be said that the last decade had seen considerable national success in the field of foreign policy. The end of the 1980s had been marked by a sense of unpredictability, with the collapse of communism and only a partial resolution of the issue of Spanish membership of NATO. The challenge for Spain in the 1990s was to reach its much vaunted potential in international affairs. Debates over Spain's relative roles in EU and NATO-led activities remained central. Security challenges came not from the Persian Gulf, where events had encouraged European institutions to develop a certain activity, but from central Europe owing to the collapse of Yugoslavia. The nature of the response demanded by the international community mirrored the dilemma faced by Spain. An initial tentative initiative by the European Union followed by the forcible application of the Dayton Accords devised by the United States generally reflected the state of international security organizations throughout the 1990s. Once again, the EU had been found lacking in its response to an international crisis. Subsequently, the Kosovo intervention reflected the supremacy of NATO in organizing responses to problems that demanded military intervention.

For Spain, the 1990s can be seen as dominated by two themes in the field of defence policy. Support would remain high for European-led initiatives in the areas of security and defence while there was also a clear attempt to settle the question of Spain's incomplete NATO membership. This study will address two key issues: Spain's enthusiasm for the development of institutions concerned with European security and the resolution of the ambiguity surrounding the country's NATO membership.

Spanish Defence Policy: An Introduction

As early as 1962, the year in which Spain unsuccessfully first sought entry to the EEC, its relationship with the US (arising out of the Madrid defence agreements of 1953) brought a degree of integration of Spanish military technology with that of the US and, by implication, NATO. Therefore, as long ago as the 1960s, there was a need to temper the demands of a military dominated by US assistance with the realities of a medium-sized European nation that traditionally had played a role of some prominence in the western Mediterranean.

However, the period since the cold war has been one of change as different institutions have sought to reassess their focus in view of the changed international situation, which was not devoid of tension between states. Spain finished the century as a full member of NATO, just as the Alliance absorbed three former Warsaw Pact countries (Poland, Hungary and the Czech Republic). Simultaneously the former Spanish foreign minister, Javier Solana, moved from the post of NATO Secretary-General to that of High Representative of the European Union for the common foreign and security policy, thus epitomizing the possible divergence of interests facing Spain.

Spain entered the 1990s as one of the NATO alliance's weaker members. It had a sizeable military and yet had one of the lowest levels of defence expenditure in the West. Spanish ambitions to exert influence in international defence matters depended not only on the institutional choices open to Madrid but also upon addressing the constraint of having a substantial yet poorly equipped military establishment. In fact, the 1990s saw a long-term decline in the pattern of defence expenditure further exacerbated.

Two observations emerge from an analysis of Spain's defence budget. First, defence has not been particularly high on the political agenda. After being made a priority in the 1980s during the early years of the Socialist government, it soon returned to its lowly status among government spending priorities (see Table 1).[2]   Second, the picture is complicated, however, by the fact that substantial parts of defence expenditure sometimes appear within the budgets of other ministries. For example, large chunks of defence expenditure on the EFA (Eurofighter) project were funded at the research and development stage by the Industry Ministry. This means, on the one hand, that defence expenditure is in fact higher than government figures suggest, and is thus not fully visible to Spanish taxpayers; and, on the other hand, that the Defence Ministry's control over defence spending is incomplete.

TABLE 1
SPANISH DEFENCE EXPENDITURE 1990–99

Year	Defence Expenditure (million pesetas)	Proportion of GDP (percentage)
1990	836,631	1.67
1991	823,180	1.50
1992	785,883	1.33
1993	757,710	1.24
1994	805,482	1.24
1995	866,499	1.24
1996	870,055	1.17
1997	869,992	1.11
1998	897,429	1.10
1999	928,172	1.00

Source: *Revista Española de Defensa* (Ministerio de Defensa, Madrid), Nov. 1996 and Feb. 1999.

The most apparent trend is that Spain's defence expenditure as a proportion of GDP declined considerably throughout the 1990s. This fall seems to have abated only towards the end of the decade, following quite considerable dissent within the armed forces. The fact remains that this was the period following the cold war and therefore could be considered a time when defence spending could realistically be reduced. The so-called 'peace dividend' was as resonant in Spain as it was in other NATO countries. However, the central conviction cannot be denied that for Spain to play a role in shaping Europe's security and foreign policy agenda, it will require a considerable level of resources and infrastructure. The levels of Spanish investment in the armed forces have lagged seriously behind those of other similarly placed countries, such as Italy and Canada.

TABLE 2
DEFENCE SPENDING PER HEAD OF POPULATION.
(IN US$ AT 1990 PRICES AND EXCHANGE RATES)

Year	Spain	Italy	Canada
1985	246	392	414
1990	233	412	415
1995	207	360	335
1998	196	356	253

Source: *NATO Review* 1 (Spring 1999), pp.31–3.

The main conclusion suggested by Table 2 is that Spain has consistently spent less on its armed forces than other similarly sized states. Even as a proportion of GDP, Spain has not matched the expenditure levels of comparable countries.

Traditionally, this situation has had the effect of maintaining a military structure that was both under-resourced and subject to external political events (namely relations with the US). A further consequence was that external defence continued to be a low priority in policy-making. Spain could aspire to being granted a support role by the US as a result of treaty obligations, yet at the same time lacked the commitments and programmes that full membership of the NATO alliance implied.

This brings us back to the demands upon Spanish defence policy at the end of the cold war. Earlier, the Spanish military had been ill-equipped for any form of modern conflict. Spain had not managed to maintain its former colonial status through the use of either military force or diplomacy, and in terms of participating in a wider conflict, doubts existed as to the efficacy of the armed forces. In order to project a more active foreign policy involving use of the defence forces, there existed a need for stronger policies of equipment procurement [Molero, 1990: 194]. Addressing this need, under the first civilian government formed by the Union of the Democratic Centre (UCD) and subsequently under the Socialist Party (PSOE), the structures of Spain's defence establishment underwent considerable reform.

Spain's defence policy during the 1980s was marked by three broad features:

- there was a domestic agenda of entry into NATO and the EC with a considerable impact upon defence policy-making within the domestic political scene;
- democratic accountability was gradually asserted over the defence establishment;
- a modernization programme extended to both defence institutions and equipment, and represented a genuine step towards a more democratic model.

Overall, there were considerable challenges for Spain with regard to modernization, the assertion of civil control over the entire Spanish armed forces (via a combination of parliamentary, executive and bureaucratic control) and a new programme seeking technical convergence with other EC and NATO member states.

In terms of the budgets and activities of the defence forces, there existed a clear divergence in Spain by the 1990s. While the military had taken on considerable responsibilities through deployments to Central America, Southern Africa and the Balkans, it now faced a steady decline in resources. In addition, fuelling the debate over conscription, there was a big rise in the number of objectors to a point where in 1992 major reforms had to be enacted in the form of a law on military service. The government opted for a shorter term of conscription (nine months, as opposed to 12 months previously) and committed itself to raising the defence budget to two per cent of GDP, deeming this sufficient for the functioning of a post-cold war military. However, by 1997 the policy had fallen short in two respects. The budget had been allowed to fall and the issue of conscription had to be revisited. In this year, a joint committee of the Senate and Congress recommended the adoption of a fully professional model.

Under the plans adopted by the Aznar administration, the size of the armed forces will fall to approximately 160,000 by 2002, having stood at 300,000 in 1990. A smaller, better-equipped force is now a model commanding a considerable degree of political consensus on what Spain seeks to achieve. The main remaining challenge is to endow it with sufficient funds. What remains to be resolved within the policy-making establishment is the problem of the systematic shortfall in the funding of this fully-professional, more flexible military institution.

NATO since the End of the Cold War

When the immediate issue of NATO membership was resolved in the referendum of 1986, the long-term question of Spain's relationship with the US-led military alliance remained unanswered. In 1986 the cold war still posed a challenge to the integrity and security of Europeans. Furthermore, alternative security institutions were still very much awaiting development and offered little scope for the creation of a European defence force in the near future. However, the need for a more complete settlement of the NATO issue was obscured by a more pressing foreign policy priority: that of successful integration with Europe.

Within a very short period of time, however, the specific agenda that had dominated Spain's foreign policy since Franco's death ceased to be adequate to new international circumstances. European accession was completed at a time of relative economic boom for Spain, thus overcoming some of the anticipated short-term problems, and encouraging ambition on the external relations front. Meanwhile, the cold war showed signs of ending: in the late 1980s the Warsaw Pact was becoming increasingly fragmented as the Soviet Union lost military and political status. The agenda of the 1970s and 1980s needed renewal in response to the emerging new post-cold war world.

For Spain, a NATO member outside the integrated military command (IMC) and only a lukewarm proponent of the Atlantic Alliance, the end of the cold war threatened to undermine the substantial consensus that had grown up around the need for NATO and EC membership. With the ending of the cold war (generally associated with the fall of the Berlin Wall in November 1989), the threat from the East to the integrity of western Europe could no longer be seen in military terms. With the questioning of a purely military analysis of the requirements of European security, Alliance unity over the role of NATO (which had never been one of the organization's strong points)[3] was almost immediately threatened by the new perspective of impending multi-polar power politics.

One issue of particular relevance for Spain arose from the West's responses to subsequent events in Yugoslavia, owing to their implications for the security of Spanish territory. Under the initial Washington Treaty that created NATO in 1949, Yugoslavia was not technically an area of Alliance responsibility. Article V of the treaty defined the area of operation in terms of maintaining the member states' own territorial integrity. Technically there existed no provision for responsibility for the defence of interests outside the North Atlantic area. As an 'out of area' issue, Yugoslavia was not NATO's responsibility. Even by the start of the 1990s, NATO's activity in Europe was based specifically on the defence of its member states. The Alliance was ill-equipped to intervene in the Balkans and there existed no precedent or consensus for this. The full significance for Spain of events in former Yugoslavia, however, relates also to the structural transformation undergone by NATO.

NATO Reforms in the 1990s

In the period 1989–99, the NATO alliance transformed its structures substantially to a point where it was able to reassert itself as the prime security institution in Europe. Within this context, it not only absorbed three former members of the Warsaw Pact but also took on the UN mandate to implement peace in Bosnia-Hercegovina and employed enormous resources in the campaign in Kosovo.

Looking back, it is easy to overlook the fact that in the early 1990s NATO's survival could not be regarded as a *fait accompli* for the Alliance. The latter consisted of a number of states that in the past had shown specific interest in NATO only as a source of protection from outside aggression. Following the disappearance of the Warsaw Pact and rapid cuts in defence spending and troop levels in central Europe, NATO faced the threat that it would be a victim of its success in confronting the eastern bloc. However, a combination of key events and active diplomacy enabled the Alliance not only to survive but also to celebrate its fiftieth anniversary with the accession of Poland, Hungary and the Czech Republic, three former Warsaw Pact members.

Within months of the fall of the Berlin Wall, NATO had begun a process of reorientating its defence posture. By the time of the London summit in July 1990, the creation of an 'Allied Rapid Reaction Corps' (ARRC) had been authorized, representing not just a continuation of the military model but a response to the changed context in the form of new types of defence forces.

NATO's 'New Strategic Concept' was approved at the Rome summit of November 1991 during the run-up to the Maastricht treaty on European Union. NATO sought to maintain a presence in Europe's changing security architecture, so much so that hopes of a common security policy for the EU were dashed, in part owing to differences of opinion between the Atlanticists (led by the UK) and Europeanists (led by France).

The creation of the Partnership for Peace (PfP) led NATO into active diplomacy with the countries of the former Warsaw Pact and Soviet Union. Much to the distrust of Russia (which later reached a separate agreement with the Alliance), the Brussels summit of January 1994 approved the PfP programme with countries that only five years previously had confronted NATO during the cold war.

In addition to the repackaging of NATO as a more open, consultative body, accessible to third parties through the creation of the concept of the Combined Joint Task Force (CJTF), this new partnership approach meant that NATO structures and equipment could be made available for use by other international organizations. Thus, by the time of the Madrid summit in 1997, the Alliance had not only managed to survive the end of the cold war but was on the verge of expanding eastwards.

Spain and the NATO Alliance

By the time of Franco's death in 1975, Spain's North African holdings had been reduced to Ceuta, Melilla and a number of tiny islands. The loss of the Spanish Sahara[4] did little to settle the status of the remaining territories and it is this, along with the region's turbulent political development, that underlies Spain's current security concerns.

Morocco consistently disputes Spain's title to Ceuta and Melilla despite the fact that both have a considerable history in Spanish hands. Both have sizeable populations in their own right (68,000 and 60,000 respectively, including troops, Moroccans and Spanish civilians). In spite of this fact, the two territories have attracted little attention from non-Spanish European observers, being small and, in the case of Melilla, some distance from the straits between Spain and Morocco.

Recent examinations of the pattern of procurement within the Spanish military point to these two enclaves consuming an inordinate amount of manpower and equipment in providing for their defence. An area of concern centres upon the long-term viability of this policy. It has been maintained in response to the long-standing Moroccan claims to the territory. This is Spain's most vulnerable border. In addition to defence expenditures, considerable resources are devoted to combating illegal immigration and contraband in this region. In recent years, bilateral relations with Morocco have been good, but the possibility of a future incursion by a hostile neighbour can never be discarded. Spain has an active interest in Moroccan stability, for this in turn influences the level of security threat to the borders of Ceuta and Melilla.

The Canary Islands are the other Spanish territory that are of significance in relation to NATO membership. Spain's long-standing sovereignty over these islands has not faced the same challenge as the North African enclaves, though the Canaries' proximity to the North African coastline has made them subject to vague threats and even a small independence movement.[5] Both the military significance of the Canaries and their distance from the Iberian peninsula account for a substantial Spanish military presence.

Unfortunately for Spain, following its belated entry into NATO and subsequent self-exclusion from the IMC, both territories in North Africa remained unprotected by the Atlantic Alliance. Moreover, despite being Spanish, the Canary Islands were part of a NATO mandate outside of Spanish control. The IBERLANT (Iberia/Atlantic) command was part of the Portuguese responsibility discharged from Lisbon and not only included the western entrance to the Straits of Gibraltar but also encompassed the Canary Islands. This command, nominally in the hands of the Portuguese military, was an issue of some contention [Maxwell, 1995: 178]. Historical rivalry between Spain and Portugal would now complicate the status of the IBERLANT mandate. While Spain remained outside the Atlantic Alliance (until 1982), this was not a problem, but with membership this became an issue between the two members.[6]

With only conditional membership of NATO from 1986, Spain had to accept only a limited extension of security in relation to its non-mainland territories. Not only did Madrid have to settle for a Portuguese mandate over a politically-sensitive area of its territory, it also had to compromise over the question of Gibraltar. The Rock, that long-standing issue in Spanish relations with the UK, was also home to a different NATO command (GIBMED), in this case in the hands of the British military.

NATO membership not only brought Spain limited prestige, but it offered little protection to the vulnerable territories of Ceuta and Melilla.

The NATO charter drawn up in 1949 was explicit in defining the Alliance area of responsibility so as to exclude any colonial conflicts affecting member states. In Spanish eyes, this policy had clearly positive implications in the conflicts that involved a number of individual NATO states (such as the US in Vietnam and the UK in the Falklands dispute), but it also meant that protection for the two North African enclaves would not be forthcoming from the US or other NATO members. In fact, in 1959, when Moroccan troops occupied Sidi Ifni, the US did not allow Spain even to use donated equipment to defeat the incursion, so wary was Washington of involvement [Cortada, 1980: 139].

The security benefits to Spain regarding these areas was therefore in doubt. NATO offered no guarantee of protection of the African territories and yet Spain clearly became a participant in the NATO effort in the cold war. Thus, with regard to Spanish territory, two main obstacles to closer integration within NATO existed. First, the North African territories were offered only marginal protection from accession to NATO. Second, both the GIBMED and IBERLANT commands lay in the hands of foreign powers.

These obstacles were of little concern while Spain lay outside the main military structure of NATO. However with the cold war ending and NATO surviving, Spain's gradual but consistent integration into the Alliance raised these issues once again. With integration into NATO's military structure imminent following the election of the Partido Popular in March 1996,[7] issues that had been considered irrelevant suddenly became the focus of media speculation.[8]

NATO's survival beyond the cold war should not, of course, be regarded as having been inevitable. By the early 1990s a number of organizations had emerged to rival NATO's hegemony in western Europe. The first was the Western European Union (WEU), a long-dormant security body that had emerged out of the post-war European Defence Community (mainly France, the UK, the Netherlands and Belgium). It had been in a form of institutional hibernation since the 1950s as NATO asserted its greater influence in European affairs. However, the WEU had re-emerged in 1984, when the Paris declaration effectively revived the concept of a European defence force. Another body that could be considered a rival to NATO's role in European security was the Conference on Security and Co-operation in Europe (CSCE).[9] This embraced all the European states as well as the US and the Russian federation.

The challenge for western Europe's security planners was to construct a model that met the security requirements of the individual states, many of which had concerns relating to an unpredictable region. In some cases, the use of NATO would not be seen as possible owing to the Article V 'out of area' restriction. Nor would it be politically expedient to opt for overtly NATO-led operations in the case of sensitive issues involving peacekeeping.

By the start of the 1990s, there was considerable overlap between a number of security institutions: NATO, the WEU and the CSCE, as well as the United Nations. All these organizations could claim a role in conflict prevention in Europe. Spain, as a member of all of them, faced a dilemma along with other EU member states.

Spain's continuation and full participation in the Alliance came about as a result of two events following the cold war: first the Gulf War of 1990–91, and second the break-up of Yugoslavia. While the Gulf War did not involve a NATO operation as such, what it did show was that any other military body was too weak to address a situation of armed incursion by a foreign power. The Spanish contribution to the liberation of Kuwait was somewhat paradoxical. Spanish public opinion was unhappy about the US use of Spanish facilities to attack Iraq. The Morón air base was used extensively to launch bombing attacks on Iraqi positions while a huge number of ships docked in Spanish ports on their way to the region. The situation was further complicated by popular Arab opinion which was anti-US. In spite of Moroccan contributions to the allied force, Spain was placed in an uncomfortable position regarding the status of Ceuta and Melilla. In response to the news that US attacks on Iraq had commenced, there was rioting by the Berber populations of these territories.

Yugoslavia's break-up followed on almost immediately after the ending of the Gulf War. Essentially, the EU response was seen as totally inadequate, as it stood by and monitored the situation before committing troops to the region under the auspices of the UN. Even then, European policy responses proved weak as differences between EU members led to disputes. Yet even in the Amsterdam Treaty of 1997,[10] the EU remained unwilling to create the foundations for really effective foreign policy action.

Despite the fact that security institutions other than NATO have generally proved ineffective thus far (with the possible exception of the WEU), there persists within Spain an ambition to help design a European defence and security identity, or at least fully participate in its result. Along with France, Spain has been a keen proponent of a non-Atlanticist security identity, in some ways influenced by the historical anti-Americanism that has tinged certain currents of Spanish nationalism. It has drawn back, however, from pushing for an exclusively European approach, and indeed in July 1997 sought a smooth completion of its NATO membership at the Madrid summit.

The NATO Madrid Summit

In the period leading up to the summit, the prospects of a relatively seamless entry into NATO's integrated command structure seemed good. In November 1996, the Cortes passed a clear resolution in support of full entry into the Alliance. Even the PSOE voted with the Aznar government to allow full membership to be achieved, although González as PSOE leader did remark that the Socialists were not offering the government a blank cheque. The final approval was opposed by the United Left (IU) and the Canary Islands Coalition (CC),[11] for very different reasons. While IU opposition was ultimately rooted in ideology, the unhappiness of the CC centred upon the awkward status of the Canary Islands and the IBERLANT command.

While NATO saw the Madrid summit as formalizing the membership invitation to Poland, Hungary and the Czech Republic, Spain had three rather different priorities in the run-up to the event. The biggest priority related to the reorganization of the NATO mandates with regard to Spain. The next main issue was the nature of Spain's contribution to the new command structure. Finally, Spain saw the Madrid summit as an attempt to develop the European Security and Defence Identity (ESDI) into a more tangible form. From the Spanish perspective, the expansion of NATO towards the East was a somewhat peripheral issue. Any challenge that could emerge to Spain's interests as a result of opening up the Alliance towards the East would be an indirect threat to the country's Mediterranean agenda. Generally, though, the impending accession of the three central European countries (not completed until May 1999) barely registered within Spain's foreign policy. This illustrates the fact that NATO as a foreign policy tool has lost its linkage to the European dimension of Spain's foreign policy. The real question relating to NATO was how Spain's military could assert influence within the structures of the Alliance.

Unfortunately for Spain, the UK remained steadfast in its insistence upon sovereignty over Gibraltar.[12] Therefore, Gibraltar remained essentially a foreign territory, notwithstanding the welcome abolition of the GIBMED command. Gibraltar is still an issue in Spain for two reasons. First, Spain objects to the colonial presence of the UK on what it sees as a Spanish land mass. Second, since the cold war, as a result of the reduction of the military contribution to the Rock's economy, Gibraltar has been involved in more and more activities that are objected to by Spain. The colony has become an off-shore financial tax haven, accused by Madrid of becoming a centre for criminal money laundering and even smuggling. The most potent symbol of discord has been the dispute between the three parties, Madrid, London and the Gibraltar 'government' over the use of the airport.

The result of this confrontation was that from 1995 rigorous border checks were implemented by the Spanish authorities in order to demonstrate governmental dissatisfaction. This policy not only affected cross-border trade with the colony but also politicized relations with the UK and even, on occasion, the EU. With these issues in mind, the Aznar government thus faced a very real threat of Britain blocking Spain's complete entry into the NATO alliance. As late as December 1997, there was speculation that UK foreign secretary Robin Cook might veto Spain's application. In addition, questions regarding the IBERLANT command were not going to enjoy much British support, particularly as Portugal has regularly enjoyed close links with the UK.

The Spanish campaign over GIBMED achieved very little. The final result was that this command was suspended while the regional command went to AFSOUTH (Allied Forces South), based in Naples. The question of Gibraltar remains topical. The UK maintains a military presence and Spain retains its sovereignty claim. NATO's jurisdiction in the dispute is non-existent, which again points to the fact that the link between NATO and the EU in Spanish foreign policy is increasingly tenuous.

The other territorial dispute within NATO, over the Canaries, cannot be seen as a vindication of Spain's strategy of expanding influence within NATO commands either. The IBERLANT command question was perhaps the most pressing of the two. On the one hand, the PP was unwilling to antagonize the Canary Islands Coalition; on the other hand, electoral support for full NATO entry in November 1996 had been conditional upon the status of the Canary Islands remaining unaltered and IBERLANT at least being administered by Spain's defence forces. Considerable defence equipment was deployed in the region, both to monitor the entrance to the straits of Gibraltar and to provide sufficient military capacity in support of any NATO requirements.[13]

After a period of intensive negotiation, the outcome provided little consolation for Spanish sensitivities. While recognizing that Spain had some justification in its demand for some form of control in an area of national interest, the Alliance resolved the issue of the IBERLANT command on the basis of wider considerations, which extended in two directions. The area was to be divided between a European command based at SHAPE (Supreme Headquarters Allied Powers in Europe) and the US, which would continue to exercise the Atlantic command (ACLANT) from Virginia on its east coast.

So far as Spain was concerned, the solution adopted at the Madrid summit was undesirable and incomplete. The US command was to extend eastwards as far as a line based on the river Guadiana at Huelva, which sits near the border with Portugal. East of the river, the space would come under European authority, shared between the commands of Portugal and Spain. Furthermore, IBERLANT was replaced, with the Canaries being designated as part of Command JSW (Joint South West), surrounded by a 'bubble' of 100 kilometres; this would not extend into Africa and would be a Spanish command. The practicality of three, if not four, countries having command over the former IBERLANT zone is dubious. With diverse command lines stretching from Virginia, Mons, Naples, Lisbon and Madrid, there is little potential for credible and serious command.

The issue of Ceuta and Melilla also did not progress particularly well for Spain. Even with Spain becoming a full member of NATO, the two enclaves did not enjoy protection under Article V of the Atlantic treaty, since they were not recognized as part of Europe. Therefore, Spain could not aspire realistically to the inclusion of these territories in NATO's areas of responsibility. Melilla, situated close to the border between Morocco and Algeria, could be seen as particularly vulnerable to regional instability. For this reason, NATO's lack of willingness to extend into the region is understandable, yet does not help to resolve the perceived security threat facing Spain in this region.

European Security Institutions and Spanish Defence Policy

The Eurocorps

Perhaps the most revealing of Spain's attitudes towards reform of its membership of NATO lies in its whole-hearted support for European-led solutions to the problems of European security. This position was emphasized virtually from the moment that Spain's membership of the EC was secured, in response to developments in the WEU from 1984. The reactivation of the latter stimulated fresh thoughts about Europe's defence provision. While the WEU was not promoted as an alternative to NATO, France's enthusiasm for it meant that there remained doubts as to the long-term aspirations of certain member states.[14] What was significant about the move was that it illustrated that the cold war constraints upon a European defence identity were starting to loosen. Just as Spain was on the verge of entering the EC and addressing membership of NATO through a referendum, possible alternatives to an Atlantic-dominated security system were being promoted.

Perhaps the most ambitious sphere of European defence that Spain has become involved in is the Eurocorps (*Eurocuerpo*). Arising from a longstanding French–German initiative to bring about greater understanding between the two nation's armed forces, in 1987 a mixed brigade was formed. By the end of 1992, a tumultuous year for Europe, agreement was reached on the formation of a division (approximately 10,000 troops) with the stated aim of attaining the proportions of a corps

(50,000 troops or more) by 1995. At this time, Spain agreed to participate by contributing a mechanized infantry brigade. In January 1998 Spain increased its contribution by offering the Brunete Armoured Division, the best equipped in the Spanish Army. By then, the Eurocorps had reached a level approaching 80,000 deployable troops. By the end of the decade, the brigade had grown into a corps many times its original size, with contributions from France, Germany, Belgium, Luxembourg and Spain.

This potential major enhancement of Europe's own military capacity was marred by a failure to fully institutionalize the new structures. The Eurocorps was marked by two key weaknesses. First, it was not adequately managed within any of the European institutions (being available to the EU but not institutionally managed by it). Second, the fact remained that countries like the UK, a major player in European defence, were at best lukewarm towards the idea of a European military capability outside of NATO's structures. The French eagerness to expand such a force remained a negative feature in the eyes of Europe's more Atlantic-leaning nations.

One possible solution to this impasse lay in the integration of the Eurocorps into the EU's 'pillar' structure. The main benefits of this would be that the European Union would at last add a military dimension to its foreign policy as developed under Article J4.1 of the Treaty on European Union. The fundamental basis of EU military action, namely having the assets to sustain a military deployment, would thus be available regardless of NATO or WEU etiquette.

Two obstacles hindered this approach. One was that the EU remained hopelessly divided over the military dimension to the CFSP. Countries like the UK and Italy fought a sustained campaign against institutionalizing a military force to enact CFSP deployments, in the face of French activism. In addition to the Atlanticist wing of the EU, there also existed neutralists like Eire that rejected membership of both NATO and the WEU. This sector was reinforced by the accession of the neutrals, Finland, Sweden and Austria, to the EU in 1995.

In the light of this three-way split over the military capacity of the EU, it is not surprising that progress in the field of a common defence capability for the European Union has been hesitant. Of interest here is Spain's own position within the debate. Of course, Spain's reluctance to embrace Atlanticism dates back much further than does the issue of European Community/Union membership. The whole debate over NATO membership was tinged with hostility towards the US military presence in Spain. Therefore Spanish enthusiasm for a European-led defence initiative was a convenient alternative to the politically-divisive question of NATO. This long-term feature of latent anti-US feeling in Spanish foreign policy goes some way to explaining Spain's enthusiasm for the idea of European defence. It also helps to explain the speed with which Spain joined the WEU in 1988.

However, the emergence of the Eurocorps resulted from more than simple concern at US hegemony in European security. The fact that Germany and France instigated the current arrangement within the concept of European integration illustrates that the corps should be seen, not only as a reaction to US/NATO hegemony, but also as a component of Europe's deepening ties. For Spain as a late entrant to the NATO alliance (1982) and even then long outside the integrated military command, European accession and military integration can be understood independently of them being an attractive alternative to the Atlantic Alliance.

The challenge for the Eurocorps and Spain in particular was just how the new security jigsaw would function. The Eurocorps sat outside the European Union's structures and also—perhaps more contentiously—those of NATO. This situation was further complicated by the renaissance of the Western European Union, which itself was not immune from controversy.

Spain faced the very real possibility that, with the end of the cold war, its carefully constructed policy towards European security and integration in general would prove inadequate, given the rapid change of events in central and eastern Europe. While its negotiated membership of NATO was generally acceptable within the context of the cold war, the end of Europe's division brought into being a new scenario that seemed likely to inspire the creation of different organizations and structures. The gradual policy of integration into NATO and the WEU was threatened now by the fact that such membership and the country's peculiarity within the confines of defence arrangements were leaving Spain somewhat marginalized. Attempts to remedy Spain's shortcomings within NATO, such as the co-ordination agreements of 1991 and 1992, were part of a wider initiative to put Spain's security demands on a higher level within its foreign policy. Other examples of this can be found in the involvement in the Spanish–Italian initiative of the Conference on Security and Co-operation in the Mediterranean (CSCM), which although unsuccessful illustrated a security gap as perceived by the EU's Mediterranean members.

Therefore Spain's enthusiasm for European-led defence initiatives goes further than a simple case of latent anti-Americanism. First, Spain could feel justified in expounding an argument that the NATO alliance would not extend to North Africa and thus Ceuta and Melilla. Second, viewed from the perspective of European integration, the concept of a common security and defence policy could be interpreted as a logical step. As Spain's enthusiastic position towards European integration is well known, this can in turn explain why Spain is such an eager proponent of common defence. Another example is provided by Spain's enthusiasm for the WEU.

Spain and the Western European Union

Spain joined the WEU at the end of 1988 when, amidst the ramifications of the 1986 NATO referendum, the relationship with the United States was finally being formalized on a more equal basis. WEU membership was seen as a boost to the European security cause as only the year before the Franco-German brigade had been formed and, according to the EC's Single European Act, the Community was now committed to the process of European Political Co-operation. Of note here was French enthusiasm for the accession of Spain and Portugal. Not only did this signify that the WEU was undergoing expansion, but Spain's much publicized divisions over the NATO question gave some credence to the idea that the WEU might supplant NATO in one way or another.

However, despite the initial success of the reborn WEU, it lacked the clear command structure that NATO possessed and was also devoid of a planning cell. Moreover, following the events of 1989 members such as the UK were unhappy at its competition with the Alliance's standing, while other countries including Denmark and Greece were not even members of the WEU.

Therefore the challenge for the WEU was not only to survive the end of the cold war, but also to maintain a sense of inclusion for countries in the EU, regardless of whether they were NATO members or not. For Spain, in turn, the challenge was also to enable the WEU to make up for the shortcomings of NATO policy. As Ceuta and Melilla were 'out of area' for the Alliance, Madrid looked briefly to the WEU to aspire to a role in this area. However, as the institution lacked a command structure, essential for it to play a role in time of conflict, the conclusion had to be drawn that, as in the case of the Eurocorps, for the time being NATO would remain hegemonic.

In spite of US hegemony, the fact remained that the WEU was a forum that would serve Spanish interests. In 1995 the creation of two bodies within the WEU, Eurofor and Euromarfor, pointed to the adoption of a Mediterranean agenda therein. Consisting of Portugal, Spain, France and Italy, both bodies now provide a military capability at the disposal of the WEU. Given the membership, a southern European dimension is inescapable. With the command based in Italy, resting on a series of high level approvals, the WEU thus developed a credible force available to the EU for operations in the Mediterranean basin. Spain's own presence in Eurofor and Euromarfor now complements its own security provision (in military terms) in the Mediterranean.

Spanish Defence Policy Summarized

Spain's defence policy has been dominated by the changes in the European security architecture since the end of the cold war. While Spain has sought to maintain NATO and has gone as far as to agree to the new command structure, the fact also remains that Madrid has pursued a strategy of participating in all efforts seeking collective security. Spain can look with some satisfaction upon its role in the WEU and Eurocorps. At the end of 1999, its adherence to the expansion of the corps was rewarded when General Juan Ortuño Such was appointed commander of its four divisions. With Javier Solana meanwhile appointed as EU High Representative, this can be seen as a successful period for Spanish diplomacy.

One area of concern is that Spain's enthusiasm for the EU to adopt a more assertive defence structure seems somewhat marginal to the concerns of larger countries such as the UK and France, although British policy evolved in the late 1990s under the Blair government. Much of Spain's early enthusiasm waned as the difficulties over the IBERLANT and GIBMED commands became evident at the Madrid summit in 1997. In turn, the effort required to maintain a reasonably high level of readiness was in contrast to the consistent downward trend in the defence budget. Although this was redressed in real terms as the century drew to a close, it remains to be seen whether defence expenditure as a proportion of GDP will return to former levels.

The peace dividend created a major opportunity for reductions in the size of armed forces across Europe, and in Spain the figure fell from 300,000 in 1990 to 160,000 by the turn of century, as a fully professional model was phased in. However, in view of additional responsibilities and the demands made upon a major western Mediterranean power, Spain needed to develop a capability consistent with its eagerness to play a more active role. Yet successive government defence ministers have appeared unable to 'protect' their budgets in the face of competing demands from other ministries.[15] In particular the Industry Ministry has enjoyed much of the control over expenditure on the EFA 2000 project. The fruits of other governmental efforts, such as the Cohesion Fund and membership of the European single currency, have not brought advantages to Spain's defence capabilities.

Conclusions

Spain has been left with a military model that still looks away from the Atlantic Alliance as NATO does not meet Spain's most pressing needs. It should be noted here, however, that traditionally NATO's other

Mediterranean members (Italy, Greece and Turkey) have also been marginal to the Alliance's security policy.

The challenge to Spanish defence policy at the turn of the century is to ensure that the gaps within its security provision left by the shortcomings of NATO and the relationship with the US are filled, namely in response to threats to the territories mentioned earlier. From a defence viewpoint, Spain is still very reliant on the US and NATO to maintain its security with regard to the Maghreb, given the enormous barriers to peace in the region. This dependence is likely to be deepened given the pattern of defence expenditure and structural features.

Ceuta and Melilla still remain outside of NATO structures, in the sense that Spain is expected to provide for its own defence in these places. While NATO commitment has always been somewhat ambiguous in the Mediterranean, the lack of Alliance protection for these enclaves can only be considered a shortcoming. The best that has emerged from lobbying by Mediterranean NATO member states has been the creation of the dialogue group in which ministers from NATO countries meet and discuss issues of concern with counterparts from Egypt, Israel, Jordan, Morocco, Tunisia and Mauritania. To quote from the *NATO Review*, this initiative:

> is not a reaction to any particular event or threat but rather is part of NATO's overall cooperative approach to security. It is a component of the broad framework of regional cooperation, complementing other international efforts such as those of the European Union (EU), Western European Union (WEU), Organisation for Cooperation and Security in Europe (OSCE), as well as the Middle East peace process … the objective of its Mediterranean Dialogue is primarily political: to increase understanding of NATO's policies and activities and get a better appreciation of the security needs of the countries involved [Bin, 1998: 4].

This gesture on the part of NATO appears of limited benefit in relation to Spain's specific security concerns. Dialogue is recognized as a key confidence-building measure, but as a mechanism for security it cannot be considered concrete in the light of Spain's experience of North African diplomacy. The exclusion of Algeria and Libya during the 1990s suggests that countries in conflict and 'pariah' states are not to be accommodated. The extent to which Spain can further a North African security agenda in NATO as yet remains unclear.

The Madrid summit resulted in only a partial foreign policy success with regard to the NATO mandates of IBERLANT and GIBMED. The abolition of the GIBMED command was somewhat offset by the transfer of the control and command facilities to AFSOUTH in Naples. The UK was able to maintain its military presence on the Rock and the actual Straits of Gibraltar came nominally under the US-led command. The fact that the CinCSouth (Commander-in-Chief South) is now a US-led position cannot be considered a victory for Spanish interests, especially in the light of France's intransigence at the Madrid summit.

The dispute over the Canary Islands' status within NATO cannot be seen as a clear-cut victory either. Not only the islands but also the approaches to the Straits of Gibraltar were originally beyond Spanish control while Spain remained outside the integrated military command. Nominally a Portuguese responsibility (as the nearest NATO member state), the transfer of control of the region to Norfolk, Virginia while leaving the Canary bubble is not a policy success for Spain. It may have resolved the immediate status of the Canary Islands, but represents a failure on the part of Spain to assume control over the Atlantic approaches to the Straits of Gibraltar. The concession on the Canary Islands was of political relief to the Aznar government, which had been under pressure from the Coalición Canarias in the Cortes. However, as a statement of confidence in Spain's ability to manage security in the region, it did not indicate much faith.

Overall, the negotiations surrounding these issues provide evidence that Spain's status within NATO is still not that of an equal in relation to several of the countries that were members of the Alliance from the start. There seems little reason to suspect that this situation will change in the near future.

NOTES

1. Reproduced in 'Objetivos de la política de defensa', *Revista Española de Defensa*, Feb. 1997, p.35.
2. Figures show a steady rise in the 1980s. In 1982, defence expenditure stood at Pta. 409,283 million; by 1989 it had reached Pta. 817,912 million (*Revista Española de Defensa*, March 1990, p.6).
3. Greek–Turkish hostility had been one traditional threat to NATO unity. France had actually withdrawn support from the IMC in 1966, thereby necessitating a move to Brussels for NATO's command. Moreover, in the 1980s certain members were hostile to the stationing of medium-range nuclear weapons in Europe and would not allow their deployment within their territory.
4. King Hassan's peaceful invasion (the Green March) during Franco's last days instigated a Spanish withdrawal following years of tension and exchanges of rhetoric between Spain and Morocco. The Spanish withdrawal was unconditional and opened a running question as to the territory's status that still existed a quarter of a century later.
5. Algeria supported broadcasts by the Canaries independence movement during the 1970s.
6. In spite of the fact that Portugal also had an authoritarian dictatorship, it managed to achieve more integration than Spain into the institutions of western Europe. At the time of Franco's death, Portugal was a member of NATO and had extensive arrangements with the US regarding military bases on both the mainland and in the Azores.
7. It is unlikely that the PSOE would have given high priority to full accession to the Alliance

if it had been re-elected in 1996. However, the party had lost a considerable amount of its old animosity towards the organization by the 1990s, to the extent that Javier Solana, a Socialist foreign minister, could be appointed Secretary-General of NATO.

8. Policy on nuclear weapons and Spain's non-participation in NATO's Nuclear Planning Group became a source of some embarrassment to the Defence Ministry in March 1997.

9. The CSCE was renamed the Organization for Security and Co-operation in Europe (OSCE) in 1994.

10. The Amsterdam summit was designed to consolidate the Maastricht Treaty of 1992. Attempts under the Finnish presidency of the EU (July–December 1999) to consolidate a common structure in defence and security affairs also proved unsuccessful.

11. The Coalición Canarias occupied four seats as a result of the 1996 election. It is a centre-right party which vigorously promotes the interests of the islands. Following the 1996 election, it wielded certain influence in the early months of the new PP government as the latter lacked an overall majority in the lower house.

12. The Treaty of Utrecht (1713) ceded Gibraltar to England. This has been a cornerstone of Gibraltar's insistence that it shall not be subject to Spanish sovereignty. Spain does not recognize the Rock's right to self-government as it is essentially a British colony. As in the case of Hong Kong's former colonial status, there exists little legal ground for autonomy. Gibraltar is either subject to British or Spanish rule.

13. The *Príncipe de Asturias* aircraft carrier, along with a substantial part of the fleet, is supposed to provide naval support in this region. This ship, the Spanish navy's most visible example of naval power, may be regarded as a very expensive tool to serve Spain's IBERLANT ambitions.

14. France had withdrawn from NATO's integrated military command in 1966 and had consistently argued for alternatives to the Atlanticist position. Even at the Madrid summit of 1997, France rejected re-entry to the IMC following the US refusal to consider allowing a European to take command of AFSOUTH (and thus control the US Sixth Fleet).

15. Efforts to offset the effects of defence cuts included the purchase of second-hand F15 fighter aircraft from Oman in 1995 and the receipt of ageing US tanks under the CFE treaty in 1991.

REFERENCES

Bin, A. (1998): 'Strengthening Cooperation in the Mediterranean: NATO's Cooperation', *NATO Review* 4, pp.24–7.

Cortada, J. (ed.) (1980): *Spain in the Twentieth Century World*, London: Aldwych Press.

Maxwell, K. (1995): *The Making of Portuguese Democracy*, Cambridge: Cambridge University Press.

Molero, J. (1990): 'Economic Aspects of the US Military Presence in Spain', in J. Sharp (ed.), *Europe after an American Withdrawal*, Oxford: Oxford University Press.

Development Co-operation and Humanitarian Action in Spanish Foreign Policy

MARIANO AGUIRRE and FRANCISCO REY

The role of development co-operation and humanitarian action in national foreign policy has undergone important changes in the last decade. In the case of Spain, an active policy of co-operation has permitted the widening and strengthening of the country's links with European colleagues and, in a different manner, with Latin American countries and the Mediterranean region. Contributions to this growth have come both from the transformation of public administration in Spain and an increasing awareness and participation on the part of society through NGOs. In a decentralized state such as Spain, the autonomous regions and many local authorities have found in development co-operation a vehicle that gives them a presence abroad. At the same time, the participation of Spain's armed forces in numerous peace missions has contributed to the legitimation of their role and improvements in their social image, as well as giving Spain a greater presence in international fora.

Over the last 50 years, development co-operation has constituted an important aspect of the foreign policy of some countries with global influence. The Marshall Plan for the reconstruction of part of Europe and the plan for the reconstruction of Japan after the Second World War coincided with the process of decolonization in Africa and Asia. In these cases development co-operation constituted a form of influence both for the nations that had triumphed in the war and for the ex-colonial powers. Although over these last 50 years this co-operation has evolved and incorporated new dimensions (human and sustainable development, gender, etc.), it has, to a greater or lesser extent, retained its character as a foreign policy instrument. Humanitarian action in the face of natural disasters or complex political and humanitarian crises became, in the 1990s, another important instrument in international relations and in the foreign policy of some EU members and of the Union itself.

The authors wish to express their thanks to Mabel González-Bustelo for her assistance in research for this contribution. Translated by Stephen MacKey.

Development Co-operation and Humanitarian Action in a New International Scenario

By definition, development co-operation – whether it be official or private, bilateral or multilateral – includes direct and indirect aid and credit on advantageous terms for the beneficiary, and excludes commercial transactions in which the donor makes no special concessions [Evans, 1998: 12]. During the cold war, co-operation was used as a strategic tool by some global powers, especially the USA, France, Britain and the former Soviet Union. With the aim of containing the USSR in order to check its potential expansion and, at the same time, to maintain or increase their influence in regions of what was then called the Third World, western countries used co-operation as an instrument in an attempt to impose political, social and economic models and combat revolutionary phenomena in general. Thus, development co-operation was previously used more to support the interests of donor states than to co-operate in the development and welfare of the beneficiaries. In turn, emergency aid during this period was strongly conditioned by the clash of interests of the cold war, and in fact counted for only a small percentage of the official development aid provided by donor countries.

Two phenomena that appeared in the 1970s influenced the evolution of official development co-operation. The first was the debt crisis, which was in fact the expression of the crisis of a model of development based on investment and international aid combined explicitly or implicitly within the dependent integration of the peripheral countries. The second was the progressive increase in the involvement of non-state bodies, particularly non-governmental organizations (NGOs), in development co-operation. This introduced a new set of tensions. On the one hand, there was a conception of co-operation as an instrument of 'realist' state interests and, on the other hand, the expression of moral concern, of a degree of commitment and solidarity by society. NGOs also began to extend their involvement in the humanitarian field, questioning the interests of states and the traditional neutrality of the classic humanitarian organizations. The near-monopoly of the International Committee of the Red Cross (ICRC) which had prevailed for many years was broken in the 1970s with the emergence of new NGOs with broader perspectives.

Various factors have played a part in the construction of an extensive and relatively loosely-structured non-governmental movement concerned about and committed to poor or endangered populations in the periphery. The end of the cold war, the crisis and collapse of numerous revolutionary movements in the periphery and depoliticization are among these factors. A similar phenomenon has occurred in peripheral countries themselves, with the NGO replacing the party and the political movement, in Central America, for example [Pearce, 1999: 51–68].

As an instrument of foreign policy and an expression of a growing moral concern, co-operation became the victim of unrealistic expectations. After several decades of co-operation, both central states and central and peripheral NGOs have serious doubts about the effectiveness of their work, at least in the way it has been carried out up to now. In the central states, this has manifested itself in so-called 'aid fatigue', or 'donor fatigue', and in the clear drop in aid figures [Alonso, 1999]. The argument goes that, in the last 20 years, adverse public opinion with regard to international aid has grown in the central states because aid has succeeded neither in reducing poverty in the Third World nor in protecting the interests of donors.

Also contributing to this adverse climate for aid has been the change in priorities in economic paradigms, especially from the promotion of the state as the central axis of development to the burgeoning of the global free market as the sole frame of reference. Thus, the development crisis was followed by the aid crisis. The end result was a drying-up of funds. Meanwhile, in the weak and fragile states of the international system there was a growth in social break-up, political crises and armed conflicts, and in some cases this led to complex humanitarian emergencies. In the face of this situation, the strong nations hovered between co-operation, caution and military intervention [Aguirre, 1996: 200–12].

In the course of the 1990s a series of crises caused the USA, EU countries, Japan and Australia to respond with diplomatic initiatives, emergency aid and in some cases military deployment. From Somalia to East Timor, situations were produced in which various states felt obliged to intervene even though their interests were not directly affected. Such interventions were also marked by tensions between the particular interests of a state and the general interests of the international community [Roberts, 1999]. The role of the UN Security Council was often ignored, as in Kosovo, while the interests of NATO or of particular states prevailed. The limitations of immediate responses, both those from the state and those from multilateral organizations or NGOs, have led some sectors to consider the need to check crises with preventive policies, which it is suggested might be structural in nature and linked to development co-operation.

However, the policies of the principal donors and international aid organizations have not considered the roots of poverty and its effects, nor of armed conflicts and their origins. On the contrary, for many decades they have placed more emphasis on plans for structural cost-cutting, the opening up of and accessibility to markets, and privatization, than on the economic impact of these policies on societies. This decrease in interest, manifest in a reduction of aid and, especially, in the abandonment of certain areas such as sub-Saharan Africa, has been accompanied by an increase in the work of private agencies and non-governmental organizations. These have been faced with the difficult task of finding effective forms of co-operation within a global framework of economic liberalization and high levels of competition which generally run counter to their projects. At the same time, in the best cases, where co-operation projects are maintained and developed, the peripheral countries have neither the time nor the capacity to find a place in the market other than by offering their natural and human resources at a low price.

This gulf between moral intentions and practical reality has led to different approaches from NGOs. While some adapt to working according to the status quo, others consider co-operation to be a practice from which to question the functioning of the international economic system and the concept of development [Sogge, 1996; Slim, 1996; Escobar, 1999]. The demonstrations in Seattle during the World Trade Organization (WTO) meeting at the end of 1999 were to some extent an expression of this questioning attitude. On the official side, the decrease in official co-operation is related to a higher level of reflection and review with regard to priorities, both on the part of some states – for example, in the White Paper issued by the British government's Department for International Development, in the Swedish Foreign Ministry's action plan on the prevention of conflicts or in the studies commissioned by the Dutch Foreign Ministry – and on the part of bodies such as the World Bank, the International Monetary Fund and the Development Aid Committee of the OECD [Rey Marcos and González-Bustelo, 1999].

It can be said, then, that in the last 50 years development co-operation has been primarily an instrument of the state. From an academic perspective and in terms of political practice, it can be considered as a part of international co-operation between states, multilateral organizations and non-state bodies. Despite the aforementioned limitations, it has been established that, without neglecting their individual national interests, in some circumstances states can co-operate with each other and with third parties in order to obtain particular and mutual benefits. It is also acknowledged that both international institutions and NGOs may constitute important elements in a plan based not only on the transfer of resources from donor to beneficiary, but that also considers other variables, including structural changes in the roots of poverty and the problems faced by the beneficiary [Martin, 1999: 51–63].

The Spanish Case

The Historical Evolution of Spanish Co-operation

In Spain, both official and non-governmental development co-operation are relatively recent phenomena, in comparison to other European countries such as Britain or France. Officially, Spain had no policy of co-operation during the Franco dictatorship, despite its paternalistic rhetoric with regard to Latin America and the Arab world and the emphasis on *hispanidad* as a unifying concept. No former Spanish colony – from Latin America to the Philippines or from Equatorial Guinea to Morocco – received special attention from Spain. On the contrary, the Franco regime established relations with the more conservative sectors in such societies. In some cases, these essentially commercial and corrupt relationships remain to this day, as in the case of Equatorial Guinea.

Moreover, Spain was a recipient of official development aid until the end of the 1970s. Furthermore, in multilateral organizations such as the World Bank it was not admitted into the group of countries that introduced international co-operation policies, and it was not made a member of the Development Aid Committee (DAC) of the OECD until 1991. Until 1979 the World Bank considered Spain to be a country that deserved international aid. But from 1975 political change brought improved external relations and a growing role for development co-operation. Co-operation policies have formed part of the relationship between Spain and the international system. From the point of view of the theory of interdependence [Nye, 1997: 161–70], development co-operation activity has permitted Spain to forge political, economic and social links with peripheral countries and with other European Union members.

A brief chronology of how Spain has incorporated co-operation into its foreign policy and adapted its administrative structure to the new challenges would read as follows [Alonso, 1992: 69-82]:

1976: Creation of the FAD (Development Aid Fund) credits, an instrument combining development aid and the promotion of commercial interests, and the setting up of an inter-ministerial commission to administer them.

1983: Creation of the Foreign Emergency Aid Group in the Ministry of Foreign Affairs.

1985: Creation of the State Secretariat for International and Ibero-American Co-operation (SECIPI), within the Foreign Ministry. First Co-operation Plan.

1986: Entry into European Community. Creation of the Inter-ministerial Co-operation Commission as a co-ordinating instrument.

1988: Creation of the Spanish International Co-operation Agency (AECI), with powers to implement programmes and projects.

1991: Spain becomes a member of the Development Aid Committee (DAC) of the OECD.

1992: Parliament recommends a schedule for increasing development aid to 0.35 per cent of GDP by 1995 and 0.7 per cent by 2000.

1994: The DAC carries out its first review of Spanish co-operation, pointing to advances but also a number of shortcomings.

1998: Passing of the International Development Co-operation Law. Publication of the second DAC review, noting substantial improvements in relation to the first review.

The passing of the International Development Co-operation Law marked the end of a long process of public and political debate and the consolidation of a model of co-operation based on a distribution of responsibilities between the ministries of the Economy and Foreign Affairs [Grasa, 1998: 66–9]. Basically, the Foreign Ministry deals with programmes, projects, technical co-operation, and so on, while Economy is responsible for FAD credits and financial co-operation. The criteria of the two ministries do not always coincide. The co-operation law, the first of its kind in the history of Spain, clearly represented a step forward, but its practical application presents problems, as demonstrated by the paralysis of the Strategic Plan owing to discrepancies between the ministries involved.

Quantitative Development

From a quantitative perspective, Spanish Official Development Aid (ODA) increased during the early 1990s, subsequently stabilized and then decreased in 1995 and 1996 (see Table 1).

As can be seen from the figures below, although Spain has not met the commitment made by its Parliament of reaching the 0.7 per cent target by the year 2000, it did succeed in maintaining stable figures for overall aid volumes at a time when those of the other DAC countries, taken as a whole, were in decline.

A more detailed analysis of the components of Spain's bilateral co-operation shows a roughly equal split between the financial component, basically FAD credits, and co-operation based around aid programmes and projects.

FAD credits and debt relief programmes are administered by the Ministry of the Economy, whilst programmes and projects are the responsibility of the Foreign Ministry's AECI agency. This division of responsibilities has given rise to incoherence and problems of co-ordination. The table also shows one of the particularities of the incipient Spanish

TABLE 1
EVOLUTION OF SPANISH OFFICIAL DEVELOPMENT AID
(in millions of pesetas)

	1993	1994	1995	1996	1997	1998
Contributions to European Union	35.734,2	44.721,9	41.184,6	34.084,4	46.964,3	55.265,7
International Financial Organizations	7.433,0	7.403,5	17.049,8	2.684,0	15.030,0	16.924,7
Non-financial International Organizations	3.757,1	8.337,8	8.319,8	9.230,1	6.719,3	8.139,5
TOTAL MULTILATERAL	**46.924,3**	**60.463,2**	**66.554,2**	**45.998,5**	**68.713,6**	**80.329,9**
FAD credits	94.925,8	80.021,0	35.291,7	41.184,4	33.021,5	31.989,1
Non-returnable:						
Foreign debt rescheduling	405,6	8.971,5	7.331,0[a]	15.261,0	13.727,2	20.342,3
Aid Programmes/Projects	14.758,0	16.649,0	31.040,0	24.005,0	30.998,0	29.902,7
Food Aid	1.184,0	534,0	432,0	1.683,0	418,5	1.814,0
Emergency Aid	368,0	511,0	2.435,0	1.611,0	2.640,6	3.971,0
Aid and subsidies to NGOs	3.102,0	3.187,0	10.073,0	10.984,0	11.245,8	11.608,0[b]
Decentralized co-operation	4.185,5	5.316,0	14.667,2	19.379,6	20.763,2	28.143,1
TOTAL BILATERAL	**118.928,9**	**115.189,5**	**101.269,9**	**114.108,0**	**112.814,8**	**127.770,2**
TOTAL ODA	**165,853,2**	**175,652,7**	**167,824,1**	**160.106,5**	**181.528,3**	**208.100,1**
Percentage ODA/GNP	0.28	0.28	0.24	0.22	0.24	0.252
GNP (in 1,000s of millions of ptas.)	60.257,8	63.507,9	69.170,8	73.661,0	76.761,7	82.650,3[c]

Notes: a Correction of debt rescheduling figures for 1995.
      b Includes only subsidies to development NGOs from the state administration, basically those of the AECI. Subsidies from regional governments and local authorities are included in the Decentralized Official Co-operation section.
      c GDP figures taken as an approximation of GNP, figures for which will be available at end of 2000.

Source: Ministerio de Asuntos Exteriores 1999.

model, namely the significant proportion of overall aid accounted for by decentralized co-operation. It was this element that was influential in preventing overall ODA from falling significantly during the latter half of the 1990s.

Decentralized Co-operation

Although the Spanish Constitution of 1978 (Article 149.1.3) defines international relations as being the exclusive responsibility of the state, in practice the Autonomous Communities and other local authorities began to participate in co-operation programmes from the 1980s onwards. These

FIGURE 1
EVOLUTION OF SPANISH OFFICIAL DEVELOPMENT AID, 1993–98
(in thousands of millions of pesetas)

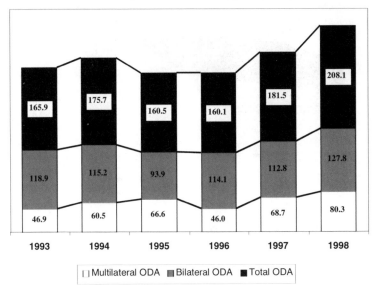

Source: Ministerio de Asuntos Exteriores 1999.

FIGURE 2
SPANISH AID COMPARED TO OTHER DAC COUNTRIES

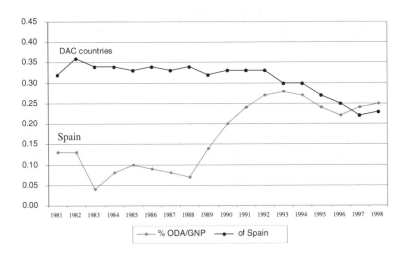

Source: Ministerio de Asuntos Exteriores 1999.

FIGURE 3
COMPONENTS OF BILATERAL ODA

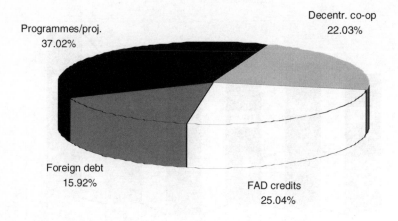

Programmes/proj.
37.02%

Decentr. co-op
22.03%

Foreign debt
15.92%

FAD credits
25.04%

Source: Ministerio de Asuntos Exteriores 1999.

tiers of government saw co-operation less as an element of the state's foreign policy and more as a demonstration of solidarity by citizens and their representative institutions. With some reluctance on the part of the state, this reality has eventually become recognized, and since 1991 the regional and local authorities have participated in the drawing-up of the Annual International Co-operation Plans.

The 1998 International Development Co-operation Law gave this participation of local authorities a stronger legal base. It also established the Inter-territorial Commission on Development Co-operation (although by the year 2000 this was still not fully operative). In 1998 decentralized co-operation constituted more than ten per cent of total Spanish ODA and 22 per cent of bilateral ODA. It was also significant in qualitative terms, since the aid budgets of the Autonomous Communities and local authorities were channelled mainly through NGOs and were thus more sensitive to citizens' demands. In terms of geographical distribution, decentralized aid followed the same pattern as co-operation carried out by the AECI. Some regions embarked on projects in direct collaboration with the European Commission, thus enabling them to enlarge the range of their activities. For example, the regional governments of Catalonia and the Basque Country have begun co-financing NGO projects with the European Commission's General Directorate for Development.

TABLE 2
DISTRIBUTION OF DECENTRALIZED OFFICIAL CO-OPERATION IN 1998

Autonomous Region	ODA (millions ptas.)	%
Andalucía	1,436.4	9.40
Aragón	315.8	2.07
Asturias	534.0	3.49
Baleares	558.2	3.65
Canarias	499.4	3.27
Cantabria	186.5	1.22
Castilla La Mancha	627.9	4.11
Castilla y León	448.9	2.94
Cataluña	1,555.1	10.17
Extremadura	308.6	2.02
Galicia	257.8	1.69
La Rioja	120.0	0.79
Madrid	1,072.6	7.02
Murcia	136.7	0.89
Navarra	1,681.9	11.00
País Vasco	4,254.5	27.83
Valencia	1,263.0	8.26
Various*	28.0	0.18
TOTAL AUTONOMOUS COMMUNITIES	15,285.1	100.00
LOCAL AUTHORITIES	12,858.0	
TOTAL DECENTRALIZED CO-OPERATION	28,143.1	

* Information from 'H' questionnaires from other public bodies.

Source: Ministerio de Asuntos Exteriores 1999.

The Geographical Distribution of Spanish Aid

For obvious historical reasons, Spanish bilateral aid is concentrated on Latin America and North Africa. The Annual International Co-operation Plan figures for 1998 are as follows:

TABLE 3
DESTINATION OF SPANISH BILATERAL AID

Latin America	37%
North Africa	11%
Sub-Saharan Africa	19.4%
Asia–Middle East	5.5%
Central Asia–Far East	6.6%
Central and Eastern Europe	2.5%
Others	The rest

Source: Ministerio de Asuntos Exteriores 1999.

Different instruments of aid (credit, programmes, food aid, etc.) are distributed in different ways in different geographical areas, but in general Latin America tends to predominate.

Civil Society and NGOs in Spanish Co-operation

Despite Spain's late arrival in the world of development co-operation, or perhaps because of it, Spanish society has made ground rapidly, and an indication of this is the vitality of the non-governmental sector. The overwhelming support in society for campaigns in 1994 and 1995 in favour of the target to raise ODA to 0.7 per cent of GDP and the incredible response to the Hurricane Mitch appeal, for which NGOs collected over 20,000 million pesetas (£100 million), and the Spanish Red Cross alone more than 13,000 million pesetas (£65 million), among other examples, demonstrate a capacity for mobilization and support that differs greatly from the situation in many other European countries. Spanish society continues to be more reactive than proactive on such issues, but is beginning to participate in a more stable way in non-governmental associative activities.

The Spanish NGO movement has developed from three sources. First, aid based on religious groups and linked to religious missions, which still retain some of their functions and prestige. Second, via political solidarity with national liberation movements. Third, and more recently, through modern, non-religious, non-political humanitarian co-operation. In some cases groups with religious or political origins have turned into organizations that fit the third model more closely; in others, the religious base has been retained, but with a more modern approach to marketing, recruitment, and the planning and development of activities. Moreover, the social prestige of non-governmental activity is on the increase, especially with regard to practical, non-political organizations such as Greenpeace, *Médicos sin Fronteras* and Amnesty International. The campaign in favour of the 0.7 per cent target encouraged debate on this issue at state level and resulted in an increase in the aid initiatives of Autonomous Communities and local authorities. More recently, and in line with the situation in other European countries, numerous NGOs have appeared that are in some way linked to political parties or trades unions and professional associations. At the same time, most of the large international NGOs and NGO networks have set up branches in Spain.

The majority of humanitarian and development aid NGOs fall under the jurisdiction of the State Co-ordinating Committee for Development Aid NGOs, which has counterparts in each of the regions. The committee is the Spanish representative on the European NGO Liaison Committee, based in Brussels. The Spanish committee, which comprised only ten NGOs in the late 1980s, now embraces over a hundred, a fact that reflects a great numerical increase within the sector. At the national level, the Council for Co-operation acts as a link between the various actors involved in development co-operation, including linkage between NGOs and the government – although it is widely recognized that this body's working mechanisms and characteristics need to be modified to make its involvement in Spanish co-operation more effective.

Since the mid-1980s, NGOs have had access to public subsidies for their projects. These subsidies increased up to 1998, when they amounted to more than 11,000 million pesetas (£55 million). Nevertheless, the model on which the relationship between NGOs and the government was based was considered unsatisfactory in the DAC report of 1998 [OECD, 1998: 36–7].

Despite all these advances, the concrete influence of the non-governmental movement on high-level political decisions was still subject to limitations. The campaigns for the 0.7 per cent target, for more generous debt relief and in relation to the Strategic Plan on Co-operation (stemming from the 1998 International Development Co-operation Law) fell short of achieving their objectives.

EU Influence on Spanish Co-operation

Since Spain's entry into the European Community in 1986, EC/EU policy on development co-operation has greatly influenced Spanish co-operation. First, in quantitative terms, since 1986 Spain has been the fifth highest contributor to the European Development Fund (EDF). In 1998 Spain's contributions to the EU's co-operation budget accounted for 26.8 per cent of total Spanish ODA and 68.8 per cent of multilateral aid. Secondly, from a more qualitative perspective, Spanish governments since the restoration of democracy have adapted both to domestic public demand and to the practices of the European Union. In the latter case, development and humanitarian action have provided Spain with a number of important diplomatic posts: Manuel Marín as a commissioner with important responsibilities for a large part of the EC aid budget; Santiago Gómez Reino and Alberto Navarro as directors of the European Community Humanitarian Office (ECHO); Carlos Westendorp as High Representative in Bosnia-Hercegovina; Miguel Angel Moratinos as the EU's Special Envoy to the Middle East peace process (this being a diplomatic post, but associated with development co-operation given the amount of aid provided by the EU to the Palestine National Authority); and senior PSOE member Javier Solana as a leading figure in EU development activities after his appointment as the first 'Mr CFSP'. Moreover, a number of other Spaniards have held important posts in the Balkans. All these cases helped raise Spain's profile in relation to development issues.

A special case in which Spain fulfilled a notable role, linking the interests of the state, the EU and NGOs, was in the creation of the Euro-Mediterranean Partnership. With the twin aim of stabilizing the region and establishing a free trade area, in its plan for the Mediterranean region the EU covered a series of issues – encompassing human rights, economic/commercial co-operation and security – to be dealt with both through multilateral agreements between states and co-operation with and between non-governmental agencies. Despite the Euro-Mediterranean Partnership's concentration far more on economic than on political and social aspects, the experience of having a multidimensional forum available, involving a wide range of protagonists, is significant. Nevertheless, a certain loss of initiative on the part of Spain was noticeable after the Euro-Mediterranean Conference in 1995 in Barcelona, and indeed a certain stagnation of the whole process.

Participation in EU fora by Spanish politicians, NGOs, civil servants and others has undoubtedly facilitated a process of learning and has brought Spanish co-operation into line with that of the other European countries. It has also helped Spain to influence EU policy toward Latin America, the Mediterranean region and other areas. Spain has played an important role in strengthening the EU's commitment to Central America, through its close involvement in the Guatemalan and Salvadoran peace processes. In the non-governmental sphere the influence of Spain's membership has also been fundamental. The participation of Spanish NGOs in the European NGO Liaison Committee and their access to finance through the European Commission budgets has been of great importance for the initial growth and subsequent stabilization of the Spanish non-governmental sector. However, the influence of Spanish NGOs on their European counterparts, in terms of encouraging more attention to be given to Latin America or North Africa, has been more limited.

Humanitarian Aid in Spanish Co-operation

If co-operation in general is, as we have seen, a quite recent phenomenon in Spain, humanitarian aid is an even later arrival. While for the DAC countries as a whole, humanitarian aid represents over five per cent of total ODA, and in some countries (such as Sweden or Austria) more than 15 per cent, in the Spanish case it accounts for only two per cent, despite having doubled in 1998. This limited share of the humanitarian component in Spanish co-operation can be explained by various factors: humanitarian aid is still seen as having a marginal role by the SECIPI and AECI; there is a lack of debate on the relationship between rehabilitation aid and development, the so-called 'continuum', in Spanish co-operation; and apart from the Red Cross and Cáritas, NGOs specializing in humanitarian work did not establish a presence in Spain until the 1980s. Nevertheless, this situation is evolving rapidly. The aborted Strategic Plan for Spanish Co-operation proposed great advances and more work in co-operation based on conflict prevention, humanitarian aid and post-conflict rehabilitation and reconstruction, within a coherent framework capable of securing stronger synergy between the various components of aid [Alonso, 1999].

The numbers of specifically humanitarian NGOs and development NGOs that also carry out humanitarian operations has increased rapidly. This owes a great deal to EU financing provided via ECHO, Spain being the third largest recipient of such subsidies. Today, Spanish humanitarian NGOs have as much experience as their European counterparts, and have considerably increased their capacity for obtaining private resources. Nevertheless, to date the participation of Spanish NGOs in debates on humanitarian issues in the European Union and in international forums has been poor. In discussions on the humanitarian aid Code of Conduct,[1] for example, or on the Sphere Project (an NGO network involved in working up proposals for co-operation and minimum standards in disaster response), Spanish NGOs and the Spanish humanitarian aid movement in general have been notable for their absence.

In this context, and despite the fact that the political and social debate on humanitarian aid within the context of Spanish co-operation has been under way for some years, there remains some conceptual confusion among the different protagonists involved. The PP government insisted on including spending on Spain's participation in peacekeeping operations as ODA, a practice expressly forbidden by the DAC. The Spanish Senate, in its Report on Spanish Policy on Development Co-operation, stated that 'at least some aspects of the UN peacekeeping missions, in which our armed forces are playing an important role in collaboration with civil personnel, will need to be considered as actions representing development co-operation, and therefore eligible to be regarded as ODA expenditure' [BOCG Senado, 1994: 86]. No specific steps have yet been taken to push forward this initiative. So far, there has been a rather muddled and opportunistic mixing of three spheres – the political, the military and the humanitarian – that should be kept apart.

From Humanitarianism to Military Intervention

Spain was given an important opportunity to become integrated into the mechanisms and institutions of the international community by the UN humanitarian missions following the cold war. Participation in peacekeeping missions allowed Spain both to find a vocation for its armed forces and to occupy a place in the community of nations. This will to participate manifested itself institutionally in the National Defence Directive of 1992, which established one aim as being to 'help to participate in United Nations initiatives for peace, disarmament and arms control, and in its peace and humanitarian aid missions' (Article 11). The International Development Co-operation Law referred to above also cites peacekeeping operations as one possible type of action of humanitarian aid (Article 12), which leads to some degree of confusion [Rey Marcos, 1998].

Since 1989, with its involvement in the independence of Namibia and in Angola, Spain has contributed forces to keep the peace in Central America (El Salvador and Guatemala) and other parts of the world. It has also carried out various military and police training missions in Central America, Angola and Mozambique, and sent naval forces in non-combat roles during the Gulf War and to the Adriatic during the Bosnian war to guarantee the arms embargo. In the Balkan wars of the 1990s the Spanish armed forces played a more active role, with a presence from November 1992 in Croatia and Bosnia as part of the UN protection force (UNPROFOR).

After the Dayton Accords, Spanish troops became part of the NATO force. In the same year Spanish and Italian military personnel worked together in Albania as a stabilizing force in the face of the imminent disintegration of the country. In 1999 the Spanish Air Force participated in the air strikes on Serbia and Serbian targets in Kosovo in order to force Belgrade to retreat from the province. The Spanish government adopted the official NATO line of the conflict in Kosovo being a 'humanitarian war', as put forward by US President Bill Clinton and British premier Tony Blair.

This discourse of humanitarian military intervention by NATO was accepted unquestioningly by the government of José María Aznar. The government's attitude provoked the first disputes between NGOs critical of armed humanitarianism and of the way NATO rode roughshod over the UN with regard to the Kosovo conflict. It is to be expected that in future humanitarian operations with a military component directed by NATO this type of confrontation will arise again.

Spanish participation in peace operations has made notable advances since it began ten years ago, in a process of internationalization of the armed forces that it is in the interests of the Ministry of Defence to support. Apart from the leading role in operations carried out in Central America, where Spanish personnel were in charge, another focus of participation has been in the conflicts in former Yugoslavia. The tasks taken on reflect the evolution of the concept of 'peacekeeping', since they include not only the demobilization and disarmament of ex-combatants and the supervision of cease-fires, but also the supervision of electoral processes, the assessment of security and public order, the distribution of humanitarian aid, and so on. For some military leaders, 'the future of the armed forces lies in

TABLE 4

SPANISH PARTICIPATION IN PEACE MISSIONS

Name of mission	Date	Spanish participation	Functions
UNAVEM-I (UN Angola Verification Mission)	1989–1991	21 military observers in relays	Verification of redeployment and retreat of Cuban troops
UNAVEM-II (Angola)	1991-1995	75 military observers in relays	Verification of ceasefire and supervision of police activity
UNTAG (UN Transition Assistance Group in Namibia)	1989–1990	250 Air Force troops; 6 C-212 Aviocar aircraft; 1 C-130 Hercules	Control and supervision of elections to ensure Namibian independence
ONUCA (UN Observers Group in Central America)	1989–1992	171 military observers in relays. Leadership of operation	Ensure halt to aid for irregular forces and insurrectional movements. Supervision of demobilisation of Nicaraguan resistance and ceasefire.
ONUSAL (UN Observers in El Salvador)	1991–1995	512 military observers in relays. Leadership of the mission.	Verification of ceasefire between FMLN and El Salvador Government
ONUVEH (Supervision Mission in Haiti)	1990	9 officers	Support Haitian Government in supervision of 1990 elections. Assessment of publ;ic order and security.
Gulf War	1991	2 corvettes and 1 frigate	Ensure Iraqi retreat from Kuwait by means of force
Operation Provide Comfort (Northern Iraq-Turkey	1991	Tactical Force with 586 ground troops. 7 helicopters, 80 vehicles, 31 trailers.	Protection of Kurdish refugees (transport, construction of camps, field hospitals, distribution of Spanish aid)
Mozambique)	1992–1995	50 military observers in relays	Guaranteeing peace accords between Government and RENAMO.
UNAMIR (UN Mission in Rwanda)	1992–1996	20 Air Force troops; 1 CN-235 aircraft	Dispatch of humanitarian aid and support for Spanish NGOs operating in the region.

TABLE 4 (cont.)

UNSCOM (UN Special Commission for Iraq)	From 1995, at intervals	5 missile experts	Control of Iraqi chemical weapons capacity
MINUGUA (UN Mission in Guatemala)	1992-date	43 military observers in 1997. Spanish leadership of the mission. Currently, 7 military advisers	Guarantee of human rights agreement between Government and URNG. Later, verification of ceasefire, demobilisation and disarmament.
UNPROFOR (UN Protection Force in Bosnia-Herzegovina)	1992-1995	19 Military observers; one tactical force of 1,200 troops; 20 officers at HQ.	Help and protect distribution of humanitarian aid. Setting-up and protection of security zones.
Operation Sharp Guard (NATO/WEU joint operation)	1992-1996	2 frigates, 1 supply ship, 1 sea patrol plane and 1 submarine.	Verification of naval embargo on ex-Yugoslavia
Operation Deny Flight	1992-1995	Air Force detachment; 6 F-18 fighters; 2 airborne refuelling planes and one intermediary plane.	Air support for UNPROFOR and IFOR
IFOR (NATO Implementation Force in Bosnia-Herzegovina)	1995-1996	1 brigade with 1,700 men; 1 frigate; 6 F-18 fighters and 3 transport planes	Continuation of UNPROFOR with aim of fulfilling military aspects of Dayton Accords
SFOR (NATO Stabilisation Force in Bosnia-Herzegovina)	1996-date	1 brigade with 1,300 men; 1 frigate; 6 F-18 fighters and 2 transport planes	Continuation of IFOR with aim of permitting fulfilment of civil aspects of Dayton Accords
ECMMY (ECSO Mission for ex- Yugoslavia)	1991-date	Maximum of 50 military and 3 diplomats. Currently 9 military and 1 diplomat	Help EU in search for lasting solution to conflict in ex- Yugoslavia.
ECTF (Special EU Force for humanitarian aid to ex-Yugoslavia)	1994-1995	3 officers at HQ in Zagreb. Spanish leadership of the mission.	Co-ordination of EU humanitarian aid in Slovenia, Croatia and Bosnia-Herzegovina
EUAM (European Union Administration in Mostar)	1994-1996	3 officers as military advisers to the EU administrator	Administration of city and demilitarisation
CIAY (Mission of the International Conference for ex- Yugoslavia for control of River Drina frontier)	1994-1995	Commanders and officers transferred from ECMMY	Verification of closure of Serbian and Montenegrin frontiers to Bosnia Serbs (except humanitarian aid)
Guarantee of Danube embargo	1993-1996	*Guardia Civil* contingent	Control of river traffic for embargo on certain goods

TABLE 4 (cont.)

			to ex-Yugoslavia
IPTF (UN Police Mission for Bosnia-Herzegovina)	1996-date	*Guardia Civil* contingent	Development of effective police structures and criminal justice procedures.
ESCO Group for Assistance to Chechnya	1995-1997	3 army officers	Promotion of respect for human rights (development of institutions). Support for distribution of humanitarian aid. Return of refugees and displaced persons.
ESCO Mission for Moldova	1996-1997	3 warrant officers	Facilitating negotiations for peaceful solution to conflict
ESCO Mission for Croatia	1995-1996	One officer	Guaranteeing protection of human rights. Promotion of reconciliation.
ESCO Mission for Georgia	1993-date	3 officers	Promotion of negotiations between parties
Operation Alba (Multinational Force for Albania)	1997	Tactical force with 325 men	Helping to establish secure environment. Ensuring rapid and secure provision of humanitarian aid.
KDOM (Kosovo Diplomatic Observation Mission)	1998	One officer	Mission dependant on ECMMY- verification and fact-finding
KVM (ESCO Kosovo Verification Mission)	1998-1999	12 military observers	Search for peaceful solution to Kosovo and Metohija situation
Operation Alpha-Charlie	1998-1999	1,000 troops. Amphibious vehicles. Medical teams. Transport planes	Humanitarian operation for reconstruction of countries affected by Hurricane Mitch
KFOR (Kosovo Multinational Security Force)	1999-date	One Light Infantry Battalion (1,200 troops); logistic support unit with transmissions; high medical level.	Prevention of resumption of hostilities; checking fulfilment of agreements; support for return of refugees and displaced persons. Provision of public security and basic civil administration

Source: Drawn up from Defence Ministry information.

humanitarian aid',[2] and the recent activity of the Defence Ministry appears to indicate agreement with this.

Conclusions

Development co-operation and humanitarian action policies have permitted Spain to increase and strengthen its links both horizontally, with its European colleagues, and vertically, with Latin America and the Mediterranean region. Co-operative and humanitarian activity is a factor that links large sectors of the Spanish population. At the same time, it is a common political factor in an increasingly depoliticized society. The majority of political groups tend to concur over the role that should be played in foreign policy by development co-operation and humanitarian aid. Neither Spain's society nor its governments have yet begun to experience the phenomenon of 'aid fatigue' found in other countries, though all the indications are that it will not be long before this happens.

After years of isolation and backwardness with respect to other European countries, Spain today has an institutional, judicial and administrative framework capable of supporting a more committed and active co-operation policy. Nevertheless, there remain serious problems with the co-ordination of responsibilities between different ministries, which affects some co-operation initiatives. The participation of regional and local authorities is one of the peculiarities of Spanish co-operation, and a demonstration of its vitality and of the social commitment that underpins it. The non-governmental movement has grown strongly both quantitatively and qualitatively, and is now comparable to those of other European countries; it can count on public support which, though unstable, is increasing.

Spain is situated geopolitically in the Mediterranean area, a zone harbouring diverse potential crises of varying intensity, from the Algerian situation to the question of immigration from Africa to Europe. At the same time, Spain is linked historically, culturally and economically to Latin America and the Caribbean. Understandably, then, Spain is particularly sensitive to development crises and potentially complex political crises, as well as natural disasters, in Latin America. The political priorities of Spanish co-operation are oriented in this direction, and there is a wide consensus in favour of such an orientation.

Spain has directed its foreign policy over the last 20 years basically towards Europe. The country's full entry into NATO implies a strong conditioning of its position in so far as the Atlantic Alliance has defined in its Strategic Concept (May 1999) a wide-ranging scope of activity that would cover everything from regional conflicts to international crime. The policies and responses Spain makes in the future, either independently or conditioned by its membership of the EU and NATO, with regard to the Mediterranean and Latin America will shape its foreign policy. The strategic question is whether this proximity to the two regions will lead Spain, in the process of constructing a foreign and European security policy, to consider individual contributions and particular perspectives, or whether it will become resigned to the leadership of the most powerful EU states and NATO's concept of extended security.

NOTES

1. A Code of Conduct relating to disaster aid for the International Red Cross and Red Crescent movements and NGOs. This has been signed by more than 150 NGOs throughout the world and also endorsed by some governments and international bodies as a point of reference for humanitarian action. It came into force in 1995.
2. Statement by Spanish Army Chief of Staff Alfonso Pardo de Santayana y Coloma in Pamplona, *El Diario de Navarra*, 15 Oct. 1999.

REFERENCES

Aguirre, M.A. (1996): 'Europe and the Challenges from the Southern Periphery', in *Brassey's Defence Yearbook 1996*, London: Brassey's.

Alonso, J.A. (1992): 'La cooperación al desarrollo en España: balance de una década', *Anuario Internacional CIDOB*, Barcelona: CIDOB, pp.69–82.

Alonso, J.A. (1999): *Estrategia para la Cooperación Española*, Madrid: Ministerio de Asuntos Exteriores.

BOCG Senado (1994): 'Informe de la ponencia de estudio de la política, española de cooperación para el desarrollo', V Legislatura, series I, no.201, 28 Nov., Madrid: Spanish Senate.

Escobar, A. (1999): 'The Invention of Development', in *Current History*, Nov., pp.382–6.

Evans, G.E. (1998): *Dictionary of International Relations,* London: Penguin.

Grasa, R. (1998): 'La ley de cooperación internacional para el desarrollo: ¿Una nueva etapa de la aportación española al desarrollo del Sur?', in *La realidad de la ayuda 1998–1999*, Barcelona: Intermón.

Martin, L.L. (1999): 'The Political Economy of International Co-operation', in P. Inge, I. Grunberg and M.S. Stern (eds.), *Global Public Goods. International Co-operation in the 21st Century*, Oxford: UNDP and Oxford University Press.

Ministerio de Asuntos Exteriores (1999): *SECIPI, Seguimiento PACI 1998*, Madrid: Oficina de Planificación y Evaluación.

Nye, Jr., J.S. (1997): *Understanding International Conflicts*, New York: Longman.

OECD (1998): *Spain, Development Co-operation Review Series*, Paris: OECD.

OECD (1998): *Conflict, Peace and Development Co-operation on the Threshold of the 21st Century*, Paris: OECD.

Pearce, J.P. (1999): 'Peace-building in the Periphery: Lessons from Central America', *Third World Quarterly* 20/1, pp.51–68.

Rey Marcos, F. (1998): 'Visiones de la acción humanitaria en 1997', in M. Aguirre (ed.), *Anuario CIP 1998*, Barcelona: Icaria.

Rey Marcos, F. and M. González-Bustelo (1999): 'Comité de la Ayuda al Desarrollo (CAD) de la OECD y los conflictos, la paz y la cooperación para el desarrollo', Madrid: Centro de Investigación para la Paz (unpublished).

Roberts, A. *et al.* (1999): *Desafíos de la acción humanitaria*, Icaria with MSF/Universidad de Deusto and CIP.

Slim, H. (1996): 'What is Development?', in M.B. Anderson (ed.), *Development and Social Diversity*, Oxford: Oxfam.

Sogge, D. (ed.) (1996): *Compassion and Calculation*; London: Pluto Press/TNI.

Conclusion

RICHARD YOUNGS

To many outside observers, the evolution of Spain's external relations during the 1980s and into the early 1990s was of prime interest in so far as it constituted one of the most notable case studies of a state seeking fundamentally to restructure its international identity around incrementally-accumulating norms of European co-operation. This reshaping was neither a finite process nor an end in itself. Rather, once Spain had successfully remoulded itself into a standard European-oriented state by the early 1990s, it became pertinent to analyse how this long-coveted framework would be employed and managed in order to advance perceived national interests. Spain might have become a fully European democracy, but the point was to assess the implications of this, the opportunities but also the responsibilities it would bring in its wake. The contributions to this volume explore the way in which the reshaped or redefined framework of Spain's external relations was harnessed as the 1990s progressed. The preceding chapters offer a range of perspectives on Spain's performance in this regard. In broad terms, a distinction can be made between largely positive assessments of Spain's role in internal EU developments, on the one hand, and chapters offering a more critical assessment of Spain's response to wider international challenges, on the other hand.

Mainstream EU Status and the Assertion of National Interests

The volume's contributions demonstrate that, following the period of adaptation in the late 1980s and early 1990s, Spain could be viewed as fully incorporated into the European arena as the principal debates of the 1990s were addressed. If 'normalization' was the much-used lietmotif of Spanish foreign policy objectives during the 1980s, the complexity and variety of debates within the EU now cast doubt on the term's ability fully to capture the nature of Spain's status once the broad redefinition of the country's external relations had apparently been secured. None the less, Spain had clearly obtained a basic kind of 'mainstream' status, in Esther Barbé's terminology, by the mid-1990s. This status did not preclude the possibility of divergence from European partners, but certainly denoted a situation where the nature and determinants of Spain's external policies were not qualitatively different from those of other EU states. To the extent that Spain joined the EC with a distinctive pattern of international relations and a self-declared priority of establishing itself as a co-operative team player rather than of maximizing specific short-term outcomes, such a difference was widely held to have prevailed prior to the early 1990s (even if there were contrasting opinions on just how significant that difference was). To an overwhelming degree, the contributions to this volume proceed from an acknowledgement that this was no longer the case by the mid-1990s, taking this understanding as the starting point for analyzing the nature of Spain's external policies over the latter part of the decade. Co-ordination with European partners over this period was assisted additionally by the fact that many of the big issues of principle had been determined by the mid-1990s and debates within EU fora consequently centred on detailed second-order issues of fine-tuning institutional structures and existing policy commitments. Important questions remained outstanding, however, and the very incremental accumulation of EU integrative dynamics represented by such fine-tuning ensured that Spain's domestic policies were increasingly inseparable from developments at the European level.

This absence of fundamental qualitative divergence was manifest in Spain's relatively smooth and seemingly successful incorporation into EMU. As Keith Salmon points out, both the prospect and then the early functioning of EMU drove ongoing structural reform and did, as many had predicted and/or hoped when the commitment to monetary union was made at Maastricht, ensure further convergence around European best practice in the fields of business regulation and economic governance. After slipping back during the recession of the early 1990s, Spain resumed progress in closing the gap between its level of wealth and the EU average. In addition, there was strong evidence for concluding that Spain's business cycle had become more strongly aligned with those of the bigger EU economies (even if ECB rates during EMU's first year could have offered greater assistance in quelling modest inflationary pressures in Spain). The convergence of the Spanish economy's basic structure around EU norms gathered pace over the 1990s, with the proportion of the workforce engaged in agriculture falling dramatically and those employed in services continuing to increase. While some continued to question the longer-term sustainability of EMU membership, its apparent success in shielding Spain from the ensuing global financial crisis seemed to imply that Spanish economic and monetary policy was appropriately and adequately adapted to its new Europeanized framework.

In many areas, 'mainstream' status reflected an increasingly intricate balancing of, on the one hand, short-term interests and, on the other hand, the more diffuse gains from co-operative approaches to alliance building within the EU. A slightly more cautious or 'realist' approach to integration emerged during the early 1990s, in particular as a result of the costs of seeking to meet the EMU convergence criteria in the midst of a deep recession. While the economy recovered and, contrary to the predictions of the mid-1990s, the convergence targets were met without widespread social and political instability, this realism persisted and in some areas deepened. In this sense, European policy under the PP should be interpreted as the incremental unfolding of a trend initiated under the PSOE government. An increasing robustness in defending national interests was witnessed in relation to a number of sectoral policies (especially agriculture and fishing), the government's resistance to widespread extensions of majority voting during the 1996–97 IGC and in the PP's preference for a minimal agenda for the IGC starting in 2000. However, it was, of course, in relation to enlargement that Spanish positions were under closest scrutiny.

Angel Viñas argues in this volume that it would be wrong to categorize Spain as having been difficult or unenthusiastic over the prospect of eastern enlargement. Rather, he suggests that Spain defended its interests - in particular, the retention of cohesion funds - in no different a manner to the way that other states dug in over those aspects of the Agenda 2000 reform package of particular importance to them. This remains a subject of debate. For some Madrid demonstrated an unreasonable degree of intransigence, while others have highlighted the compromise that was involved (the setting of an upper limit to future transfers from the EU to Spain). Some have suggested that the 'success' in deferring the cessation of cohesion receipts was bought at the price of weakening Spain's alliances within the EU [Sahagún, 2000]. Spain certainly resisted the degree of reform pressed upon it by other states. However, in so far as the long term untenability of Spain remaining a net beneficiary of the EU was increasingly acknowledged, Viñas hints that Spain, in the Agenda 2000 negotiations, did take a limited first step towards assuming the heavier responsibilities of a more leading role within the soon-to-be expanded EU.

In other areas, the pursuit of 'positive realism' manifest itself in less acutely combative fashion. In the foreign policy sphere, Esther Barbé highlights how this approach was expressed in Spain's increasingly firm adherence to intergovernmentalism within CFSP. Such gradualism brought Spain into line with the larger member states' instrumental perspective on CFSP, the latter being seen as an adjunct to, not a replacement of, national diplomacy. In relation to third pillar issues, it translated into a high-profile proactive strategy to deepen European co-operation on anti-terrorist work, culminating, with some success, in the agreement at the Tampere summit in October 1999 to create a Common Judicial Space. A similar agenda-setting role was exercised, in particular through an alliance between José María

Aznar and Tony Blair, in relation to exploring possibilities for EU co-operation on competitiveness and employment policies, which culminated in the Lisbon summit in March 2000. These examples demonstrated Spain's willingness strongly to assert perceived national interests, in both proactive and defensive fashion, and suggested that its mark on the European agenda was undoubtedly more visible at the end of the 1990s than it had been at the conclusion of the previous decade.

The European Imperative, Global Change and Domestic Constraints

Notwithstanding the more assertive or 'realist' pursuit of some perceived interests within European fora, the expanding competences of the EU simultaneously appeared incrementally to set tighter constraints on national policy options as the 1990s progressed. A major theme running through the various contributions to this volume is that, in key areas, the centrality of the European imperative deepened under the Aznar government. Absolute priority was attached to gaining entry into EMU and positioning Spain for reform to the structure of the integration project at a defining moment in the EU's development. It would be hard not to conclude from many of the preceding studies that, in this sense, the evolution of commitments at the European level established itself even more firmly as the most potent determinant of Spain's external policies. Several contributions point, either implicitly or explicitly, to a degree of self-generating 'spill-over' momentum driving Spanish European policies. Francisco Granell, for example, points out how participation in the euro began to firm up Spain's desire to secure more far-reaching progress on related aspects of economic union. In this sense, the increased resistance to co-operation witnessed in some sectors co-existed with, and, arguably, deflected attention away from, a persistent accumulation of the underlying trend of Europeanization underpinning Spain's foreign policies.

However, some authors' work quite clearly cautions against overstating the potency of specifically European factors in determining Spain's external orientations. Indeed, what emerges from a number of the contributions is that the construction of foreign policy choices took place within a more complex and shifting international environment, increasing the saliency of broader global developments. It became of key importance to understand the way in which broader structural shifts interacted with the dynamics of European co-operation. If European dynamics were strong, they could not be seen as having absolute explanatory primacy for all that was significant in the evolution of Spanish external choices. The initial orientation towards Europe had occurred within a stable and familiar external environment - bipolarity - and a domestic environment that gave the PSOE government considerable autonomy over European and other external policies. Both these factors changed during the 1990s. External choices not only became increasingly constrained by (if also benefiting from) European developments, but also had to juggle with significant and challenging developments at the global and domestic levels.

The importance of fundamental structural shifts was seen most clearly in the fields of defence and security. As Crispin Coates argues, Spain's growing commitment to the European Security and Defence Identity (ESDI) was, to the extent that the PP government saw it within the context of a broad approach to integration, partly a standard spill-over from integration in other sectors. Principally, however, he suggests it was a calculated and specific response to very concrete security needs in the changed post-cold war environment - brought about, that is, by the shift in the overall structure of the international system, the adaptation of security policy to a different geographical focus and the USA's more relaxed attitude towards some degree of autonomous European defence and security competences. These developments both facilitated and rendered more necessary Spain's full entry into NATO. As NATO took on new roles, central to the new post-cold war security concerns, Madrid – like Paris – began to feel increasingly isolated. Hence, in the defence and security arena, Spanish policies can clearly be seen to have resulted from broad structural changes simultaneously facilitated by an existing base of European co-operation and understanding. Global and European imperatives similarly reinforced each other in the field of monetary policy: the Asian financial crisis engendered more profound fears over globalization and further encouraged Spain, as other member states, to see a complete emasculation within European structures as the only feasible means of securing some protection from the increasing vicissitudes of the international financial system.

Such systemic shifts were paralleled by shifts in the nature of domestic debates over external relations. As Antonio Alaminos notes, European policy gradually became more intertwined with domestic party identification and was no longer seen as a topic entirely separate from national-level divisions. He points out that public opinion became more discerning, remaining broadly pro-European but increasingly keen that the Spanish governments battle hard for particular national interests. Domestic reactions were factored into policy-making in a way that was not the case prior to the 1990s. This conditioned the nature of party political debate, which became more divisive during the 1990s. Beyond a broad continuity and convergence of views between the PSOE and PP, the Socialists criticized the PP government in almost identical fashion to the nature in which they themselves had been berated by the *populares* prior to 1996. This reflected the structuring of debate, as elsewhere in the EU, around the division between incumbents and opposition rather than any apparent fundamental ideological cleavages.

Many of the criticisms put forward by the PP opposition before 1996 formed part of the PSOE's attack on the PP government after Aznar took office. In opposition the PSOE was critical of the PP for putting at risk key alliances for the sake of narrow sectoral concerns, but at the same time was ready to highlight concessions made in individual policy areas as a means of berating the government. The PSOE was, for instance, critical of the PP both for unduly holding up eastern enlargement and for not defending Spanish interests sufficiently robustly in the Agenda 2000 negotiations. The significance of all this was that, as Europe became an increasingly 'normal' party issue, the PP government could no longer appeal to Euro-idealism as a convenient scapegoat or as a means of deflecting domestic debate. As in other states, the government had to engage in traditional doubled-edged diplomacy, balancing the cultivation of international alliances with the protection of short-term national interests, under ever-closer scrutiny from a domestic political environment more critically engaged than hitherto. In Spain, this scrutiny would have been more intense if both the PSOE and IU, the latter momentarily having picked up support in the mid-1990s for its opposition to the EMU convergence criteria and NATO, had not both been immersed in internal difficulties.

Arguably, the more interesting elements of the domestic debate were unfolding beyond the debate between the two principal Spanish parties. There was a more fundamental division between the state-wide parties, on the one hand, and the regional parties, on the other hand, over the model of European integration. The former were united in seeing integration as a state-managed process increasing the capacity of the national state to fulfil policy commitments, while regional parties saw it as a more profound transformation transcending the role of the nation state. As some of the regions sought to establish greater protagonism in foreign affairs, the complexity of the policy-making process increased. The regions' activities in this area were a double-edged sword. They took on responsibilities for co-ordinating and managing an increasing proportion of the total aid budget, thus reinforcing central government's policies. On occasions, however, the risk of conflict became apparent – as, for example, when the Basque government invited the Kurdish government-in-exile to use its parliamentary facilities at the very moment when Madrid was seeking to strengthen relations with Ankara. Another significant trend was the increasing engagement and influence of NGOs, in particular over some aspects of development and immigration policy. Mariano Aguirre and Francisco Rey contend here that, from a relatively low base, by the end of the 1990s the Spanish NGO sector had become one of the most active in

Europe. As the analysis of Spain's Latin American policy here makes clear, governmental and NGO priorities did not always coincide. The influence of these trends in the nature of the policy-making process again demonstrated the way in which a number of PP policies were rooted in the pre-1996 period to a greater extent than they represented conjunctural shifts on the basis of distinctive ideological preferences.

Europeanization on the World Stage: Opportunities and Constraints

The preceding studies catalogue many instances where Spain became progressively more successful in Europeanizing its national concerns during the 1990s. A number of authors suggest that European co-operation was increasingly valued in these instrumental - rather than idealistic - terms. Aznar's protagonism in advancing co-operation within the EU's third pillar, which culminated in the Tampere agreement, was perhaps the most notable case of Spain seeking to harness the EU to further its specifically national goals - not only on counter-terrorism but also immigration and asylum policy. Spain's pressure for EU mechanisms to provide financial support for states hosting incoming refugees in effect sought northern European solidarity in assisting with North African migrants arriving in the Iberian peninsula. Again, perspectives differ on these actions: for some, Spain made skilful use of its negotiating power and diplomacy to ensure progress on these issues, based on a genuine argument that such concerns generated within a national context should be seen as 'European' problems; for others, they highlighted the continuing weakness of Spanish influence (the proposed funds being reduced by Germany).

As Felipe Sahagún highlights, Europeanization was especially influential in the context of relations with the US. Spain, with its sometimes difficult bilateral relationship with Washington, extracted considerable 'free-rider' benefit from the EU's New Transatlantic Agenda. Moreover, Madrid was the principal beneficiary of the EU's steadfast opposition to the US Congress's Helms-Burton legislation. As, by some margin, Europe's leading investor in Cuba, the Helms-Burton legislation was of particular concern to Spain. The EU's success in at least temporarily ensuring that sanctions would not be applied to European investors in Cuba constituted one of the clearest examples of the Fifteen's combined international weight producing a concrete result of considerable and disproportionate benefit to Spain which could not have been obtained through bilateral channels. Crispin Coates outlines how Spain enjoyed some success in ensuring that the incipient ESDI was atuned to Spanish concerns, in compensation for the fact that NATO's revamped remit continued to exclude issues of primary importance to Madrid. Spain's strong interest in the sustainable containment of Algeria and Libya meant it was particularly disappointed with these two countries' exclusion from NATO's new Mediterranean Dialogue. In this context, the creation of Eurofor and Euromarfor in 1995 under the WEU umbrella, was seen as a notable development.

Conversely, Jesús Núñez's account of the evolution of Spain's policies in the Mediterranean suggests some of the potential dangers of such Europeanization. It is widely acknowledged that the greater priority accorded by the EU to the Mediterranean in the early 1990s owed much to Spanish protagonism. Núñez describes how, after the 1995 Barcelona Conference, Spain failed to maintain such a prominent role in the region and argues that, to some degree, Madrid's very success in securing a European framework addressing an area of particular national concern encouraged a perception among some Spanish policy-makers that this would somehow provide cover for subsequently diminished Spanish activism. In this sense, the upgraded European commitment to the Mediterranean provided an unwarranted sense of comfort to the PP government. Subsequent efforts on Spain's part to secure a new CFSP Common Strategy covering the Mediterranean suggested some renewed urgency in this area of policy. On the other hand, as battles over the MEDA II financial protocol demonstrated – northern states resisting in 1999 any significant increase in funding of the sort they had consented to earlier in the decade – it was not clear to what extent European resources would continue to fund Spanish concerns in the Mediterranean.

Elsewhere, several authors make reference to Spain taking advantage of the continued scope for distinctive bilateral action, in such cases the relative lack of 'Europeanized' competences being useful for national diplomacy. This was most obviously and dramatically the case in Latin America. There, Spain succeeded in pushing other states into a range of new policy commitments towards the region, but also pursued a more intensive agenda outside the scope of joint EU policies. The scope for national diplomatic manoeuvrability was also exercised in the decision to allow the use of bases in Spain for the air attacks on Iraq and Kosovo, such support contrasting with the scepticism over these operations expressed by some other European states. Distinctive bilateral action was also witnessed in relation to Turkey, where a package of measures – including a new bilateral diplomatic forum, additional loans, development assistance and trade and investment incentives – were used to circumvent Greek (and others') unwillingness to make any significant move towards allowing for Turkish accession to the EU. In relation to the Middle East peace process, Spain pursued the common EU line while adding its own distinctive input by channelling, in contrast to the US and other EU states, a large slice of its aid in the Mediterranean to the Palestinian Territories. Here, as in Latin America, historical influences counterbalanced the dynamics of European convergence. In the economic sphere, as Keith Salmon points out, Spain took advantage of limits to EU merger and competition regulations actively to promote domestic fusions, facilitating national champions capable of establishing an international presence.

Selective or Global Protagonism?

As neither 'big player' nor 'small' member state, the extent of Spain's potential capabilities in foreign affairs has been less self-evident than that of other EU countries. There is much in this volume to corroborate claims that Spain's political and economic presence and prestige on the international stage strengthened dramatically during the 1990s. However, there is also evidence suggesting that Spain has not yet come significantly closer to developing a truly global reach to its external relations. Indeed, in some senses it appears to have concluded that the resources at its disposal can most profitably be concentrated within a limited number of key areas and issues. It is this kind of international protagonism that appears to have been accepted as most appropriate to Spain's distinctive medium-sized status within the EU. This profile has sometimes resulted from an express policy preference, sometimes from a frustrating inability to exercise more significant control over a particular policy agenda.

The concentration of investment outflows, development assistance and diplomatic initiatives in Latin America is the factor that most clearly gave Spain a distinctive international profile. The counterbalance, as a number of contributors suggest, was the relative weakness of Spain's presence in other parts of the world. Felipe Sahagún laments the limits to the non-military elements of Spain's relations with the US: in contrast to many EU states, the proportion of Spain's trade and investment carried out with the US declined during the 1990s; Spanish public opinion remained more ambivalent over seeking stronger ties to the US than nearly all other EU populations; and unlike most other EU states, Madrid established no high-level bilateral diplomatic channels with Washington. Crispin Coates expresses doubts over the compatibility between Spain's military capacity and its oft-stated desire to be a 'core' player within the new ESDI and conflict management competences: the Spanish defence budget fell as a proportion of GDP during the 1990s (although with a slight turn around in the real level of expenditure at the end of the decade) and was significantly less than that of Italy, a key comparison for Madrid.

Notwithstanding policy-makers' rhetoric insisting on the region's priority status for Madrid, the substance to Spain's presence in the southern Mediterranean was limited. Spanish investors demonstrated less interest in the region than those of several northern European countries, the former's plans limited to Morocco and a small number of big investments in the Algerian energy sector. Bilateral diplomatic efforts weakened after 1996, and were still concentrated overwhelmingly in the Maghreb. A declining proportion of Spanish aid went to the Mediterranean. As a limited aid donor and one of the prime opponents of granting extra-Community Mediterranean agricultural produce greater access to the European market, Spain's willingness to assume the responsibilities of leadership in the Mediterranean was increasingly doubted by the northern European states, themselves called upon by Madrid to fund the EU's policies in the region. Jesús Núñez argues that the PP's Mediterranean policy represents a clear example of the limits to Spanish external ambition. If, during the early 1990s, the PSOE was panicked into pushing for new Mediterranean policies by the alarmist prophecies of mass migration, anti-western Islamic government and endemic 'civilizational conflict', the PP judged such destabilization to be less likely by the latter half of the decade. Madrid appeared to be either unwilling or unable to secure a sustained lead protagonism in the Mediterranean. Only with the death of Hassan II were efforts with Morocco re-intensified, Spain at this juncture having to juggle its desire to pressurize Morocco into agreeing to new fishing provisions, on the one hand, and not to upset the fragile moment for democratization in Morocco, on the other hand.

Despite its determination to be among the 'core' countries involved in new defence and security competences, Spain was marginal to the most dramatic step forward in the European defence and security framework. The December 1999 Helsinki agreement to move towards the establishment of a European Rapid Reaction Force was worked up on the basis of an initial bilateral agreement between France and the UK, to which Germany and Italy then signed up. Esther Barbé points out that, within CFSP, Spain has thus far taken a very low profile in defining and operationalizing EU policy towards Russia and the Ukraine. Despite being keen to demonstrate its value as a new mainstream NATO member in Kosovo, Spain was unable to secure a permanent presence in the Contact Group defining overall policy on Yugoslavia. In East Timor, Madrid made no more than a small financial contribution and donated only a single unit of civil guards, in stark contrast to the heavy presence of Spanish diplomats and military officials involved in peace process work in Central America. Mariano Aguirre and Francisco Rey highlight the limits to Spain's input into broader debates on humanitarian and peacekeeping operations during the 1990s.

Such limits to Madrid's international protagonism were underpinned and compounded by the continuing structural weaknesses of the Spanish economy, outlined by Keith Salmon. Despite considerable progress towards becoming a fully 'normal' EU economy, at the end of the century Spain still had a level of wealth 15 points below the EU average; it also suffered from particular weaknesses in hi-technology sectors and had a higher proportion of its workers on short-term fixed contracts than any other European economy. In addition, as Angel Viñas points out, Spanish companies were less focused on preparing themselves for the opportunities of eastern enlargement than those of other EU states. These observations return us to one of the most salient factors to have emerged from this study: namely, the far-reaching interactions between the different arenas of Spain's increasingly multi-layered external policies. The impact of EU commitments affected the outlook of domestic actors in relation to issues and areas beyond Europe; issues which in turn rebounded to affect the EU context conditioning Spanish policy. Such complexity has, in some sense, given the Spanish government more levers to pull in pursuing its external objectives, but has also often placed tighter constraints on policy-making.

Of course, such limitations measure Spain's international protagonism against the big players with whom it cannot realistically aspire to compete, at least in the short to medium term. Such a comparison is useful, nevertheless, as a means of furthering our understanding of precisely what Spain's 'medium player' status entails, exactly what it lacks in relation to the EU's three major foreign policy players (France, Britain and Germany). As this volume makes clear, as the century turned Spain had undoubtedly come a long way since the first moves of repositioning that took place in the early 1980s and its presence and achievements during the 1990s were notable in many respects. The country navigated many of the challenges of the 1990s with skill and increasing self-assurance, and began to make more notable contributions to resolving global problems. The possibility of Spain's international protagonism developing further was suggested by Aznar's claim, made during the 2000 election campaign, that the country increasingly merited a place in both the G8 and UN Security Council. If it is the case that Spain has established itself as the 'seventh world power', this clearly implies a notable presence but still not one with a truly global reach. If other European states have come to seek a greater 'global burden-sharing' from Spain [Sahagún, 2000], this is both a sign of Spain's considerable potential, success and prestige, but also a symptom of new tensions and pressure within the EU. The challenge of maximizing the opportunities of 'medium player' protagonism, while deflecting responsibilities that it feels unable to meet, was fast becoming Spain's distinctive dilemma as the twenty-first century commenced.

REFERENCE

Sahagún, F. (2000): 'La política exterior española 2000',s *Anuario Internacional CIDOB*, Barcelona: Centre d'Informació I Documentació Internacionals a Barcelona, forthcoming.

Notes on Contributors

Mariano Aguirre is Director of the Centro de Investigaciones para la Paz (CIP) in Madrid, a researcher for the Transnational Institute (Amsterdam) and a member of the Humanitarian Action Unit created by Médècins sans Frontieres-Spain, the University of Deusto and the CIP.

Antonio Alaminos is Lecturer in Sociology at the University of Alicante.

Esther Barbé is Professor of International Relations at the Universitat Autònoma de Barcelona.

Crispin Coates is a doctoral candidate at the University of Nottingham.

Richard Gillespie is Professor of Politics at the University of Liverpool.

Francisco Granell is Chief Adviser for Development at the European Commission and a professor at the Universitat Autònoma de Barcelona.

Jesús Núñez Villaverde is based at the Centro de Investigación para la Paz (CIP), Madrid.

Francisco Rey is Director of the Study and Analysis Unit of the Spanish Red Cross and a member of the CIP and Humanitarian Action Unit.

Felipe Sahagún is 'Professor Titular' in International Affairs at Madrid's Complutense University and an editorial writer for the Spanish daily, *El Mundo*.

Keith Salmon is a Senior Lecturer at the University of Luton.

Angel Viñas is Director for Multilateral Relations at the European Commission and professor at the Universidad Complutense, Madrid.

Richard Youngs is a Senior Research Fellow based at the Centre for European Studies Research (CESR) at the University of Portsmouth.

Index

Books of Related Interest

Politics and Policy in Democratic Spain
No Longer Different?
Paul Heywood, *University of Nottingham* (Ed)

> *'This assessment of Spain's transition from forty years of stagnation to a dynamic and successful democracy provides much insight into exactly how this was accomplished and what it portends for the future'*
>
> **Contemporary Review**

'Spain is different' was a favourite tourist board slogan of the Franco dictatorship. But is Spain still different? Spain's 1978 Constitution marked the formal establishment of democracy, following nearly 40 years of dictatorial rule, but what shape has Spanish democracy taken? This volume provides an original series of analyses of the development of politics in Spain since the remarkable success of the transition to democracy. Drawing on the latest research by both established and younger scholars, most of them Spanish, the book offers an up-to-date assessment of democracy in the least studied of Europe's major states. It will be essential reading for those who want to understand politics in contemporary Spain.

248 pages 1999
0 7146 4910 4 cloth   0 7146 4467 6 paper
A special issue of the journal West European Politics

The Barcelona Process
Towards a Euro-Mediterranean Regional Community
George Joffé, *School of Oriental and African Studies, University of London* (Ed)

The Euro-Mediterranean Partnership – the Barcelona Process – was initiated in 1995. It seeks to create economic integration in the Mediterranean basin so as to encourage economic development along the Southern Mediterranean rim. In addition there are provisions for political, security, social and cultural cooperation. This volume, written by experts from around Europe and the South Mediterranean, seeks to take a critical look at the problems the Process faces and its likelihood of success.

180 pages 2000
0 7146 5109 5 cloth   0 7146 8128 8 paper
A special issue of Mediterranean Politics

FRANK CASS PUBLISHERS
Newbury House, 900 Eastern Avenue, Newbury Park, Ilford, Essex IG2 7HH
Tel: +44 (0)20 8599 8866 Fax: +44 (0)20 8599 0984 E-mail: info@frankcass.com
NORTH AMERICA
c/o ISBS, 5824 NE Hassalo Street, Portland, OR 97213 3644, USA
Tel: 800 944 6190 Fax: 503 280 8832 E-mail: cass@isbs.com
Website: www.frankcass.com

'Europeanization' and the Southern Periphery

Kevin Featherstone and **George Kazamias**, *both at the University of Bradford* (Eds)

'Europeanization' is a term increasingly used in the social sciences to describe the impact, convergence or response of actors and institutions in relation to the European Union. Its increasing currency is a symptom of the broadening and deepening of the European integration process at the turn of the century. Its usage implies a common understanding, yet it is applied in a variety of different ways. This volume explores the concept in a variety of different settings in order to clarify its meaning.

176 pages 2000
0 7146 5087 0 cloth   0 7146 8128 8 paper
A special issue of the journal South European Society & Politics

Perspectives on Development
The Euro-Mediterranean Partnership
George Joffé, *School of Oriental and African Studies, University of London* (Ed)

The Euro-Mediterranean Partnership Initiative, launched by the Barcelona Conference in 1995, is the most ambitious project to date directed at comprehensive prosperity and security in the Mediterranean region. Yet the assumptions on which it is based are untried and untested. This study seeks to analyse what they are and to draw some conclusions as to the potential of the Initiative for success by comparing it with other experiences of regional development.

288 pages 1999
0 7146 4939 2 cloth   0 7146 4499 4 paper
A special issue of the Journal of North African Studies

The Euro-Mediterranean Partnership
Political and Economic Perspectives
Richard Gillespie, *University of Portsmouth* (Ed)

The economic dimension of the Barcelona process has been its most tangible thus far. Will the North African economies be able to cope with the liberation of market forces or will greater social and political unrest ensue? Can the Mediterranean partners expect to benefit from an initiative in which Europeans set the agenda? These are two of the crucial questions addressed in these pages by economists, political scientists and international relations specialists.

200 pages 1997
0 7146 4822 1 cloth   0 7146 4370 X paper
A special issue of the journal Mediterranean Politics

FRANK CASS PUBLISHERS
Newbury House, 900 Eastern Avenue, Newbury Park, Ilford, Essex IG2 7HH
Tel: +44 (0)20 8599 8866 Fax: +44 (0)20 8599 0984 E-mail: info@frankcass.com
NORTH AMERICA
c/o ISBS, 5824 NE Hassalo Street, Portland, OR 97213 3644, USA
Tel: 800 944 6190 Fax: 503 280 8832 E-mail: cass@isbs.com
Website: www.frankcass.com